From the Library of:

Dawnings

Finding God's Light in the Darkness

Dawnings
Finding God's Light in the Darkness

Edited by
PHYLLIS HOBE

GUIDEPOSTS   CARMEL, NEW YORK 10512

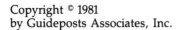

Book design by Elizabeth Woll

Photographs by J. Gerard Smith
    (Elizabeth Woll pages 53, 72 and 107)

Cover design by Elizabeth Woll
Cover photograph by J. Gerard Smith

Acknowledgments

Grateful acknowledgment is hereby expressed to all who have contributed to this volume. Any inadvertent omission of credit will be gladly corrected in future editions.

The essay in "Memories" by Charles L. Allen is used by permission of the author./ "The World's Most Beautiful Rose," "The Ugly Duckling," and "The Little Match Girl" are all from THE COMPLETE FAIRY TALES AND STORIES by Hans Christian Andersen, translated by Erik Christian Haugaard. Translation copyright © 1974 by Erik Christian Haugaard. Reprinted by permission of Doubleday & Company, Inc./ Pages 37-41 in THE DAY CHRIST WAS BORN by Jim Bishop. Copyright © 1959, 1960 by Jim Bishop. Reprinted by permission of Harper & Row, Publishers, Inc./ The essay in "Steadfastness" by Charles W. Colson is used by permission of the author./ "Sheer Joy" and "The Secret" from SPIRITUAL HILLTOPS, by Ralph Spaulding Cushman, and "Lonesome" from HILLTOP VERSES AND PRAYERS, published by Abingdon Press./ "Forgive," "Golden Rays of Hope," "Another Look," "Sunset Symphony," "Bring Tomorrow's Dawning," "The Magic of a Smile," "Faith," "To God With Love," "Meditation" are from BECAUSE I LOVE YOU by Alice Joyce Davidson. Copyright © 1982 by Alice Joyce Davidson. Published by Fleming H. Revell Company. Used by permission./ An excerpt from "What Is a Man?" is from STRAIGHT TALK TO MEN AND THEIR WIVES, by James C. Dobson. Used by permission of the author and Word Books, publisher, Waco, Texas./ "The Butterfly" is from JONI by Joni Eareckson and Joe Musser. Used by permission of Zondervan Publishing House./ An abridgment of "A Place of Safety" by Elisabeth Elliot is used by permission of Elisabeth Elliot./ The essay in "Trials and Triumphs by Colleen Townsend Evans is used by permission of the author./ An excerpt from TEACHING YOUR CHILD TO PRAY by Colleen Townsend Evans is used by permission of Doubleday & Company, Inc./ An excerpt from START LOVING by Colleen Townsend Evans is used by permission of Doubleday & Company, Inc./ "The Give-and-Take of Forgiveness" is an abridgment from the book START LOVING by Colleen Townsend Evans. Copyright © 1976 by Colleen Townsend Evans and Laura Hobe. Reprinted by permission of Doubleday & Company, Inc./ "The Miraculous Staircase" by Arthur Gordon, Guideposts, December 1966. Used by permission of the author and Guideposts./ "The Night the Stars Fell" is from A TOUCH OF WONDER by Arthur Gordon. Copyright © 1974 by Fleming H. Revell Company. Used by permission./ The essay in "De-

votion" by Ruth Graham is used by permission of the author./ "Myself" by Edgar Guest, reprinted from THE COLLECTED VERSE OF EDGAR GUEST, © 1934, p. 724, with the permission of Contemporary Books, Inc., Chicago./ The essay in "Humility" by Russell T. Hitt is used by permission of the author./ The essay in "Contentment" by Marjorie Holmes is used by permission of the author./ "Keep Me At It," "The Unexpected," "The Message" and "Night Duty" from I'VE GOT TO TALK TO SOMEBODY, GOD by Marjorie Holmes. Copyright © 1968, 1969 by Marjorie Holmes Mighell. Reprinted by permission of Doubleday & Company, Inc./ "Child in Trouble," "Go With Me to Work Today" and "The Radiant Company" from WHO AM I, GOD? by Marjorie Holmes. Copyright © 1970, 1971 by Marjorie Holmes Mighell. Reprinted by permission of Doubleday & Company, Inc./ The essay in "Compassion" by Sue Monk Kidd is used by permission of the author./ Excerpts from MERE CHRISTIANITY by C. S. Lewis. Copyright © 1943, 1945, 1952 by Macmillan Publishing Co., Inc. Copyrights renewed. Used by permission of the publisher./ The essay in "Character" by Catherine Marshall is from MEETING GOD AT EVERY TURN by Catherine Marshall, Fleming H. Revell Company, publisher. Used by permission./ "Can You…?" "The Tap on the Shoulder" and "Whispering Voices" excerpted from MR. JONES, MEET THE MASTER: The Sermons and Prayers of Peter Marshall. Edited by Catherine Marshall. Copyright © 1949, 1959 by Fleming H. Revell Company. Renewed 1976, 1977 by Catherine Marshall LeSourd. Used by permission./ "The Boy With Five Barley Loaves" and "Magdalene" from TOUCHED BY CHRIST by Louis G. Miller, C.SS.R. Copyright © 1978 by Liguori Publications, One Liguori Drive, Liguori, Missouri 63057./ Dodd, Mead & Company for permission to reprint "Cradle Song" from THE SCEPTRED FLUTE by Saronjini Naidu./ The essay in "Truth" by Lloyd John Ogilvie is used by permission of the author./ "Finding Your Personal Power" and "A Lesson From Grandma" are from A GUIDE TO CONFIDENT LIVING by Norman Vincent Peale. Copyright © 1948 by Prentice-Hall, Inc. Published by Prentice-Hall, Inc., Englewood Cliffs, N.J. 07632./ An adaptation from DYNAMIC IMAGING by Norman Vincent Peale. Copyright © 1982 by Norman Vincent Peale. Published by Fleming H. Revell Company. Used by permission./ "Faith Is Undefeatable" and "A Whole Man" are from YOU CAN IF YOU THINK YOU CAN by Norman Vincent Peale. Copyright © 1974 by Norman Vincent Peale. Published by Prentice-Hall, Inc., Englewood Cliffs, N.J.

07632./ Excerpts from THE ADVENTURE OF BEING A WIFE by Mrs. Norman Vincent Peale. Copyright © 1971 by Ruth S. Peale and Arthur Gordon. Published by Prentice-Hall, Inc., Englewood Cliffs, N.J. 07632./ The essay in "Loyalty" by Eugenia Price is used by permission of the author./ An excerpt from IN THE VINEYARD OF THE LORD by Helen Steiner Rice as told to Fred Bauer. Copyright © 1979 by Helen Steiner Rice and Fred Bauer. Published by Fleming H. Revell Company. Used by permission./ The poems of Helen Steiner Rice are reprinted by permission of the author and by permission of Gibson Greeting Cards, Inc./ The essay in "Consolation" by Elaine St. Johns is used by permission of the author./ An excerpt from THE MAN BORN TO BE KING by Dorothy L. Sayers, Wm. B. Eerdmans Publishing Co., © 1943 Dorothy L. Sayers, renewed by Anthony Fleming. Used by permission./ "Something That Grows" by Dorothy L. Sayers is from THE POETRY OF SEARCH AND THE POETRY OF STATEMENT. Published by Victor Gollancz, London./ "Thought" by Dorothy L. Sayers is from BEGIN HERE: a WARTIME ESSAY. Published by Victor Gollancz, London./ "Simile" by Clyta Shaw. © 1962, The Billy Graham Evangelistic Association./ Excerpts from THE CHRISTIAN'S SECRET OF A HAPPY LIFE by Hannah Whitall Smith are used by permission of the publisher, Fleming H. Revell Company./ Excerpts from GITANJALI by Rabindranath Tagore. Copyright © 1913 by Macmillan Publishing Co., Inc. Used by permission of the publisher./ Excerpts from TRAMP FOR THE LORD by Corrie ten Boom. Copyright © 1974 by Corrie ten Boom and Jamie Buckingham. Published cooperatively by Christian Literature Crusade and Fleming H. Revell Compa-

ny. Used by permission./ "February Twilight" by Sara Teasdale is reprinted by permission of Macmillan Publishing Co., Inc. from COLLECTED POEMS by Sara Teasdale. Copyright © 1926 by Macmillan Publishing Co., Inc., renewed 1954 by Mamie T. Wheless./ "Night" and "The Falling Star" by Sara Teasdale are reprinted by permission of Macmillan Publishing Co., Inc. from COLLECTED POEMS by Sara Teasdale. Copyright © 1930 by Sara Teasdale Filsinger, renewed 1958 by Guaranty Trust Co. of New York, Exr./ Henry van Dyke, "America for Me" and "Prayer" from THE POEMS OF HENRY VAN DYKE. Copyright © 1911 by Charles Scribner's Sons. Copyright renewed. Reprinted with the permission of Charles Scribner's Sons./ Henry van Dyke, "Salute to the Trees" from SONGS OUT OF DOORS. Copyright © 1922 by Charles Scribner's Sons: copyright renewed. Reprinted with the permission of Charles Scribner's Sons.

The following authors we have been unable to locate: Amelia Josephine Burr, "Rain in the Night"/ Mary Carolyn Davies, "The Day Before April"/ Arthur J. Peel, "Shadows"/ Caryl Porter, "Wonder Lies In a Round Rainbow"/ Elizabeth Yates, "The Pigeon That Went to Church." The publisher and editor will appreciate any information made available so that proper credit can be given in future editions.

Diligent effort has been made to locate and secure permission for the inclusion of all copyrighted material in this book. If any such acknowledgments have been inadvertently omitted, or if such were not received by the time of publication, the compiler and publisher would appreciate receiving full information so that proper credit may be given in future editions.

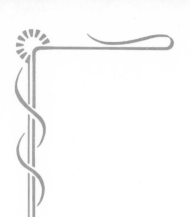

A Dedication

This book is lovingly dedicated to the memory of

HELEN STEINER RICE,

dear friend, generous teacher,
gentle servant of Almighty God.

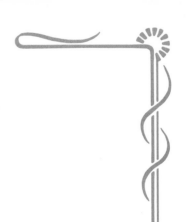

Preface

IN EVERY LIFE there are times of darkness. Times when we can't see where we are going. When we feel terribly alone, out of touch even with those we know and love. Darkness makes us wonder if anyone is there to help us. Does anyone really care?

Each of us knows what it is to spend a sleepless night, troubled by problems that seem overpowering. Each of us remembers how long those hours of darkness can be. It's a time when tears sting the eyes, and the heart aches more than we ever believed it could.

But then, just when we think the darkness will never end, we see something — there, along the distant horizon. Something is happening to the darkness! A faint glimmer of pale light is pushing the night away and bringing in the dawn of a new day. And as we watch this miracle, we realize that we are not alone. That God is there, that he is always there, even in the darkness. That he cares deeply what happens to us. And he will always come to us in our time of need.

In these pages we will meet others who have walked in darkness and found God's light…a proud, stubborn woman who discovers her lifelong enemy is her dearest friend, a child whose generosity is returned in a way that saves her life, a young doctor desperately trying to save a patient he has learned to love, a mother's prayer for a runaway child, a penniless father's priceless gift to his heartbroken daughter, a lonely widow's journey back into the past, a memory of quiet moments by a fireside, an appreciation of God's beautiful world…in all of them a message of hope and cheer and encouragement.

And we understand, as we share these poignant human experiences, that God sends his light to us in many ways — in the assurance that there is nothing to fear, in strength we didn't know we had, in a helping hand we didn't know was there, in an unexpected point of view, in the warmth of a smile, and in the certainty that God is close beside us along the way.

Yes, there will always be times of darkness in our lives. But, as the writers in this book reveal, we need never go through them alone. God will always comfort us. His light will always find us. And no matter how long the night, we must watch for that miracle on the horizon.

This is no ordinary light. Nor is it a light we can see with our eyes. It isn't like the sun, wonderful as the sun is. It isn't like the lamp we turn on to banish the shadows at sunset. This is the light of God's love, and we see it with our faith. It finds us wherever we are. It penetrates the deepest darkness. It illuminates the most difficult path.

Look over there, beyond the darkness, and you will surely see the dawning!

PHYLLIS HOBE

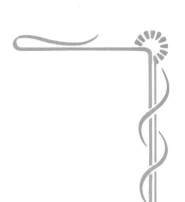

Table of Contents

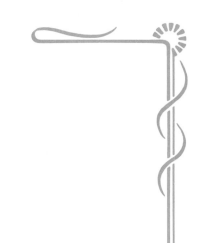

Guidance

BEING TREATED AS SPECIAL and unique may be some people's cup of tea, but it has never been mine, because, frankly, I've never felt that unique. Furthermore, prima donnas are big bores and after their moment in the sun most end up feeling depressed and bitter.

From the beginning, I've longed for permanence. I suspect it is in my genes. People with whom I grew up didn't cotton to those who were phonies or thought more of themselves than they should have.

I've always sought things of substance — lasting things — which is why I count my faith the most important thing in my life. Following my love of God is my love of the friends who provide life with depth and meaning.

Nothing that has come from whatever fame I've achieved in the last twenty years has given me more satisfaction than the people who have come into my life as a result of that "fame."

Thousands, no, *tens* of thousands have told me in person, called, or written me to say how much they have received from my writings.

What they don't realize is that the greatest thrill I receive is learning about their appreciation. That is because every time someone tells me that my words have given them strength or guidance or inspiration, I realize God has opened another door for me, and I thank Him each time for the privilege of being a small part of His plan.

Nothing could be clearer than that all of the things that have happened to me are part of a divine plan. The events are too preposterous for me to believe differently. Think of it. How could some person with my background, a woman without position or wealth or family name, a woman with only a high-school education, be given the role in life that I have received? The only answer I have ever been able to find is that I have been a willing servant, and God uses willing disciples in fantastic ways. The Bible tells us what happened to Peter and Andrew when they left their nets and followed Christ. Exciting things always happen to anyone who is willing to follow Him without reservation.

HELEN STEINER RICE

Prayer

HENRY VAN DYKE

Lord, the newness of this day
Calls me to an untried way:
Let me gladly take the road,
Give me strength to bear my load,
Thou my guide and helper be —
I will travel through with Thee.

*Our help is in the name of the Lord, Who
made heaven and earth.*   Psalm 124:8

This Day Is a Gift

GRACE NOLL CROWELL

This day is a gift from the outflung hand of
    God:
The gift of an untrod road for our feet to
    tread
As we journey onward toward the
    beckoning days
That swim in a shimmering mist of the year
    ahead.
Shadows are there that we but dimly see,
And there will be many a rugged hill to
    climb,
But we carry with us a Book that makes it
    clear
That the way will be safe if we take it a day
    at a time.

It tells of a Friend who will walk with us all
    the way.
The Comrade who builds the road for our
    pilgrim feet.
If gratefully we accept His company,
He will be our guide down each lane and
    city street,
And the way we go will be bright to the
    farthest end,
If we have for companion this wise and
    gracious Friend.

This Thing Called Guidance

RUTH STAFFORD PEALE

It was a Sunday that had been a happy day
from morning until night, and then —! After
church we went to lunch with some friends
and had a relaxed and enjoyable visit. The
day was, you might say, one grand, sweet
song. In the afternoon we did some other
interesting things and finally got home
about seven P.M. to find a message to call a
surgeon at the North Carolina University
Hospital in Chapel Hill.

Our son, John, was completing his studies
for a doctorate of philosophy degree at the
university. We made the call. The surgeon
said, "Your son came into this hospital today
in an emergency, suffering great agony.
We've tested him throughout the afternoon
and we've arrived at a diagnosis of inflamed
gallbladder with probably pancreatic complications." He continued, "We're medicat-
ing him, trying to delay operating, because
he has a hot gallbladder [that's what he
called it]. It's dangerous to operate with the
gallbladder in this condition. We hope to
reduce the infection and bring down his
temperature first and operate on him later."

"Well, doctor," I said, "he is in your hands
and he is in God's hands. You do what you
think is best." We immediately went into
prayer, praying for the doctor, praying for
our only son. At 11:15 that night the doctor
called back and said, "John hasn't responded to medication. The situation is becoming
very serious. I do not like to operate under
these conditions — it's dangerous to operate; but it's more dangerous not to. So I must
operate."

Again I said, "Doctor, he is in your hands
and in God's hands. Dr. Peale and I will be
with you in prayer. Bring him through for
us."

"I'll try mighty hard," he said.

So then we faced each other. This is our
only son. We knew he was in great danger.
But all our lives we have practiced to the best
of our ability the idea of letting go and letting
God. But it is very hard to let go of your own

son when everything within you draws him to yourself, but I believe we achieved it.

The doctor had said he would call us back in about two to three hours, that being the time he thought the operation would require.

But he didn't call us back. Four hours passed; then five hours. Six hours went by. We literally prayed all night long. Even though no word had come from the surgeon, at about 3:30 in the morning I had a strong conviction that it was going to be all right with John and that I could leave him in the hands of God. I told this to Norman. He said, "I had the same feeling a few moments ago."

At six o'clock in the morning the doctor called. He said, "I'm glad to report that John came through the operation successfully. He's a very sick boy, but he is also a good healthy boy. He has lived a clean life, and that counts when the chips are down. I feel that he will be all right."

Not in years have I had so great a sense of the greatness and the goodness and the love of God as I did that night.

Later I learned that at about three A.M. the situation became so serious that they brought the hospital's chief surgeon in to take part in the operation. I also told the doctor I had been praying for my son all night. He said, "I always try to work in partnership with God."

In this deeply human crisis, which occurs in every family in one form or another, we learned once again that you can trust this thing called guidance.

January Snow

ALMA ROBISON HIGBEE

The heart leans on its silence,
And God, with a gentle hand
Writes with the chalk of winter
On the blackboard of the land.

Our Father, Our Friend

BENJAMIN FRANKLIN

And have we now forgotten that powerful Friend? Or do we imagine we no longer need His assistance? I have lived a long time; and the longer I live, the more convincing proofs I see of this truth: that God governs in the affairs of men. And if a sparrow cannot fall to the ground without His notice, is it probable that an empire can rise without His aid?

Stay Thy Heart on Me

AMY CARMICHAEL

I am the God of the stars,
They do not lose their way,
Not one do I mislay,
Their times are in My hand,
They move at My command.

I am the God of the stars,
Today as yesterday,
The God of thee and thine,
Less thine they are than Mine;
And shall Mine go astray?

I am the God of the stars,
Lift up thine eyes and see
As far as mortal may
Into Eternity;
And stay thy heart on Me.

Let Go and Let God!

HELEN STEINER RICE

When you're troubled and worried and sick
    at heart
And your plans are upset and your world
    falls apart,
Remember God's ready and waiting to share
The burden you find much too heavy to
    bear —
So with faith, "LET GO" and "LET GOD"
    lead the way
Into a brighter and less troubled day.

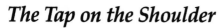

The Tap on the Shoulder

PETER MARSHALL

…I never knew my father, as other boys know their father, for he died when I was four, leaving my mother with two children, my sister being only a few months old.

Three years after my father's death, I acquired a stepfather, and my boyhood was profoundly affected by this new relationship.

I soon learned to fear my stepfather, for he was a jealous man with a violent temper.

…I had few toys.
Birthdays came and went unnoticed.
We never had a Christmas tree.
My mother's relatives never visited us, for it was too unpleasant after they left.

All references to my father or to my father's family were forbidden.
It was an unnatural situation, in which repressions were the rule.

I was quite unhappy, and began at an early age to think about some escape.

Like every British boy, I had a strong love of the sea.
On a still night one could hear the deep bassoon of ships' sirens as they warped into the docks of Glasgow or slipped down the Clyde for distant ports.

I began to think of the sea and to dream of it.
The books I read were tales of the sea.

With pen and pencil, and later with water colors,
I had sketched and scribbled, and always it had been ships.

How I longed to get off to sea.…

I had just turned fourteen when I ran off to join the Royal Navy. At that time the Navy

signed boys at fifteen and nine months. I said farewell to my friends in high school and to my teachers, and the next morning walked most of the way to the naval recruiting station ten miles away.

My career in the Navy was short-lived, for my parents secured my release because of my age.
And then I very foolishly refused to go back to school, since I had told my friends I was off to sea.

There was nothing left to do but to start working.
I began as an office boy, and enrolled in night school to study mechanical engineering.

I became a junior clerk
and then a time keeper.

For two years I worked in an accountant's office.
Then I became a machinist in an iron and steel tube works.

I had six years of night school in technical college, and now had three years' practical engineering experience, operating machines of all kinds.

Then came the climax of an intolerable home life in a harangue and a violent scene when my stepfather, under the influence of drink, gave me an ultimatum to leave the house.

How could I have known, at this time of severe crisis in my life, that even this would work out to the glory of God, and that in the years ahead there was to be a complete reconciliation with my stepfather?

At the time I was earning thirty-eight shillings per week, and the outlook was none too encouraging, for I had given my mother my pay envelope every pay day and had no money saved. I had no financial resources.

My mother's faith was simple and strong, and as I made plans to secure lodgings elsewhere, she said,

> "*Dinna* worry, son, the Lord will
> provide.
> He'll open up the way."

Well do I remember the Monday morning I left home with my overalls under my arm. That very morning, after I had been at my machine about two hours, I was summoned to the manager's office and informed that I was promoted to be a foreman of a section in another part of the plant, at twice the salary I had.

Thus, from the beginning, God was providing for my material needs.

That fall, a missionary returned from China and spoke in our church to the young people.
He was not seeking money — but volunteers for the mission field.

I volunteered for foreign service.
I was free.
I had no responsibilities
and I was obeying some impulse to offer my life.

…Whatever the impulse, from that time on, I knew that my call was for whole-time Christian service.

…Now, if you were walking down the street, and someone came up behind you and tapped you on the shoulder…what would you do?

Naturally, you would turn around.

Well, that is exactly what happens in the spiritual world. A man walks on through life — with the external call ringing in his ears but with no response stirring in his heart, and then suddenly, without any warning, the Spirit taps him on the shoulder.

What happens? He turns round.
The word "repentance" means "turning round."
He repents and believes and is saved.

"Give Us This Day Our Daily Bread"

MALTBIE D. BABCOCK

Back of the loaf is the snowy flour,
    And back of the flour the mill,
And back of the mill is the wheat and
        the shower,
And the sun and the Father's will.

Life is a pure flame, and we live by an invisible sun within us.
Thomas Browne

Everlasting Light

AUTHOR UNKNOWN

Almighty God, whose light is of Eternity and knoweth no setting, shine forth and be our safeguard through the night; and though the earth be wrapped in darkness and the heavens be veiled from our sight, let Thy brightness be about our beds, and Thy peace within our souls, and Thy Fatherly blessing upon our sleep this night. Amen.

God has given you a spirit with wings on which to soar into the spacious firmament of Love and Freedom.　　　　Kahlil Gibran

*God knows the secret plan
Of the things he will do for the world,
Using my hand.*　　　　Toyohiko Kagawa

This Is My Father's World

MALTBIE D. BABCOCK

This is my Father's world;
The birds their carols raise,
The morning light, the lily white,
Declare their Maker's praise.
This is my Father's world;
He shines in all that's fair;
In the rustling grass I hear him pass;
He speaks to me everywhere.

His Tender Mercies

LYMAN ABBOTT

I neither know nor wish to know what the future life has for me. I would not, if I could, stand at the open window and peer into the unknown beyond. I am sure that He whose mercies are new every morning and fresh every evening, who brings into every epoch of my life a new surprise, and makes in every experience a new disclosure of His love, who sweetens gladness with gratitude, and sorrow with comfort, who gives the lark for the morning and the nightingale for the twilight, who makes every year better than the year preceding, and every new experience an experience of His marvelous skill in gift-giving, has for me some future of glad surprise which I would not forecast if I could.

Go with Me to Work Today

MARJORIE HOLMES

God, please go with me to work today.

I am tired, troubled, discouraged.

There are so many problems at home, so many worries. Yet I must not carry them with me. I must be pleasant and poised, keep smiling. I must produce. I must earn my pay.

Thank you that you will help me. You will sustain me, sweep me free of these problems until I am able to think about them again, focus my entire attention on them.

Lord, I put my worries into your hands. I turn my family over to you now for blessing and safekeeping. I know that you will be with them, loving and directing them wherever they are, all through this day.

And I know that you will be with me.

As I go on with my work, I am suddenly thankful that I have it. I can lose myself in it, forget some of these problems. I won't be able to brood on them, and make the mistakes that come from idle brooding.

I can withdraw and get perspective. And when I return to all these situations in the family, I'll be better able to handle things.

Thank you for this reassurance. Thank you for going to work with me today.

Prayer

MARGARET BAILEY

God, give me sympathy and sense
　　And help me keep my courage high.
God, give me calm and confidence —
　　And, please — a twinkle in my eye.

Dreams and Deeds

JOHN HUNTER

Dear Master, in whose life I see
All that I long and fail to be;
Let thy clear light forever shine.
To shame and guide this life of mine.

Though what I dream and what I do
In my poor days are always two,
Help me, oppressed by things undone,
O thou, whose dreams and deeds were
    one.

We walk by faith, not by sight.
    II Corinthians 5:7, King James Version

Word of Life

WOODROW WILSON

The Bible is the Word of Life. I beg you will read it and find this out for yourself — read, not little snatches here and there, but long passages that will really be the road to the heart of it.

You will not only find it full of real men and women, but also of things you have wondered about and been troubled about all your life, as men have been always, and the more you read, the more will it become plain to you what things are worthwhile and what are not; what things make men happy — loyalty, right dealing, speaking the truth, readiness to give everything for what they think their duty, and, most of all, the wish that they may have the real approval of the Christ, who gave everything for them; and the things that are guaranteed to make men unhappy — selfishness, cowardice, greed, and everything that is low and mean.

When you have read the Bible, you will know that it is the Word of God, because you will have found it the key to your own heart, your own happiness, and your own duty.

Jeanie's Christmas Journey

MARGARET E. SANGSTER

Little Jeanie's bright eyes have a look of the
    morn,
And her sunny hair shines like the gloss of
    the corn.
When the eyes shall be dim and the locks
    shall be gray,
I think she'll remember a strange Christmas
    day
She had in her life when her birthdays were
    few,
And little of danger or sorrow she knew.

With Father and Mother away at the West,
The child was as lone as a bird in the nest,
Uncared for, untended, though Aunty was
    there —
An Aunty whose kisses were frosty and
    rare,
Who had meetings to go to and people to
    see,
And to all Jeanie's questions would answer
    "Dear me!
Just do as you please, pet, and keep out of
    harm";
Then, over the work of the letters whose
    charm
Enchanted her heart, would forget the poor
    child,
Who was left very much like a weed to run
    wild.

It was late in December, and Christmas was
    near,
When home should be bubbling with mirth
    and good cheer;
But no one seemed thinking of Christmas a
    bit,
And much Jeanie marvelled and puzzled,
    till it
Grew plain to her mind that no Christmas
    could come
To a child without father and mother at
    home,
And dear brother Tom — oh, she couldn't
    tell where —

Every night she asked God to keep Tom in
    His care,
And to let him be found soon; for Aunty
    had said
That he had been naughty, and so he had
    fled.
Had Jeanie been naughty, she'd never have
    stayed
Away from dear Mother, ashamed and
    afraid.
So, "Jesus, forgive him, and make him be
    good,"
Prayed Jeanie, the darling, and did what
    she could.

The day before Christmas, nor cedar, nor
    pine,
Nor red-berried holly had Jeanie to twine.
"You may hang up your stocking," her
    Aunty had said.
But not of herself mused the fair drooping
    head.
Her swift little fingers were aching to sew
On something for Mother; but hours would
    go,
While Aunty thought nothing of presents
    to make,
And the fond little heart felt as though it
    would break.
"At least," she concluded, "I'll do what I
    can:
My Father would say 'twas a beautiful plan:
I'll give my best things to some child who
    has none,
And I'll not even save the prettiest one.
I'll go out with my gifts now, and make
    someone glad,
And then perhaps Jesus will see that I'm
    sad,
And show me the way to my Father and
    Mother,
And help me to find, where he's hidden,
    my brother."

In her warm Mother Hubbard and cunning
    gray poke,
A mite of a thing in the hat and the cloak,
With a doll in her arm, and a basket quite
    full,

She tripped in to Aunty, just home from a
    school
Where poor little children were brought
    from the street,
And fed, and taught verses, and given a
    treat
On the bright Christmas-eve. Now Aunty
    was tired;
The day had not been as she planned and
    desired.
So, scarcely attending to what Jeanie asked,
In the glow of the grate as she cozily
    basked.
"Yes, run away, little one," quickly she said,
"But be back before tea," and away Jeanie
    sped.

She knew where, far up on a steep winding
    stair,
A poor crippled Hetty no pleasures could
    share,
Save what from her window she caught as
    they passed —
Procession or pageant moving too fast.
"I never," mused Jeanie, with face growing
    grave,
And brown eyes with look burning earnest
    and brave —
"I never had 'sperience' of trouble before,
And here's Hetty cannot step out of the
    door;
I'll give her my dolly, my own precious
    child."
At the stair foot she kissed it, then cried,
    and then smiled,
Climbed up to the attic — she knew it, you
    see;
For Mother had been there in days that
    were free
From the "sperience" of trouble; flashed in
    like a beam
Of gay winter sunshine; flashed out like a
    dream;
And Hetty with rapture was clasping a doll
That could walk and could laugh and a ditty
    could troll.
'Twas gathering dusk, and beginning to
    snow,

And the small Mother Hubbard skipped
    quick to and fro —
Skipped over the sidewalk, and tried a
    blithe race —
Such fun! — with the white floating
    feathers to chase.
Her basket was heavy, so, one at a time,
She dropped little gifts, caring not for the
    grime
Of the poor beggar's hand, thinking only to
    please
These children who looked as if ready to
    freeze.

There was left in her basket one treasure
    most dear:
To make it had taken her more than a year,
And now it was dark, but the streets were
    ablaze,
And crowded with shoppers, and scarce
    through the maze,
In the fast-growing gloom, could Jeanie
    proceed.
She *must* give the bright scrap-book to some
    one in need
Of pictures and stories and verses so sweet.
The gay dancing measure went out of her
    feet,
For Jeanie was weary, and deep was the
    snow.
Alas! tea was over — oh, long, long ago.
And Aunty, now frightened, sent this way
    and that
For a wee Mother Hubbard and Greenaway
    hat.
And neighbors were searching, and soon
    the police
Would be hunting a child with a soft golden
    fleece
And eager brown eyes, through the cold
    and the storm.
Oh! where could be loitering the dear little
    form?

Meanwhile little Jeanie had come to a place
Where the yellow lamps flared on full many
    a face
With homesickness written in every hard
    line.

There were women with brows that were
    patient and fine,
And rosy-cheeked girls, cheery, honest,
    and true,
Who would shrink from no labor their
    hands found to do;
There were old men, with beards that hung
    low on the breast,
And lads looking forth to the green, ample
    West;
There were flaxen-haired babies, and
    children blue-eyed,
In shawls and odd kerchiefs that primly
    were tied,
And Jeanie looked round for the one who
    should fold
To her bosom the book that was better than
    gold.

Such a tiny, quaint woman she picked from
    the throng,
A child with a face that was gleeful and
    strong.
"Merry Christmas!" cried Jeanie, and gave
    her the book.
Then right in her eyes saw so happy a look
That she pressed through the crowd, lest
    the chance she should miss,
And with arms round her neck, gave the
    stranger a kiss.

"All aboard!" rang the order. With hurry
    and rout
Were the travellers marshalled, spectators
    sent out.
"All aboard!" rang the shout, then were
    whistles amain,
And steamed from the station the emigrant
    train.
And somehow, hand clasped in the dear
    Norway girl's,
The pretty hat crushed o'er the cloud of her
    curls,
Little Jeanie went too, with a heart
    throbbing fast,
And a passionate feeling of freedom at last,
Quite sure it was Jesus had led her along,
And made her a place in this strange-
    speaking throng.

"Dear Saviour!" she whispered, with lowly
　　bent head —
"Please keep me all safe, like a lamb of Thy
　　fold;
Please think of my name when the names
　　are all told,
And take me, I pray, to my Father and
　　Mother
To-morrow, and help us find Tom, my dear
　　brother!"

Then softly and safely — for Jesus would
　　keep
The dear trustful child — she fell soundly
　　asleep;
And Gretchen's mamma, seeing some great
　　mistake,
Such care as she could then decided to take;
And covered her snugly till night wore its
　　way
To the dawn of the Christmas — earth's
　　holiest day.
I think, on this night the bright angels
　　above
Recall in their music that errand of love
When the hills of Judea were kindled to
　　flame,
And heaven taught earth to repeat the blest
　　name
Of the mighty Redeemer, the conquering
　　One,
Divine and eternal, yet Mary's fair Son.

Little Jean slept all night, and when
　　morning had broke,
By signs to a uniformed man Gretchen
　　spoke,
And Gretchen's mamma; and with angry
　　surprise
He fastened on Jeanie a keen pair of eyes,
The dress, the distinction, the bright little
　　face
In this rabble of peasants he knew had no
　　place.
Yet tenderly, too (he'd a child of his own),
He lifted her up, and with arm round her
　　thrown,

Said: "Where did you come from? Who are
　　you, my dear?
I see you are lost; but, pray, who brought
　　you here?"
"I think it was Jesus," the little one said.
"I am going out West" — with a nod of her
　　head.
"It's Christmas, you know, and I'm going to
　　Mother
And Father, and maybe to Tom, my big
　　brother."

"Well! well!" said the man, very crusty and
　　cross,
But he carried her high on his shoulder; "a
　　loss
Like this was enough just to drive her folks
　　wild,"
He muttered. "They should have looked
　　after the child."

The train slackened speed, and went slowly
　　and stopped,
And here little Jean at a station was
　　dropped.
Her friend said "Good-bye," and a telegram
　　sent,
Which erelong gave Aunty a moment's
　　content.
The people came round, as the train
　　whirled away,
And Jeanie stood sobbing, the morn was so
　　gray,
And she was so lonesome and hungry and
　　cold,
Her hair was so tangled; the bitter tears
　　rolled
Down her cheeks one by one, a forlorn little
　　waif.
And still the dear Saviour was keeping her
　　safe.

For suddenly, swift from an incoming car
Rushed a lady whose face was as pure as a
　　star,
And caught little Jean, Mother Hubbard
　　and all,

And kissed her, and wondered, and
wrapped a great shawl
Round the shivering figure. "My daughter!
you here?
Where's Aunty? and where did you come
from, my dear?"
And Father was there, oh, so strong and so
tall!
And straightway the child forgot terror and
all
Her sadness and trouble, and laughed out
in cheer:
"Merry Christmas has come. I'm so glad
you are here.
I was going to look for you, Father and
Mother.
I thought I could help you to search for my
brother."
Ah! how they had chafed at the weary
delay,
Which had kept them enroute until dawned
Christmas-day!
And now they thanked God that their steps
had been led
To Jeanie, unhurt in a hair of her head.

'Twas a change to be whisked to a
drawingroom car,
Through great sunny windows to gaze out
afar,
Over white fields of snow, over bridges and
streams,
While people and houses rushed past her
like dreams;
And Father found somewhere a sweet Paris
doll
That was almost as lovely as Hetty's; and all
That she said Mother answered with gentle
caress,
Or a look that made up for a month of
distress.
And just as the twilight fell murky and
gray,
They came to the end of this wonderful day.
And reaching home, Aunty, as pale as a
ghost,
Cried: "Jean, of all children, you've worried
me most.

I told you, I'm certain, to stay by the door;
And here you've been flying the county
half o'er."

Many days onward passed, and from Tom
came no word;
But Jeanie felt sure that her prayers would
be heard,
And that Christ, when He saw that such
answer was best,
Would bring home the fugitive lost in the
West.

In a little log-house on a prairie's green rim
Death struggled with life for a youth, in
whose dim
Sunken eyes a fierce fever to ashes had
burned,
And life turned the scale; and, oh, wildly he
yearned
For a look, for a thought, of the far-away
home,
Neglected and scorned, he had fled from to
roam
With the vile and the wicked, in sin and in
shame,
Insulting the Saviour, forgetting His name.

A kind hand had tended him; motherly care
Had given him nursing. A child, grave and
fair,
With patience had sat by his side for long
hours,
And sometimes she brought him sweet
grasses and flowers;
And one day from folds of soft linen she
took
Her treasure of treasures, a wonderful
book.
"You may see it," she said, in her soft
broken speech.
"Be careful; don't hurt it. Ach! why!" for a
screech,
Shrill, frightened — a scream in a sob that
was lost —
Came quick from the bed, and the wan
hands were crossed,
As over a relic of saint at a shrine,

On a name written bold o'er a faint
    pencilled line.
It was "Jeanie, Tom's sister." Beneath it were
    these
Simple words — how they hurt him! —
    "Dear Lord, if You please,
Make Tom to be good; bring him home to
    our Mother;
And, oh, for Christ's sake, let us love one
    another!"

This Christmas if you at our Jeanie should
    peep,
You would see in her hands, at her side, a
    bright heap
Of playthings for Hetty, of games and of
    toys
For her pensioners cheery, the small ragged
    boys.

A remote cabin home had received a great
    box,
Which the key in dear Gretchen's letter
    unlocks.
There's a cap for mamma, there are mittens
    and hood,
And a wonderful book from the "little one
    good
Who travelled that eve on the emigrant
    train,
Whom the Christ-child took care of, as all
    might see plain."

With hundreds of gay-colored tapers
    ablaze,
Jean's Christmas-tree shines, while they
    carol their praise,
Tom, Father and Mother, and dear little girl,
To Him whose white banner 'tis bliss to
    unfurl —
To Jesus, who came when the Bethlehem
    star
Sent silvery beams to the nations afar;
To Jesus, whom Mary, the mother so sweet,
Held close, while the Wise Men were
    bowed at his feet;
To Jesus, the mighty, the conquering One,
Divine and eternal, yet Mary's fair Son.

*When the Light of Life falls upon the life of men,
secret powers begin to unfold, sleeping percep-
tions begin to awake, and the whole being becomes
alive unto God.*
        John Henry Jowett

He Is

GILES FLETCHER

He is a path, if any be misled,
He is a robe, if any naked be,
If any chance to hunger, He is bread,
If any be a bondman, He is free,
If any be but weak, how strong is He,
To dead men life He is, to sick men health,
To blind men sight, and to the needy
    wealth,
A pleasure without loss, a treasure
    without stealth.

*God's strength behind you, His concern for you,
His love within you, and His arms beneath you
are more than sufficient for the job ahead of you.*
        William Arthur Ward

Faith

ALICE JOYCE DAVIDSON

There's hope for each of us with faith,
There's hope for all who trod
Within His light, within His love,
Within the path of God,
For those of us who realize
With both our minds and hearts,
That whatever may befall us,
Whatever life imparts,
We only have to stretch our hand
To Him who dwells up high
And He will give us guidance,
He will show us by and by
That faith and trust will always
Take us through the darkest night,
And prayer that's said in earnest
Will shed the brightest light.

gramps

ANN KIEMEL

grandfather was in the backyard, and it was mid-morning. his small grandson kept begging him....

"gramps, can i fix you a hamburger?"

"no, honey, gramps is full. he just had breakfast."

"hmmmmm. can i fix you a hot dog?"

"i don't think a hot dog would mix well with the eggs inside." the child tugged on his grandfather's arms, and burst into an enormous smile.

"i know, gramps...a glass of water?"

grandfather looked into the dirt-smeared face. he wasn't thirsty, but he could see the boy's desire to do something special for the man he most admired.

"yep, i think gramps could use a drink."

the child ran into the kitchen. he happened to pick up a dirty glass from the sink instead of a clean one. he turned on the hot water tap, instead of the cold. as he ran out the door with the water, the mud from his hands smeared over the outside of the glass, dribbled inside, and clouded the hot water.

"here you are, gramps." (oh, his enthusiasm)

gramps looked at the awful glass of water, and caught the sparkle in the small face. he drank it all, and wrapped his arms around the lad.

"you know, that was the best glass of water gramps ever had."

sometimes my very best, however supported by enthusiasm, turns out not to be so good after all. like "gramps," God's love overlooks the muddiness and dirt, sees down under to my heart.

with time, He teaches me the difference between a good glass of water and a bad one. He smooths my rough edges if i let Him...

even when it hurts   terribly. He mellows me.

the motto of my life is YES, LORD. anytime. anywhere.

"yes" to whatever He wants, wherever He leads.

sometimes i have kind of died inside, saying "yes." it has meant, "God, you can put anything in or take anything out of my life... anything You wish...if you will help me."

*you will seek me and you will find me
when you search for me with all your heart.*

His Ways

ESTHER GUYOT

God has a thousand ways
Where I can see not one;
When all my means have reached their end
Then His have just begun.

Evensong

ROBERT LOUIS STEVENSON

The embers of the day are red
Beyond the murky hill.
The kitchen smokes; the bed
In the darkling house is spread:
The great sky darkens overhead,
And the great woods are shrill.
So far have I been led,
Lord, by Thy will:
So far I have followed, Lord, and
wondered still.
The breeze from the embalmed land
Blows sudden towards the shore,
And claps my cottage door.
I hear the signal, Lord — I understand.
The night at Thy command
Comes. I will eat and sleep and will not
question more.

Heritage

DURING THE CHRISTMAS SEASON 1969, my father's two surviving brothers and his sister gathered in California for a family reunion. And on that happy occasion, they spent the better part of five days reminiscing about their childhood and early home life. One of the grandchildren had enough initiative to record the discussions on cassette tapes, and I was privileged to obtain a complete set. What a rich heritage this provided, granting insight into my grandparents' home and the early experiences of my dad.

While all the conversations were of interest to me, there was a common thread that was especially significant throughout the week. It focused on the *respect* with which these four siblings addressed the memory of their father (my grandfather). He died in 1935, a year before my birth, yet they spoke of him with an unmistakable awe more than thirty-four year later. He still lived in their minds as a man of enormous character and strength.

When I asked them to explain the quality they admired so greatly, my dad provided the best evidence by writing his recollection of Grandfather Dobson's death, which I've reproduced below. Flowing throughout this narrative is the impact of a great man on his family, even three decades after his demise.

THE LAST DAYS OF R. L. DOBSON

The attack that took his life occurred when he was sixty-nine years of age, and resulted ultimately in the breakup of the family circle. For many years after his death, I could not pass Tri-State Hospital without noting one particular window. It stood out from the rest, hallowed because it represented the room where he had suffered so much. The details of those tragic days and nights remain in my memory, unchanged by the passage of time.

We had been three days and three nights practically without sleep, listening to him struggle for breath, hearing the sounds of approaching death, smelling the smells of death. Dad lay in a deep coma. His heavy breathing could be heard up and down the corridor. We walked the halls of that old hospital for hours listening to the ceaseless struggle which now was becoming fainter and fainter. Several times the nurse had called us in and we had said the last "good-bye" — had gone through the agony of giving him up, only to have his heart rally, and then the endless vigil would begin all over again. Finally, we had gone into an adjoining room not prepared for sleep, but some in the chairs and some across the beds, we had fallen into the sleep of utter exhaustion.

At five minutes to four o'clock the nurse came in and awakened one of my twin brothers. Robert roused with a start. "Is he gone?" he asked.

"No, but if you boys want to see your dad one more time while he is alive, you'd better come, now."

The word quickly passed around and we filed into the room to stand around his bed for the last time. I remember that I stood at his left side: I smoothed back the hair from his forehead, and laid my hand on his big old red hand, so very much like my own. I felt the fever that precedes death: 105. While I was standing there a change came over me. Instead of being a grown man (I was twenty-four at the time) I became a little boy again. They say this often happens to adults who witness the death of a parent. I thought I was in the Union Train Station in Shreveport, Louisiana, in the late afternoon, and I was watching for his return. The old Kansas City Southern passenger train was backing into the station and I saw it come 'round the curve. My heart swelled with pride. I turned to the little boy standing next to me and said, "You see that big man standing on the back of the train, one hand on the air brake and the other on the little whistle with which he signals the engineer? That big man is my dad!" He set the air brakes and I heard the wheels grind to a stop. I saw him step off that last coach. I ran and jumped into his arms. I gave him a tight hug and I smelled the train smoke on his clothes. "Daddy, I love you," I said.

It all comes back. I patted that big hand and said "Good-bye, Dad," as he was sinking fast, now. "We haven't forgotten how hard you worked to send five boys and one girl through college: how you wore those old conductor uniforms until they were slick — doing without — that we might have things that we didn't really need...."

At three minutes to four o'clock, like a stately ship moving slowly out of time's harbor into eternity's sea, he breathed his last. The nurse motioned us to leave, and pulled the sheet over his head, a gesture that struck terror to my heart, and we turned with silent weeping to leave the room. Then an incident occurred that I will never forget. Just as we got to the door, I put my arm around my little mother and said, "Mama, this is awful."

Dabbing at her eyes with her handkerchief, she said, "Yes, Jimmy,

but there is one thing Mother wants you to remember, now. We have said 'good night' down here, but one of these days we are going to say 'good morning' up there."

I believe she did say "good morning" too, eleven years later, and I know he met her "just inside the Eastern gate."

JAMES C. DOBSON

The great man is he who does not lose his child's heart.
Mencius

Out of the Vast

AUGUSTUS WRIGHT BAMBERGER

There's part of the sun in an apple,
    There's part of the moon in a rose;
There's part of the flaming Pleiades
    In every leaf that grows.
Out of the vast comes nearness;
    For the God whose love we sing
Lends a little of his heaven
    To every living thing.

Whatever Is — Is Best

ELLA WHEELER WILCOX

I know, as my life grows older,
    And mine eyes have clearer sight,
That under each rank wrong somewhere
    There lies the root of Right:

That each sorrow has its purpose,
    By the sorrowing oft unguessed;

But as sure as the sun brings morning,
    Whatever is — is best.

I know that each sinful action,
    As sure as the night brings shade,
Is somewhere, sometime punished,
    Tho' the hour be long delayed.
I know that the soul is aided
    Sometimes by the heart's unrest,
And to grow means often to suffer —
    But whatever is — is best.

I know there are no errors,
    In the great Eternal plan,
And all things work together
    For the final good of man.
And I know when my soul speeds onward,
    In its grand Eternal quest,
I shall say as I look back earthward,
    Whatever is — is best.

Faith and Sight

MARY GARDNER BRAINARD

So I go on, not knowing,
    — I would not, if I might —
I would rather walk in the dark with God
    Than go alone in the light;
I would rather walk with Him by faith
    Than walk alone by sight.

The Old Oaken Bucket

SAMUEL WOODWORTH

How dear to this heart are the scenes of my
    childhood,
      When fond recollection presents them
      to view! —
The orchard, the meadow, the
    deep-tangled wildwood,
      And every loved spot which my
      infancy knew!
The wide-spreading pond, and the mill that
    stood by it;
      The bridge, and the rock where the
      cataract fell;
The cot of my father, the dairy-house
    nigh it;
      And e'en the rude bucket that hung in
      the well.
The old oaken bucket, the iron-bound
    bucket,
      The moss-covered bucket, which hung
      in the well.

That moss-covered vessel I hailed as a
    treasure;
      For often at noon, when returned from
      the field,
I found it the source of an exquisite
    pleasure —
      The purest and sweetest that Nature
      can yield.
How ardent I seized it, with hands that
    were glowing,
      And quick to the white-pebbled bottom
      it fell!
Then soon, with the emblem of truth
    overflowing,
      And dripping with coolness, it rose
      from the well —
The old oaken bucket, the iron-bound
    bucket.
      The moss-covered bucket arose from
      the well.

How sweet from the green, mossy brim to
    receive it,
      As, poised on the curb, it inclined to
      my lips!

Not a full, blushing goblet could tempt me
    to leave it,
      The brightest that beauty or revelry
      sips.
And now, far removed from the loved
    habitation,
      The tear of regret will intrusively swell,
As Fancy reverts to my father's plantation,
      And sighs for the bucket that hangs in
      the well —
The old oaken bucket, the iron-bound
    bucket,
The moss-covered bucket that hangs in
    the well!

Bless This House

HELEN TAYLOR

Bless this house, O Lord, we pray,
    Make it safe by night and day;
Bless these walls, so firm and stout,
    Keeping want and trouble out;
Bless the roof and chimneys tall,
    Let thy peace lie over all;
Bless this door, that it may prove
    Ever open to joy and love.

*Look well to the hearthstone; there all hope for
America lies.*   Calvin Coolidge

With This Faith

JERRY LIPMAN

Home has to be the place where
    a man has a purpose;
    where he belongs;
Where he is loved and needed
    and respected;
Where he has a job to do,
    a cause,
And loyalties that lead him
    to discover
A meaning for his life.

The Family

ALAN BECK

The family is a storehouse in which the world's finest treasures are kept. Yet the only gold you'll find is golden laughter. The only silver is in the hair of Dad and Mom. The family's only real diamond is on Mother's left hand. Yet can it sparkle like children's eyes at Christmas or shine half as bright as the candles on a birthday cake?

A Mother's Prayer

MARGARET E. SANGSTER

Father in Heaven, make me wise,
 So that my gaze may never meet
A question in my children's eyes;
 God keep me always kind and sweet,

And patient, too, before their need;
 Let each vexation know its place,
Let gentleness be all my creed,
 Let laughter live upon my face!

A mother's day is very long,
 There are so many things to do!
But never let me lose my song
 Before the hardest day is through.

Beatitudes for the Home

THEODORE F. ADAMS

Blessed is the home where God is at home
 and where the spirit of Christ rules.
Blessed is the home where children are
 welcomed and given their rightful
 place.
Blessed is the home having a church home
 where father, mother, and children
 worship regularly together.
Blessed is the home where each puts the
 other's happiness first.

Blessed is the home where all show their
 love in ways that mean the most to
 those they love.
Blessed is the home where each seeks to
 bring out the best in the other and to
 show his own best self at all times.
Blessed is the home where all have learned
 to face their daily problems in a
 Christian spirit and to disagree
 without being disagreeable.
Blessed is the home where children grow
 up and grown-ups do not act like
 children.
Blessed is the home having the assurance of
 a heavenly home.

From *The Prophet*

KAHLIL GIBRAN

Your children are not your children.
 They are the sons and daughters of Life's longing for itself.
 They come through you but not from you,
 And though they are with you, yet they belong not to you.
 You may give them your love but not your thoughts.
 For they have their own thoughts.
 You may house their bodies but not their souls,
 For their souls dwell in the house of tomorrow, which you cannot visit, not even in your dreams.
 You may strive to be like them, but seek not to make them like you.
 For life goes not backward nor tarries with yesterday.

Our families in Thine arms enfold
As Thou didst keep Thy folk of old.
          Oliver Wendell Holmes

Lonely Farm

LOIS KINGSLEY PELTON

The whirling snow, like huge, white petals
    blown
From heaven's tree, lay piled on fence and
    road.
The house was old and gray, and all alone,
And past it, storm-winds, roaring hoarsely,
    strode.

The fields were harvested, and now lay
    bare.
It seemed a wild, deserted place to me,
That windy evening through the frosted air,
A sad old house beneath a leafless tree.
But, when I entered — what a change I
    found!

The farmer sat within a clean, warm room,
A rugged man whom summer days had
    browned.
In catalogues, he read when plants would
    bloom,
And talked of fertile fields, of sun and seed,
And all the hungry that his land could feed.

America for Me

HENRY VAN DYKE

'Tis fine to see the old World, and travel up
    and down
Among the famous palaces and cities of
    renown,
To admire the crumbly castles and the
    statues of the kings, —
But now I think I've had enough of
    antiquated things.

So it's home again, America for me!
My heart is turning home again, and there I
*   long to be,*
In the land of youth and freedom beyond the
*   ocean bars,*
Where the air is full of sunlight and the flag
*   is full of stars.*

Oh, London is a man's town, there's power
    in the air;
And Paris is a woman's town, with flowers
    in her hair;
And it's sweet to dream in Venice, and it's
    great to study Rome;
But when it comes to living there is no place
    like home.

I like the German fir-woods, in green
    battalions drilled;
I like the gardens of Versailles with flashing
    fountains filled;
But, oh, to take your hand, my dear, and
    ramble for a day
In the friendly western woodland where
    Nature has her way!

I know that Europe's wonderful, yet
    something seems to lack;
The Past is too much with her, and the
    people looking back.
But the glory of the Present is to make the
    Future free. —
We love our land for what she is and what
    she is to be.

Oh, it's home again, and home again,
*   America for me!*
I want a ship that's westward bound to
*   plough the rolling sea,*
To the blessed Land of Room Enough beyond
*   the ocean bars,*
Where the air is full of sunlight and the flag
*   is full of stars.*

An Old Church

HANNAH KAHN

The walls which now
Are crumbling lime
Could not withstand
The urge of time.

The wood has rotted
On the doors;
Rain has ravished
Roof and floors....

And yet because
Men worshipped here,
Something holy
And austere

Lingers on
And fills the air,
Like echoes
Of a quiet prayer.

When God began creating the heavens and the earth, the earth was at first a shapeless, chaotic mass, with the Spirit of God brooding over the dark vapors.

Then God said, "Let there be light." And light appeared. And God was pleased with it, and divided the light from the dark.

Genesis 1:1-5, Living Bible

In the Beginning

EUGENIA PRICE

One day we may be able to stand on another planet and look through a powerful telescope at the Earth. If and when this day comes, it will be hard to believe that there was once a time when there was no such thing as the planet Earth. Just as it is hard to imagine as we look at the other planets now, that once there was nothing but space, not only in our universe, but in all the others.

Once there was no place to stand at all. Once there was nothing to look at. More than this, there was no one to look.

Then one day in deepest heaven a great light broke. Brighter than the great light already there. Every shining mountain and every bright angel leaned expectantly toward the light and listened.

God was about to speak.

A deep rhythm swelled and subsided, and God said: "Let us make man in our own image."

He did not speak to the angels or to the shining mountains. He spoke to Someone else. Someone who was a part of Himself.

"Let Us make man in Our image — after Our likeness.... "

In God's heart was so much love that He needed to create other beings for His own sake. Beings who would be completely dependent upon His love. And so that these new creatures would have a place to live, God began to create the heavens and the Earth, and all that is in both.

Into space He flung the stars and the suns and the moons.

Over the dark waters that hung in one particular part of that trackless space, His Spirit brooded, and there was dry land. The mountains, valleys, little hills and meadows of the planet Earth.

Between the stretches of dry land, God limited the rivers to their banks and the big oceans to their shores. And when rivers began to run their courses and when oceans met shores, a new rhythm was born on the earth. A rhythm that met and mingled with the rhythm of the wind that blew the clouds, and the rain that fell when the thunder came across the sky.

Then under the sound of this rhythm which we can hear, another sound we cannot hear was born. The sound of seeds cracking in the dark ground, and the sound of little green sprouts pushing their way toward the sun. Little sprouts which became great trees and bright fragrant flowers and grass.

In the seas, God put fish.

In the skies, He put birds.

On the dry land, big and little horned and

furry animals began to roam and scamper and chatter and roar.

God was busy creating the heavens and the Earth for love of the man He would create and watch over forever.

…whatever is good and perfect comes to us from God, the Creator of all light, and he shines forever without change or shadow.

James 1:17, Living Bible

I have no fear that the candle lighted in Palestine years ago will ever be put out. William R. Inge

Consolation

IT DOES NOT TAKE LONG for a car to go over a cliff. One instant the convertible in which I was a passenger was right side up on the night-black, mountainous Topanga Canyon Road between the bright lights of the San Fernando Valley and the beach houses on the Pacific Ocean. The next instant it was upside down in a tangle of scrub and brush far below. And I was pinned under the car, fully conscious, paralyzed from the neck down.

It should have been one of the darkest moments of my life.
But it wasn't.

For between that one instant and the next, I had actually felt God's presence. It came as an inner voice repeating three times the beautiful promise, "Lo, I am with you alway" (Matthew 28:20). Simultaneously I entered into a timeless moment where the love of God was a substance — comforting, warm, light-bright, peace-filled, enveloping.

The moment passed, but the peace, His peace, remained.

Subsequent events unfolded rapidly. I smelled gas fumes. I called to my driver-companion — he had been thrown clear and was confused, but unhurt — to turn off the ignition. All at once, although I had no medical competence, I knew my neck was "broken." I asked my companion to pull me out from under the wreckage firmly, steadily, holding both feet. As he did so, the spinal cord was released from pressure. Feeling returned. (Later we were told how dangerous this procedure was, to be attempted only in surgery after a series of X-rays, and then not always successful.)

A car came along the lonely road, stopped, two men carried me carefully up the cliff, drove me to a hospital, and disappeared. (Again, a most dangerous procedure, yet it could have been hours before we were discovered, and, since we were in a no-man's-land which was in controversy between ambulances from the Valley and the coast — more hours before help arrived.)

At the hospital the doctors waited for me to go into shock. I never did. Nor did I lose my calm during the medical crises and emergencies of the ensuing weeks.

All this, the hospital staff decided, was a series of minor miracles. I knew it wasn't. It was the result of one great miracle, that moment in which I experienced God's love.

I had labored long, sometimes very discouraged, in an effort to receive Christ's work "in an honest and good heart, and bring forth fruit with patience" (Luke 8:15). Too often it seemed that patience itself was to be the chief fruitage. Then, in a moment of extremity, when I could do nothing of myself, when I had no time to labor, or pray, or even think, the fruitage appeared as instant grace — "Lo, I am with you always."

And He was.

ELAINE ST. JOHNS

The darkness now seems absolute. Men before us have forgotten that it hides the morning star.
Irwin Edman

Love comforteth like sunshine after rain.
William Shakespeare

Broken Things
VANCE HAVNER

God uses broken things. It takes broken soil to produce a crop, broken clouds to give rain, broken grain to give bread, broken bread to give strength. It is the broken alabaster box that gives forth perfume.... It is Peter, weeping bitterly, who returns to greater power than ever.

The Butterfly

JONI EARECKSON

Just before Christmas that year, Donald and I had our first argument. We'd been spending a lot of time together, and I began to become possessive. I was even upset when he had to work. I wanted to spend all my time with him; I wanted his life to center around me.

When pretty young girls from church or youth groups came to visit, I was jealous when he laughed and chatted with them. I became envious that I wasn't on my feet to compete for his attention....

Donald reacted vocally and forcefully. He reminded me that I was acting foolish — like a possessive schoolgirl. I told him I was sorry, that I wouldn't be so demanding of his time and affections; but for some reason, I'd still give in to these unreasonable fears.

Donald decided we both needed a vacation from each other, so he planned to take a trip to Europe in January, 1972. I resisted, taking his plans as a personal rebuke, as if he wanted to get away from me for some reason....

When he returned from Europe, he exploded into the house. "I missed you so much, I couldn't wait to get back," he exclaimed. He did come back — more loving and sensitive than ever.

Donald and I began talking about the possibility of my being healed. Until now, I'd accepted my situation. But my desire to be a complete woman led me to fiercely claim promises I felt the Lord had put in His Word for me. *After all*, I reasoned, *He allows us to have experiences of suffering and sickness to teach us. I've learned an enormous amount through my accident. But now that I've learned what He had for me to learn, He might heal me!* This was to be a new adventure of faith — the next phase of spiritual development for me....

"We're absolutely convinced that God wants me healed!" I told Diana.

"Joni, this whole thing is getting out of hand. You're twisting God's arm — blackmailing Him. You're not being realistic about this," she replied.

"Diana, I'm surprised that you'd say that. I thought you'd have more faith than that. You must have faith that God really does want to heal me," I said by way of rebuke....

With all the faith, devotion, and spiritual commitment we could discover through our own inner resources, Donald and I prayed and trusted.

I wasn't anticipating immediate healing, but expected a slow recovery, since my rehabilitation alone had taken nearly two years. It was logical to think God would restore me gradually, I reasoned.

But after several attempts and many healing services, it became obvious that I wasn't going to be healed. I was able to accept the reality of the situation, but I was frustrated — probably more for Donald than myself. Donald was quiet, yet intense. He seemed to be questioning everything, reevaluating all that had happened. It was awkward, especially for him, after pinning so much to that prayer of faith which went "unanswered." His introspection was guarded, and he began spending more time away from me. I resented this, again jealous of his time....

Then one day when Donald came, I sensed an awkward quiet, a tenseness. Finally, in a low voice, he said, "Joni, I'm going to be counseling this summer up in New York at a *Young Life* camp. I'm leaving tomorrow. I just wanted to come and say good-bye."

I thought, *That's good. Things have been a bit sour in our relationship lately. We both need a breather from each other — like the Europe trip.* But I was puzzled about the decisive inflection Donald gave to the word *good-bye*.

"What do you mean, good-bye? You'll be gone for several weeks, but —"

"No, Joni. This is it. I'm sorry. We never should have allowed this relationship to develop the way it has. I never should have kissed you. We never should have shared the things we shared. We never should have talked and dreamed of marriage. It was all a mistake."

"A mistake! What do you mean? You were the one who encouraged me! I was the one who didn't want to get involved. You've kissed me and held me. I went from fear to hope because you told me you loved me and wanted us to build a life together! Donald — I've shared things so deeply with you — more than I've shared with my own family. And you're just going to walk away, just like that? Now you're saying it's a mistake — that you were just leading me along?" My voice faltered as I desperately tried to put words and thoughts together.

Hot tears of rage and frustration made me want to throw myself on him and beat him with my fists. All I could do was sit there and sob.

"I wasn't leading you along, I swear it," Donald said firmly. "I sincerely thought I could do it. But I was wrong. It's impossible. It's all a mistake."

"Oh, dear God, what is this? Is it really happening?" Panic swept over me as I thought of Donald standing across the room saying good-bye. *What happened?* He came into my life and made me feel so attractive and useful — a *woman*. I didn't think anyone would ever care for me as much as he had. I didn't think it possible I could love anyone as deeply as I loved him.

I tried to stop crying. "Maybe you need time to reconsider —"

"No, Joni. I've thought seriously about what I'm doing. There's no turning back. It's over. I'm sorry." With that, he turned and walked to the door.

"Donald! Don't leave me! Donald, wait!"

"Good-bye, Joni," he said quietly and closed the door behind him.

"No! Oh, my God — why are You letting this happen? Why are You hurting me like this?"

I'd been warned not to let my feelings for Donald get out of hand. Jay and Diane had urged me many times to be careful, but I didn't listen. Now my hopes and dreams for marriage were hopelessly crushed....

How can I describe my feelings? For a year my mind had been working toward fulfillment of an ideal — my marriage to Donald; I had believed that our plans were part of God's perfect will for us. Then, in one brief day, my dream disintegrated before my eyes so completely that there was not a flicker of hope that it could be revived....

It was hard for me to accept the fact that Donald was not God's will, God's best for me. "But, Lord, if not Donald, I believe You have someone or something better for me. I will trust You to bring it into my life." I recalled hearing a preacher say *God never closes a door without opening a window — He always gives us something better when He takes something away....*

One day, while sitting outside in my wheelchair, I was quietly reflecting over these thoughts. *Lord*, I prayed, *I wish I could have seen this earlier — wish I'd have remembered that Your grace is sufficient for me.* As I sat there on the quiet wooded lawn, verse after verse came to mind to comfort me. *Please, Lord, make Yourself real to me just now.*

Peace of mind and inner joy flooded my mind and soul. Then I looked up. Almost as a symbol of God's love and reassurance, a butterfly from high among the trees fluttered within inches of me. It was both startling and beautiful....

It was a slow transition, but not as difficult as I had expected. I saw Donald in a new light, with greater understanding. He had done what was right and best, even if it hurt us both, for I know now that it hurt him as much as it hurt me.

We were both blind to the serious consequences of what such a relationship would mean. When we're in love, our love takes expression in actions. If there is nowhere to go in reality, then wishful thinking and fantasy convince us that "everything will work out." People warn us, but we choose not to believe them....

I look back now and thank God for our relationship. There are so many things I never would have learned if Donald had not come into my life and left me, and so I thank the Lord for this experience. I'm especially grateful God helped me deal with our separation without lingering feelings of bitterness or despair.

I even accepted Donald's new love with honest joy that he, too, had at last found God's perfect will for his life. At Bible study one evening, a friend came up to me. Hesitantly, he said, "Uh — Joni, I want to tell you something before you hear it from someone else."

"Jimmy, you don't have to say anything more. I know."

"You do? You've already heard that Donald is engaged? How?"

"I don't know," I smiled. "I guess I just knew it, that's all."

I was shocked at how easily God helped me meet what should have been a hurtful, difficult meeting. And when Donald brought Sandy, a beautiful, young widow who had lost her husband in an accident, to Bible study three weeks later, we were seated next to one another.

She knew about me. In any other situation, this would have been awkward, to say the least. But I turned to her, a tall, lovely woman whose dark features complemented Donald's own good looks, and said, "Sandy, I'm really glad to meet you. I want you to know how genuinely happy I am for you and Donald...."

Friends and family members who knew how deeply Donald and I had cared for one another were amazed at my attitude. They had expected me to fall apart. And I probably would have gone to pieces if I had not allowed God to handle the situation.

I really began to see suffering in a new light — not as trials to avoid, but as opportunities to "grab," because God gives so much of His love, grace, and goodness to those who do.

My life changed more during the last half of 1972 than any other period of my life — even my previous five years in the chair.

When Donald walked out of my life, there was no one in whom I could put my trust — except God. And since the Lord had always proved Himself faithful before, I trusted Him now.

Look on the Sunny Side

HELEN STEINER RICE

There are always two sides,
    the GOOD and the BAD,
The DARK and the LIGHT,
    the SAD and the GLAD —
But in looking back over
    the GOOD and the BAD
We're aware of the number
    of GOOD THINGS we've had —
And in counting our blessings
    we find when we're through
We've no reason at all
    to complain or be blue —
So thank God for GOOD things
    He has already done;
And be grateful to Him
    for the battles you've won,
And know that the same God
    who helped you before
Is ready and willing
    to help you once more —
Then with faith in your heart
    reach out for God's Hand
And accept what He sends,
    though you can't understand —
For OUR FATHER in heaven
    always knows what is best,
And if you trust in His wisdom
    your life will be blest,
For always remember
    that whatever betides you,
You are never alone
    for God is beside you.

What God Hath Promised

ANNIE JOHNSON FLINT

God hath not promised
    Skies always blue,
Flower-strewn pathways
    All our lives through;
God hath not promised
    Sun without rain,
Joy without sorrow,
    Peace without pain.

But God hath promised
    Strength for the day,
Rest for the labor,
    Light for the way,
Grace for the trials,
    Help from above,
Unfailing sympathy,
    Undying love.

Steady

DAVID A. REDDING

Steady me
Now, my Father,
With faith that goes
A little farther
Into the night.
Brace my belief,
Make me a good traveler
In rough weather,
So this trouble
I'm having
Will not seem like
The last straw,
Only a mean time.
Show me how to let
My grief
Open up for faith —
Wide enough for the sky
To fall in,
Full of
God.

Amen.

Put Your Burden on the Lord

HANNAH WHITALL SMITH

I knew a Christian lady who had a very heavy temporal burden. It took away her sleep and her appetite, and there was danger of her health breaking down under it. One day, when it seemed especially heavy, she noticed lying on the table near her a little tract called "Hannah's Faith." Attracted by the title, she picked it up and began to read it, little knowing, however, that it was to create a revolution in her whole experience. The story was of a poor woman who had been carried triumphantly through a life of unusual sorrow. She was giving the history of her life to a kind visitor on one occasion, and at the close the visitor said feelingly, "Oh, Hannah, I do not see how you could bear so much sorrow!" "I did not bear it," was the quick reply; "the Lord bore it for me." "Yes," said the visitor, "that is the right way. We must take our troubles to the Lord." "Yes," replied Hannah, "but we must do more than that: we must *leave* them there. Most people," she continued, "take their burdens to Him, but they bring them away with them again, and are just as worried and unhappy as ever. But I take mine, and I leave them with Him, and come away and forget them. If the worry comes back, I take it to Him again; and I do this over and over, until at last I just forget I have any worries, and am at perfect rest."

My friend was very much struck with this plan, and resolved to try it. The circumstances of her life she could not alter, but she took them to the Lord, and handed them over into His management; and then she believed that He took it, and she left all the responsibility and the worry and anxiety with Him. As often as the anxieties returned, she took them back, and the result was that, although the circumstances remained unchanged, her soul was kept in perfect peace in the midst of them. She felt that she had found out a practical secret; and from that time she sought never to carry her own burdens, nor to manage her own affairs, but to hand them over, as fast as they arose, to the Divine Burden-bearer.

This same secret, also, which she had found to be so effectual in her outward life, proved to be still more effectual in her inward life, which was in truth evermore utterly unmanageable. She abandoned her whole self to the Lord, with all that she was and all that she had, and, believing that He took that which she had committed to Him, she ceased to fret and worry, and her life became all sunshine in the gladness of belonging to Him. It was a very simple secret she found out: only this, that it was possible to obey God's commandment contained in those words, "Be careful for nothing; but in everything by prayer and supplication, with thanksgiving, let your requests be made known unto God"; and that, in obeying it, the "peace of God which passeth all understanding shall keep your hearts and minds through Christ Jesus."

Truly the light is sweet, and a pleasant thing it is for the eyes to behold the sun.

Ecclesiastes 11:7, King James Version

Milton's Prayer for Patience

ELIZABETH LLOYD HOWELL

Thy glorious face
Is leaning toward me; and its holy light
Shines in upon my lonely dwelling
        place, —
    And there is no more night.

This Too Will Pass Away

HELEN STEINER RICE

If I can endure for this minute
Whatever is happening to me,
No matter how heavy my heart is
Or how "dark" the moment may be —
If I can but keep on believing
What I know in my heart to be true,
That "darkness will fade with the morning"
And that THIS WILL PASS AWAY, TOO —
Then nothing can ever disturb me
Or fill me with uncertain fear,
For as sure as NIGHT BRINGS THE
        DAWNING
"MY MORNING" is bound to appear.

Do Not Worry

GEORGE MACDONALD

It has been well said that no man ever sank under the burden of the day. It is when tomorrow's burden is added to the burden of today that the weight is more than a man can bear. Never load yourselves so, my friends. If you find yourselves so loaded, at least remember this: it is your own doing, not God's. He begs you to leave the future to Him, and mind the present.

Night

SARA TEASDALE

Stars over snow,
    And in the west a planet
Swinging below a star —
    Look for a lovely thing and you will
        find it,
It is not far —
    It never will be far.

Wonder Lies in a Round Rainbow

CARYL PORTER

That year I was ten. My father was the minister of a small church in a Midwestern town. This was already my third school, and I was in the fifth grade. I hoped we wouldn't have to move again.

One day Celia spoke to me. She was the jeweler's daughter. They lived in a big white house and went to the stone church on their side of town.

"See my diamond ring?" Tossing her long black hair like a restless pony, she stretched out her hand. On her little finger was a thin gold band set with a diamond. Colors flashed, and I saw the sky and the green of leaves reflected in the stone.

"It's only a little one." She tossed her hair again. "Daddy says I can have a big one when I graduate from high school." I couldn't think of anything to say. Celia laughed and walked away with two of her friends.

One day after school I told my father, "I don't have any friends." I knew I was going to cry and before I knew what I was saying, I sobbed, "Celia has a diamond ring." He was sitting at the desk in his big, high-backed chair. "Come, Caryl." He motioned to the chair across from him. "Come, let us read together."

He handed me a volume of German poetry. I took the heavy brown book. It smelled of old leather and its thin pages made soft whispering sounds as I turned them. Through my tears I began to read aloud.

"That is good, Caryl," my father said, "but turn the *r* more on your tongue. Like a bird's note."

All the while my father and I read, I knew he was seeing, from some window of his memory, towers on the Rhine, the flowing river; breathing the golden air of his homeland. I looked at the rows of books on the walls, thinking that my father knew every-thing in all of them. I wondered whether someday I would acquire all knowledge available to mankind as he had done.

That year my mother and I wore clothes that came in missionary boxes. Mother did not enjoy sewing, but she altered the clothes so we could wear them. She cut down a gray coat for me. It was the right length when she finished, but it was broad in the shoulders and roomy in the sleeves. She pinned a red flower on the lapel.

The dresses I wore to school were sometimes crepe or satin. I knew I was different. The other girls knew it, too. But in the evenings my father would wind up the old phonograph and put on a record. He would smile at my mother and me and say, "Now. Mozart." Then everything was all right, and we were safe there together with the music, with one another.

One spring day the girls were talking about Celia's birthday party. "Remember the clown last year?" one girl said. "I love circus parties!"

"I liked the one before that when they took us all to the movies," said another girl. "What is it going to be this year, Celia?"

Celia laughed. "It's a secret," she said, looking at us as we stood there in a ring around her. "It's going to be the best one of all. I'm sending the invitations in the mail. Everybody's invitation will come in the mail."

I told my mother about it. I told her I wished I could have a new dress for the party. A real dress. A dress of my own. "What can I give Celia?" I asked my mother. What can you give a girl who has a diamond ring?

I did not get a new dress. Not really. Mother cut down a white cotton and I felt almost right in it. She made an apron and helped me embroider Celia on the pocket in little blue letters. I thought it was beautiful.

At school the girls talked about the invitations they had received. I heard them talking to each other, but they would change the subject when I came near. I had a sick feeling that Celia was not going to ask me, that I would be the only one not going to her party.

But she seemed friendly to me. She said, "Caryl, I wish I could write a poem like the one you wrote. The one Miss Jameson read in class yesterday."

I hoped again. If she liked my poem, maybe she liked me, too. Three days before the party I called to my mother when I came home from school. "Mother, has my invitation come yet?"

Father answered. "Your mother is not at home, *Liebchen*. There was no mail." As he looked at me, he seemed to know what I was thinking. "Do this for me, please," he said. "I have not yet seen the new dress. Put it on, that I may see how you look in it."

I went to my room and put on the white dress. I combed my straight hair and stared at myself, solemn and pale in the shadowy mirror. Then I went downstairs and stood before my father.

"Turn around." I revolved before him slowly. "Like a flower," he said. "Like a snowdrop. But are those the shoes to wear with such a dress?" I wore my brown oxfords. "Come," he said, "come." Together we went down into the town.

When my mother came home, I heard them talking, but I couldn't hear all they said. I was in my room with my new shoes. I had never had black patent-leather slippers before. I stroked the surface of them, mirror bright. I smelled the fresh new smell of them. I felt them smooth and strong against the skin of my fingers, and then, princess-like on my feet. For my father I would have walked on swords, like the little mermaid. But in my new shoes there were only shafts of love.

On the day of the party my invitation still had not come. That Saturday afternoon was balmy with spring. I put on my white dress and my new shoes and sat on the back porch to wait for the mailman. Celia's package was beside me. My mother came out and stood by me.

"Do you suppose I will ever have a dia-mond ring?" I asked her. I took her hand, the one with the ring on it, and looked into the diamond. It was smaller than Celia's and I could not see the myriad colors I had seen in Celia's ring; only a hint of red, a shadow of blue.

Then I saw Mr. Elliot, the mailman, walk past the corner. I went into the house and watched from the hall window. He didn't even pause. He walked right by our mail-box. And then I knew for sure.

I went up to my room and shut the door. Tearing the wrapping off Celia's apron, I crumpled it into a ball and threw it on the floor. I took off my white dress and put on my Saturday clothes. I started to take off my new shoes, but then the tears came. I lay on my bed with my face in the pillow and I cried for a long time. My throat hurt and it was hard to breathe. After a while, though, the tears stopped. I smoothed out the apron, washed my face, and went down to the back porch again.

Soon my father came out and placed a bowl of soapy water beside me. He laid a piece of an old woolen mitten on the step. I had worn those mittens the year I was four. Mother had knit them. Then he put a wooden bubble pipe on my lap. I looked at it and held it against my face. The wood was smooth and tan, and it touched me comfortably, like my father's hand.

I dipped into the soapsuds and blew a family of small bubbles which flew away on the soft wind. The bubble pipe tasted woody and tart, faintly tinged with soap.

Holding the woolen mitten on my left hand, I began to blow a large bubble. Evenly letting out my breath in tiny wisps of air, I watched it grow. There were little windows in it. When it was ripe, I flicked it carefully from the bowl of my pipe to the piece of wool and held it while it quivered and shim-mered. There would never again be one just like it. I made it myself, and when it left me it would go where all bubbles go.

As I looked at it, just before it burst, I saw the most lovely colors. I saw the sky and the

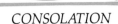

budding trees. I saw the back door of my house, and although I did not see my parents, I knew they were there. I saw all the fragile wonders of the world. And when at last my bubble burst, I felt the cool and gentle moisture on my cheek.

The Miracle of Love

JOHN KENDRICK BANGS

I never knew a night so black
Light failed to follow on its track.
I never knew a storm so gray
It failed to have its clearing day.
I never knew such bleak despair
That there was not a rift somewhere.
I never knew an hour so drear
Love could not fill it full of cheer!

The Magic of a Smile

ALICE JOYCE DAVIDSON

A smile is
a magic thing

you can keep it
and pass it on to others
at the same time

a smile can
erase sadness
alleviate loneliness
and even cure a headache

a smile is
a ray of sun
a show of love
a gift that comes right back to you
a blessing from above!

Angel's Hand

ERNEST TEMPLE HARGROVE

The gloom of the world is but a shadow. Behind it, and yet within our reach, is joy. There is radiance and glory in darkness could we but see; and to see we have only to look. Life is so generous a giver, but we, judging its gifts by their covering, cast them away as ugly, or heavy, or hard. Remove the covering and you will find beneath it a living splendor woven of love, by wisdom, with power. Welcome it, grasp it, and you touch the angel's hand that brings it to you. Everything that we call a trial, a sorrow, or a duty — believe me, that angel's hand is there; the gift is there, and the wonder of an overshadowing Presence.

Beware of desperate steps; the darkest day,
Lived till tomorrow, will have passed away.
William Cowper

God's Delays

GRACE E. TROY

God's delays are not denials,
    He has heard your prayer,
He knows all about your trials,
    He knows your every care.

God's delays are not denials,
    Help is on the way.
He is watching o'er life's dials,
    Bringing forth the day.

God's delays are not denials,
    You will find Him true;
Working through the darkest trials,
    What is best for you.

Symbol

DAVID MORTON

My faith is all a doubtful thing,
 Wove on a doubtful loom —
Until there comes each showery spring,
 A cherry-tree in bloom.

And Christ who died upon a tree
 That death had stricken bare
Comes beautifully back to me
 In blossoms, everywhere.

They...

DOROTHY L. SAYERS

They mocked and railed on Him and smote Him, they scourged and crucified Him. Well, they were people very remote from ourselves, and no doubt it was all done in the noblest and most beautiful manner. We should not like to think otherwise.

Unhappily, if we think about it at all, we must think otherwise. God was executed by people painfully like us, in a society very similar to our own — in the over-ripeness of the most splendid and sophisticated Empire the world has ever seen. In a nation famous for its religious genius and under a government renowned for its efficiency, He was executed by a corrupt church, a timid politician, and a fickle proletariat led by professional agitators. His executioners made vulgar jokes about Him, called Him filthy names, taunted Him, smacked Him in the face, flogged Him with the cat, and hanged Him on the common gibbet — a bloody, dusty, sweaty, and sordid business.

...It is curious that people who are filled with horrified indignation whenever a cat kills a sparrow can hear that story of the killing of God told Sunday after Sunday and not experience any shock at all.

*...if the while I think on thee, dear friend,
All losses are restored and sorrows end.*
William Shakespeare

The Resurrection and the Life

CHARLES L. ALLEN

Here on this earth we are gathered together in families. Our loved ones become inexpressibly precious to us. We live in intimate associations. One gets so close to mother and father, wife or husband, sons and daughters, that they literally become a part of one's life. Then comes a day when a strange change comes over one we love.

He is transformed before our very eyes. The light of life goes out of him. He cannot speak to us nor we to him. He is gone and we are left stunned and heartbroken. An emptiness and loneliness comes into our hearts. We broken-heartedly say, "That one whom I loved is dead." It is such a cold, hopeless thing to realize.

Then, out of the very depths of our despair, like the melody of music coming from a mighty organ, like the refreshing sound of rippling waters, comes that marvelous declaration of our Lord. "I am the resurrection, and the life: he that believeth in me, though he were dead, yet shall he live: and whosoever liveth and believeth in me shall never die."

Then we know! We *know* we have not lost our loved ones who have died. We have been separated, and so long as we live there will be an empty place left in our hearts. To some extent, the loneliness will always be there. But when we really know that one is not forever lost, it does take away the sorrow. There is a vast difference between precious memories, loneliness, the pain of separation, on the one hand, and a sorrow that ruins and blights our lives, on the other hand.

When my heart was seamed with sorrow and I thought the sun could never shine again, my church drew me to the Friend of all the weary and whispered to me the hope of another morning, eternal and tearless.
William H. Boddy

The Message

MARJORIE HOLMES

Oh God, my God, you have taken my mother away and I am numb with shock.

I see her apron still hanging behind the kitchen door. I see her dresses still in the closet, and her dear shoes there upon the floor.

Her house is filled with her presence. The things she so recently used and touched and loved. The pans in the cupboard. The refrigerator still humming and recent with her food. The flowers she had cut still bright in their bowl upon the table.

How quickly you called her, how mercifully. She simply stopped what she was doing and looked up — and you were there.

Golden Rays of Hope

ALICE JOYCE DAVIDSON

When your heart is sorely aching,
When you've too much to endure,
When you're weary of your burdens
And you're looking for a cure...
Put your faith in God who loves you
And with golden rays of hope,
He will comfort you and give you strength
To climb the steepest slope!

A More Enduring Light

SENECA

Do not grudge your brother his rest. He has at last become free, safe and immortal, and ranges joyous through the boundless heavens; he has left this lowlying region and has soared upwards to that place which receives in its happy bosom the souls set free from the chains of matter. Your brother has not lost the light of day, but has obtained a more enduring light. He has not left us, but has gone on before.

When Jesus comes, the shadows depart.
Author Unknown

The Empty Tomb

EUGENIA PRICE

Before dawn on Sunday, the first day of the new week, three sorrowing women hurried through the still silent streets of Jerusalem. They carried boxes of aromatic spices and vials of oil and rose water. This would be the last thing they could do for Him, whom they loved so deeply.

Mary, His mother, walked between Magdalene and Salome, leaning on them for strength. As they trudged across the wide field outside the city, toward the garden tomb, His mother murmured over and over:

"Who will roll the stone from the mouth of the tomb for us?"

The two women with her could only press her arm and answer her nothing. They didn't know either. But go they must, all of them. They were driven by their hearts.

"Surely the guards will help us," Magdalene said finally, when Mary kept repeating her piteous question. There wasn't much more hope of help from the tough Roman soldiers, but they had to try.

His dear body must be cared for by loving hands.

Down the flower-bordered path to the tomb, they walked single file now, expecting to be halted any moment by the gruff voice of one of the soldiers stationed at the tomb.

A bird began to wake up in the trees above them.

Still no other sound in the quiet, fragrant garden. Magdalene walked in front, down the path. She saw it first!

The stone was rolled away.

His mother stumbled, then lifted her heavy mourning veil to see more clearly. Magdalene and Salome threw back their veils, too. Slowly the three women moved toward the open grave.

It smelled of the spices and ointments with which Nicodemus and Joseph had rubbed His body. Magdalene stooped to look inside. Then she ventured in all the way, the others following her.

Salome screamed!

There, to their right, sat a young man dressed in a snow-white robe.

"Do not be terrified!" The young man's voice was quiet and reassuring. "You are looking for Jesus of Nazareth, who was crucified."

"Yes!"

"He is risen! He is not here — see the place where they laid Him!" His young voice echoed exultantly in the empty tomb. "But go now, tell His disciples — and Peter — that He precedes you into Galilee."

"Galilee?" His mother whispered.

"Yes, there you will see Him, just as He told you."

Then the young man was gone. The women hurried outside, their hearts pounding. The trees seemed filled with awakened birds now.

"Go back to rest awhile," Magdalene urged Mary. "I will run ahead to tell Peter and John!"

"What's the matter with you, woman?" Peter rubbed his eyes, forcing himself awake. "What's there to make you beat on a man's door like that?"

"They — they've taken the Lord out of the tomb!" Magdalene blurted. "Or, He's risen as He said — His mother and Salome and I were just there and He's gone!"

"What?" John demanded, joining them.

"It's true, and we do not know where they have laid Him!"

Both men ran all the way to the garden tomb. Younger and lighter on his feet, John reached the grave first, and looked inside. Peter pounded up behind him, panting.

"What do you see, John?" he cried.

"He's gone, Peter! But His grave linen is still there!"

Peter pushed past John and went inside the empty tomb. There were the linens — and the handkerchief which had covered His face and head, still wrapped as though it had never been disturbed!

"Where is He?" Mary demanded, when she, too, had reached the tomb again.

The two disciples did not answer her, but walked away home, not knowing what to think. Knowing only that now they did not even have His body!

Magdalene stood alone in the spring sunlight which filtered through the tall cedar trees and picked out the dew which still clung to the rows of pale blue flowers along the path to the tomb. When she and the other women had seen the white-robed young man earlier, their hearts had almost lost the dread weight. Now, she didn't know what to think. After all, Peter and John were two of His closest disciples. If they just turned and went home, what was she to think?

The weight rolled back on her heart. Was she to be deprived of even this last chance to show Him her love, her gratitude for all He had done for her?

For several minutes she stood like a helpless child, weeping. Then her heart drew her down toward the entrance to the empty tomb once more. Had the grief become too much for her mind? She clutched her head with both hands.

There, one sitting at the head, and one at the foot of the place where they had laid Him, were two angels in white. Together, as one lovely voice, they said to her:

"Woman, why are you crying?"

"Because they have taken away my Lord and I do not know what they have done with Him!" she sobbed.

Suddenly the tomb seemed to stifle her. She turned and flung herself out into the clear, sweet air. She breathed deeply, filled with revulsion at the thought of the blood- and spice-encrusted tomb!

Outside there was light, and it drew her to itself. The sweet scent of lilacs and white myrtle gave her the earth again and with it, life.

But what was her life now, with the Master gone? How could she ever believe in anything good again? All He had ever done was good. All He had ever been was kind and unselfish and good. All He had ever done was to give new life to twisted, scarred creatures like herself. All He had ever done was to heal and bless and forgive. Now, she had seen with her own tormented eyes all they had done to Him!

Again her weeping filled the quiet garden.

Suddenly she knew someone else was there. She whirled around and heard the same question the two angels had asked her inside the tomb!

"Woman, why are you crying? Whom do you seek?"

It must be the gardener, she thought absently. But it was someone, and she did need help.

"Sir, if you've carried Him away, tell me where you've put Him, and I'll take Him!"

"Mary!" Jesus' voice spoke her name tenderly, reassuringly.

She threw back her veil and looked full in His face. It was He! Everything stood still.

"Master! My Master!"

He *was* alive! Walking the earth, with His goodness and gentleness and love. Her Saviour was alive! She dropped to her knees, and reached for His hand to kiss it and bathe it with tears of joy.

"Do not cling to me, Mary," He said gently. "For I have not yet ascended to My Father."

She still had to learn that she had not received Him back, like another Lazarus, merely restored to natural life. She must let Him go first, in order that she could have Him back forever — everywhere she would go. In everything she would do. Magdalene still had this to learn, but she obeyed Him and did not try to touch Him further. He was there. She could see His dear face. She could hear His voice. For now, that was enough.

He was talking to her again. "Go now, Mary, to my brothers and tell them that I said, 'I ascend to My Father and your Father, to My God and your God.'"

Mary went, her feet flying, her heart on wings. He had come to *her* first, calling her name, because she could not bear to give Him up!

Prayer for Your Tomorrow

ROBERT H. SCHULLER

May God bless you with
    a clear dawning,
    a cool morning,
    a warm noonday,
    a golden sunset,
    a gentle twilight,
    a starlit night,
and if clouds should cross your sky,
may God give you the faith to look for
the silver lining.

Have courage for the great sorrows of life and patience for the small ones; and when you have laboriously accomplished your task, go to sleep. God is awake.
Victor Hugo

The Little Match Girl

HANS CHRISTIAN ANDERSEN

It was dreadfully cold, snowing, and turning dark. It was the last evening of the year, New Year's Eve. In this cold and darkness walked a little girl. She was poor and both her head and feet were bare. Oh, she had had a pair of slippers when she left home; but they had been too big for her — in truth, they had belonged to her mother. The little one had lost them while hurrying across the street to get out of the way of two carriages that had been driving along awfully fast. One of the slippers she could not find, and the other had been snatched by a boy who, laughingly, shouted that he would use it as a cradle when he had a child of his own.

Now the little girl walked barefoot through the streets. Her feet were swollen and red from the cold. She was carrying a little bundle of matches in her hand and had more in her apron pocket. No one had bought any all day, or given her so much as a penny. Cold and hungry, she walked through the city; cowed by life, the poor thing!

The snowflakes fell on her long yellow hair that curled so prettily at the neck, but to such things she never gave a thought. From every window of every house, light shone, and one could smell the geese roasting all the way out in the street. It was, after all, New Year's Eve; and this she did think about.

In a little recess between two houses she sat down and tucked her feet under her. But now she was even colder. She didn't dare go home because she had sold no matches and was frightened that her father might beat her. Besides, her home was almost as cold as the street. She lived in an attic, right under a tile roof. The wind whistled through it, even though they had tried to close the worst of the holes and cracks with straw and old rags.

Her little hands were numb from cold. If only she dared strike a match, she could warm them a little. She took one and struck it against the brick wall of the house; it lighted! Oh, how warm it was and how clearly it burned like a little candle. She held her hand around it. How strange! It seemed that the match had become a big iron stove with brass fixtures. Oh, how blessedly warm it was! She stretched out her legs so that they, too, could get warm, but at that moment the stove disappeared and she was sitting alone with a burned-out match in her hand.

She struck another match. Its flame illuminated the wall and it became as transparent as a veil: she could see right into the house. She saw the table spread with a damask cloth and set with the finest porcelain. In the center, on a dish, lay a roasted goose stuffed with apples and prunes! But what was even more wonderful: the goose — although a fork and knife were stuck in its back — had jumped off the table and was waddling toward her. The little girl stretched out her arms and the match burned out. Her hands touched the cold, solid walls of the house.

She lit a third match. The flame flared up and she was sitting under a Christmas tree that was much larger and more beautifully decorated than the one she had seen through the glass doors at the rich merchant's on Christmas Eve. Thousands of candles burned on its green branches, and colorful pictures like the ones you can see in store windows were looking down at her. She smiled up at them; but then the match burned itself out, and the candles of the Christmas tree became the stars in the sky. A shooting star drew a line of fire across the dark heaven.

"Someone is dying," whispered the little girl. Her grandmother, who was dead, was the only person who had ever loved or been kind to the child; and she had told her that a shooting star was the soul of a human being traveling to God.

She struck yet another match against the wall and in its blaze she saw her grandmother, so sweet, so blessedly kind.

"Grandmother!" shouted the little one. "Take me with you! I know you will disappear when the match goes out, just like the warm stove, the goose, and the beautiful Christmas tree." Quickly, she lighted all the matches she had left in her hand, so that her grandmother could not leave. And the matches burned with such a clear, strong flame that the night became as light as day. Never had her grandmother looked so beautiful. She lifted the little girl in her arms and flew with her to where there is neither cold nor hunger nor fear: up to God.

In the cold morning the little girl was found. Her cheeks were red and she was smiling. She was dead. She had frozen to death on the last evening of the old year. The sun on New Year's Day shone down on the little corpse; her lap filled with burned-out matches.

"She had been trying to warm herself," people said. And no one knew the sweet visions she had seen, or in what glory she and her grandmother had passed into a truly new year.

"Lift Up Thine Eyes..."
GRACE NOLL CROWELL

As clearly as a trumpet blown, the shout
Rings out today as certainly as when
They found the Christ had risen, without
        doubt,

To walk once more along the ways of men.
Here in these troubled times the words
        have power
To bring the glorious sunburst of the dawn
That was delayed through many a
        darkened hour —
They bid us hopefully move up and on.

The Christ is risen! Rejoicing voices spell
The hope of earth and heaven through each
        word.
Oh, may we go on joyous feet to tell
The blessed news to those who have not
        heard!
Dear anxious ones, lift up your eyes and see
The assurance of our immortality.

It's Me Again, God
HELEN STEINER RICE

REMEMBER ME, GOD?
I come every day
Just to talk with You, Lord,
And to learn how to pray...
You make me feel welcome,
You reach out Your hand,
I need never explain
For YOU understand...
I come to You frightened
And burdened with care
So lonely and lost
And so filled with despair,
And suddenly, Lord,
I'm no longer afraid,
My burden is lighter
And the dark shadows fade...
Oh, God, what a comfort
To know when I seek You
YOU WILL ALWAYS BE THERE!

Truth

IT WAS IN the early years of my ministry when it happened. At first it was almost impossible. Then it became alarming. I was running out of steam. It was the darkest moment in my life.

Longingly, I recalled my college days when I became a Christian, when I wanted more than anything else to serve Jesus Christ. He was my Lord and my Savior. He was the very meaning of my life, and my ambition was to spend my future telling people how wonderful He was. There was no end to my enthusiasm in those days!

But now, I felt empty inside.

I couldn't understand it. Here I was, successful by all the usual standards, the pastor of a large and growing church, respected as a preacher and a teacher of God's Word. I had accomplished much of what I had set out to do, and now I had to continue in that direction. Why did the road ahead of me look so bleak, so gray? There were still so many men and women who didn't know Him. There was still work for me to do. What happened to all my eagerness?

It was summer and I had some time off, so I decided to go to the seashore and study. Alone. Well, not really. I wanted to be alone — with God. We had things to talk about. I wasn't sure what they were, but I knew I needed to be alone with Him for a while.

I was lying in the sand one day, feeling the sun warming me down to my bones, comforted by the steady rhythm of the waves curling up on the shore. I had been reading John 10:10 — "I am come that they might have life, and that they might have it abundantly" — when I felt something stirring inside me. I closed my eyes, close to tears, and I began telling God how I felt. There wasn't any light left in me, I told Him. It was all dim and dark. And in the darkness, I couldn't see where I was going, or know what I was supposed to do.

That was when I knew I had to go back to my Bible — back to John 10:10 — and take another look. And there it was! Why hadn't I seen it before?

What John was telling us in this verse is that Christianity is a two-part blessing. When we accept Christ as our Savior, when we open our hearts and lives to Him, we become part of Him. But — He

also becomes part of us! And that second half of the blessing was the one I had overlooked.

I had been doing what a lot of other Christians do. I had been trying to live the way Christ lived — but on my own strength. And I didn't have the power to achieve that goal. I was burned out. Exhausted. Out of steam. And the reason was that I hadn't allowed Christ to live *through me*. I hadn't allowed His strength, His power, His energies to work their way into me.

Now I can look back on those moments of darkness, and thank God for them. Because that was how I discovered an "inner splendor" — a radiance — I had never known before. It constantly brightens my view of the road ahead. It reminds me that the key to abundant living is not what we do for our Lord, but what Our Lord Jesus Christ does in — and *through* — us.

LLOYD JOHN OGILVIE

Can You...

PETER MARSHALL

Can you, by worrying, keep something
unpleasant from happening?
  Do you soften the blow
    ease the burden
      or lessen the pain?
Of course not, but you stand a good chance
of reducing your ability to take it.

Time Is

HENRY VAN DYKE

Too Slow for those who Wait,
Too Swift for those who Fear,
Too Long for those who Grieve,
Too Short for those who Rejoice;

But for those who Love,
  Time is Eternity.

In darkness there is no choice. It is light that enables us to see the difference between things; and it is Christ that gives us light.

Julius Charles Hare

Proof

ETHEL ROMIG FULLER

If radio's slim fingers
    Can pluck a melody
From night and toss it over
    A continent or sea;
If songs, like crimson roses,
    Are culled from thin, blue air,
Why should mortals wonder
    If God can hear their prayer?

God Does Do Such Wonderful Things!

ANGELA MORGAN

God does do such wonderful things!
How can we doubt He'll see us through?
He has proved Himself through a million
  springs,
Yet still we wonder: "What shall we do?"
The world is black with war and woe —
But look where the pussy willows grow,
And hear the songs and see the wings…
God does do such wonderful things!

Unfinished Work

VICTOR HUGO

For half a century I have been writing my thoughts in prose and in verse — history, philosophy, drama, romance, tradition, satire, ode, and song. I have tried all. But I feel I have not said the thousandth part of what is in me. When I go down to the grave I can say, like many others, "I have finished my day's work!" But I cannot say, "I have finished my life." The tomb is not a blind alley; it is a thoroughfare. It closes on the twilight, it opens on the dawn.

Great works are performed not by strength but by perseverance.

Samuel Johnson

A Whole Man

NORMAN VINCENT PEALE

In Tokyo I met an American, an inspiring man, from Pennsylvania. Crippled from some form of paralysis, he was on an around-the-world journey in a wheelchair, getting a huge kick out of all his experiences. I commented that nothing seemed to get him down. His reply was a classic: "It's only my body that is paralyzed. The paralysis never got into my mind."

How many unhappy people suffer the mental paralysis of fear, self-doubt, inferiority and inadequacy! Dark thoughts blind them to the possible outcomes which the mind is able to produce. But optimism infuses the mind with confidence and builds up belief in oneself. Result? The revitalized mind, newly energized, comes to grips with problems. Keep the paralysis of unhealthy thoughts out of that incomparable instrument, your mind.

God Doesn't Expect Us to Do Everything

CHARLIE W. SHEDD

Grandpa was working on the gate when a small boy appeared. He puzzled a while as small boys will. Then he asked, "Whatcha' doin', grandpa?"

To which the aged sage replied, "Sonny, there are five kinds of broken things in this old world.

"There's the kind which, when they are broken, can never be fixed.

"Then there's the kind that'll fix themselves if you leave them alone.

"There's also the kind which are none of my business. Somebody else has got to fix them.

"There's the kind which, when they are broken, you should never worry about. Them only God can fix.

"And then there's the kind I got to fix. That's what I'm doing. Fixin' this gate."

Wouldn't it be fine if my grandchildren could also learn this from me:

> God doesn't expect
> us to do everything.

What We Are

AMY CARMICHAEL

Fragrance is like light. It cannot be hidden. It is like love: intangible, invisible, but always at once recognized. Though it is neither to be touched, nor heard, nor seen, we know that it is there. And its opposite is just as impossible to hide. This brings us to a solemn truth: it is what we *are* that tells.

Reflections

CYRUS E. ALBERTSON

In a puddle by the roadside
Left by the warm, spring rain,
Its waters dark and muddy
With the brown earth stain,
I saw a glorious mountain
That stood up bold and high
Reflected in the water,
With a patch of cloud-decked sky.

Sometimes in folk around me
With burdens, hurts and fears;
Through joyful, happy hours
And often through their tears:
In some loving acts of kindness
As they show how much they care —
In the lives of folk around me
I find God reflected there.

A faithful friend is a sturdy shelter.
He that has found one
Has found a treasure.   Ecclesiasticus 6:14

Making Life Worth While

GEORGE ELIOT

Every soul that touches yours —
Be it the slightest contact —
Gets there from some good;
Some little grace; one kindly thought;
One aspiration yet unfelt;
One bit of courage
For the darkening sky;
One gleam of faith
To brace the thickening ills of life;
One glimpse of brighter skies —
To make this life worthwhile
And heaven a surer heritage.

If You Could Only Know

PHILLIPS BROOKS

You who are letting miserable misunderstandings run on from year to year, meaning to clear them up some day;

You who are keeping wretched quarrels alive because you cannot quite make up your mind that now is the day to sacrifice your pride and kill them;

You who are passing men sullenly upon the street, not speaking to them out of some silly spite, and yet knowing that it would fill you with shame and remorse if you heard that one of those men were dead tomorrow morning;

You who are letting your neighbor starve, till you hear that he is dying of starvation;

Or letting your friend's heart ache for a word of appreciation or sympathy, which you mean to give him someday;

If you only could know and see and feel, all of a sudden, that *"the time is short,"* how it would break the spell! How you would go instantly and do the thing which you might never have another chance to do.

A person completely wrapped up in himself makes a small package.   Harry Emerson Fosdick

Upon every face is written the record of the life the man has led; the prayers, the aspirations, the disappointments, all he hoped to be and was not — all are written there; nothing is hidden, nor indeed can be.   Elbert Hubbard

The Significant Hours

ALBERT SCHWEITZER

I always think that we live, spiritually, by what others have given us in the significant hours of our life. These significant hours do not announce themselves as coming, but arrive unexpected. Nor do they make a great show of themselves; they pass almost unperceived. Often, indeed, their significance comes home to us first as we look back, just as the beauty of a piece of music or of a landscape often strikes us first in our recollection of it. Much that has become our own in gentleness, modesty, kindness, willingness to forgive, in veracity, loyalty, resignation under suffering, we owe to people in whom we have seen or experienced these virtues at work, sometimes in a great matter, sometimes in a small. A thought which had become an act sprang into us like a spark, and lighted a new flame within us.

Whatever of love has touched a man's life has been touched by God.   Eugenia Price

My Friends

ELIZABETH WHITTEMORE

My friends are little lamps to me,
    Their radiance warms and cheers my
       ways,
And all the pathway dark and lone
    Is brightened by their rays.

I try to keep them bright by faith,
    And never let them dim with doubt;
For every time I lose a friend
    A little lamp goes out.

Something That Grows

DOROTHY L. SAYERS

"The Kingdom of Heaven," said the Lord Christ, "is among you." But what, precisely, is the Kingdom of Heaven? You cannot point to existing specimens, saying, "Lo, here!" or "Lo, there!" You can only experience it. But what is it like, so that when we experience it we may recognize it? Well, it is a change, like being born again and re-learning everything from the start. It is secret, living power — like yeast. It is something that grows, like seed. It is precious like buried treasure, like rich pearl, and you have to pay for it.

The Greatest of These...

ST. PAUL (I CORINTHIANS 13)

Though I speak with the tongues of men and of angels, and have not love, I am become as sounding brass, or a tinkling cymbal.

And though I have the gift of prophecy, and understand all mysteries, and all knowledge; and though I have all faith, so that I could remove mountains, and have not love, I am nothing.

And though I bestow all my goods to feed the poor, and though I give my body to be burned, and have not love, it profiteth me nothing.

Love suffereth long, and is kind; love envieth not; love vaunteth not itself, is not puffed up.

Doth not behave itself unseemly, seeketh not her own, is not easily provoked, thinketh no evil;

Rejoiceth not in iniquity, but rejoiceth in the truth;

Beareth all things, believeth all things, hopeth all things, endureth all things.

Love never faileth: but whether there be prophecies, they shall fail; whether there be tongues, they shall cease; whether there be knowledge, it shall vanish away.

For we know in part, and we prophesy in part.

But when that which is perfect is come, then that which is in part shall be done away.

When I was a child, I spake as a child, I understood as a child, I thought as a child; but when I became a man, I put away childish things.

For now we see through a glass, darkly; but then face to face: now I know in part; but then shall I know even as also I am known.

And now abideth faith, hope, love, these three; but the greatest of these is love.

More Truth and Light

JOHN ROBINSON

I am confident
　　the Lord hath more truth
　　　　and light
　　yet to break forth
　　　　out of His Word.

Simile

CLYTA SHAW

Truth is love —
bright as sunlight
clear as living water
soft as moonlight
old as time
sure as eternity.

The heavens declare the glory of God...
Psalm 19:1, King James Version

From *The Day Christ Was Born*

JIM BISHOP

It had been said by the elders that when the saviour came to earth, he could be expected on a great white cloud, sitting in august kingliness, listening to the trumpets and songs of hosts of angels surrounding his throne as he ruled over heaven and earth. Tonight, the angels seemed to be an afterthought. It was as though his birth had been so insignificant, so humble, that the angels had to come down to summon a few lonely men to go to the stable and worship him.

A stable? God? Could he not at least have been born in the great palace of Herod the King? Or perhaps in the Holy of Holies of the great Temple of Herod? A manger, the angel said. They understood the word. It meant a sort of trough out of which animals ate grain. It would have the sweet odor of old oats and barley, and the sides would be chewed and chipped. A salt cake would lie in the bottom.

The shepherds reached the top of the eminence and walked among the dozing pilgrims of Bethlehem, asking where the Messiah might be found. Most of the men turned away from them in silence. A few asked what Messiah; the shepherds asked if anyone had seen the angels. What angels? Some of the wayfarers were rude: they asked the shepherds if they had become mad through too much grape.

Abuse was not unbearable or new to the herders. They had known it before. Patiently, they continued their rounds, asking here and there and finally confining their questions to this: Where can we find a newborn baby in this town? Someone told them to try the inn. The innkeeper, exhausted with his labors, remembered the young man and pregnant young lady going to the cave beneath the inn.

The shepherds approached timidly. They moved down the path in their sandals, whispering. As they approached the lighted aperture, they crouched and coughed. Joseph came out. He studied them solemnly, without rancor, and the leaders told him that they had seen angels in the valley, and one angel had said that a Messiah had been born this night in the town of David. They had — well, if it wasn't too soon — they had come to worship him.

Mary heard, and told Joseph to permit the men to come in. Joseph had some tools in his hand. His spouse told him that the nights would be too cold to permit the infant to travel until after the circumcision. They would have to continue to live in the stable for eight days. Joseph had gone into town and awakened a carpenter and explained the circumstances. Now he had tools and, with the permission of the owner of the inn, he was using sides of stalls to build a small, almost private room for his Mary and baby.

The shepherds came in, the cowls down off their heads. Their hair was long and ringleted, the beards trembled with murmured prayer, the hands were clasped piously before their chests. In the flickering yellow light of the oil lamp, they saw the childmother, seated on straw. She was looking over the side of an old manger. The men lifted themselves a little on their toes to peer over the sides. Inside was an abundance of white swaddling clothes. An aura of light seemed to radiate from it.

Without looking up, the mother knew that they were trying to see her precious baby, so she stuck a finger into the white cloth and pulled it away from the infant's face. The men looked, with mouths open, and fell to their knees. They adored the baby, and thanked him for coming to save the nation. They recited some of the formal prayers. Joseph, standing aside, was amazed that so many strangers now knew the secret.

The shepherds were torn between wonderment and happiness. This little baby was God and the Son of God, but he was also a helpless, lovable infant. Their hearts welled with joy and the stern, deeply bronzed faces kept melting into big grins, which were quickly erased as the sheep men recalled that they were in the presence of the King of All Kings.

The scene in a chilly manger, warmed by the bodies and breathing of the animals, was, to the shepherds, closer to their hearts than if the Messiah had come on a big cloud with trumpeting angels. They understood babies, and they understood animals and they murmured with delight that God would see fit to come to earth in an abode only slightly less worthy than their own homes in the hills.

They remained kneeling, clasping and un-clasping their hands, and staring at the face of the infant, as though trying to etch on their memories the peaceful scene, the tiny ruddy face, the serenity of the mother, who, by the grace of God, had had her baby with-out pain. They were men of such poverty and humility that their colored threadbare cloaks spoke more eloquently than their ton-gues. Their adoration came from full hearts.

If there was any wonderment in Mary's heart, she did not show it. After a while, the shepherds stood and, in the manner of the Jews, apologized for intruding. They ad-dressed their remarks to Joseph because to speak to Mary would have been immodest. They asked Joseph if he had seen the angels and he said no. They related all that had happened to them in the valley. Joseph shook his head. Mary nodded toward the sleeping baby, as though she and he alone understood that this was only the first of many great world events.

The shepherds left, praising God, and in their joy awakening people to tell them that the promised Messiah had come. Every-thing, they said, had been revealed exactly as the angel in the sky had said it would be. Most of their audience ordered them to go in peace. Thus, if one can say that the place of birth was small, humble, a place of animals and odors, then one can say that the first apostles were the most humble and scorned of men.

The Builders
R.L. SHARPE

Isn't it strange
That princes and kings,
And clowns that caper
In sawdust rings,
And common people
Like you and me
Are builders for eternity?

Each is given a bag of tools,
A shapeless mass,
A book of rules;
And each must make —
Ere life is flown —
A stumbling block
Or a steppingstone.

The Seekers
GRACE NOLL CROWELL

The Holy Word says "Seek and ye shall
    find";
Much undiscovered riches lie ahead:
The soil still holds a further healing power,
The dock is near the nettle. Any hour
The earnest prayerful seeking one may find
Some new resource to benefit mankind.
There is music yet to write that will inspire
The dullest heart. There are words that will
    set fire
In others when great poets pen their lines.
There will be generated light that shines
From unearthed metals, and new warmth
    will glow
From sources which as yet we do not know.
But for these, the sincere seekers on earth's
    sod,
The greatest of all discoveries is God.

From *Walking on Water*

MADELEINE L'ENGLE

We are all asked to do more than we can do. Every hero and heroine of the Bible does more than he would have thought it possible to do, from Gideon to Esther to Mary. Jacob, one of my favorite characters, certainly wasn't qualified. He was a liar and a cheat; and yet he was given the extraordinary vision of angels and archangels ascending and descending a ladder which reached from earth to heaven.

In the first chapter of John's Gospel, Nathanael is given a glimpse of what Jacob saw, or a promise of it, and he wasn't qualified, either. He was narrow-minded and unimaginative, and when Philip told him that Jesus of Nazareth was the one they sought, his rather cynical response was, "Can anything good come out of Nazareth?" And yet it was to Nathanael that Jesus promised the vision of angels and archangels ascending and descending upon the son of man.

Moses wasn't qualified (as I run over my favorite characters in both Old and New Testaments, I can't find one who was in any worldly way qualified to do the job which was nevertheless accomplished); Moses was past middle age when God called him to lead his children out of Egypt, and he spoke with a stutter. He was reluctant and unwilling and he couldn't control his temper. But he saw the bush that burned and was not consumed. He spoke with God in the cloud on Mount Sinai, and afterwards his face glowed with such brilliant light that the people could not bear to look at him.

In a very real sense not one of us is qualified, but it seems that God continually chooses the most unqualified to do his work, to bear his glory. If we are qualified, we tend to think that we have done the job ourselves. If we are forced to accept our evident lack of qualification, then there's no danger that we will confuse God's work with our own, or God's glory with our own.

The Miraculous Staircase

ARTHUR GORDON

Every now and then a reporter comes across a fact, or a set of facts, for which there is no satisfactory or logical explanation. One way to handle such a paradox is to ignore it. Another — more fun — is to let your imagination try to supply the missing ingredients. Then, of course, you are dealing with myth, or legend, or even fiction. But sometimes legend can be a shimmering cloak for truth.

I came across a hidden story like that one time in Santa Fe. I thought about it for a while, and eventually it turned out like this....

On that cool December morning in 1878, sunlight lay like an amber rug across the dusty streets and adobe houses of Santa Fe. It glinted on the bright tile roof of the almost completed Chapel of Our Lady of Light and on the nearby windows of the convent school run by the Sisters of Loretto. Inside the convent, the Mother Superior looked up from her packing as a tap came on her door.

"It's *another* carpenter, Reverend Mother," said Sister Francis Louise, her round face apologetic. "I told him that you're leaving right away, that you haven't time to see him, but he says.... "

"I know what he says," Mother Magdalene said, going on resolutely with her packing. "That he's heard about our problem with the new chapel. That he's the best carpenter in all of New Mexico. That he can build us a staircase to the choir loft despite the fact that the brilliant architect in Paris who drew the plans failed to leave any space for one. And despite the fact that five master carpenters have already tried and failed. You're quite right, Sister; I don't have time to listen to that story again."

"But he seems such a nice man," said Sister Francis Louise wistfully, "and he's out there with his burro, and.... "

"I'm sure," said Mother Magdalene with a smile, "that he's a charming man, and that his burro is a charming donkey. But there's sickness down at the Santo Domingo Pueblo, and it may be cholera. Sister Mary Helen and I are the only ones here who've had cholera. So we have to go. And you have to stay and run the school. And that's that!" Then she called, "Manuela!"

A young Indian girl of twelve or thirteen, black-haired and smiling, came in quietly on moccasined feet. She was a mute. She could hear and understand, but the sisters had been unable to teach her to speak. The Mother Superior spoke to her gently: "Take my things down to the wagon, child. I'll be right there." And to Sister Francis Louise: "You'd better tell your carpenter friend to come back in two or three weeks. I'll see him then."

"Two or three weeks! Surely you'll be home for Christmas?"

"If it's the Lord's will, Sister. I hope so."

In the street, beyond the waiting wagon, Mother Magdalene could see the carpenter, a bearded man, strongly built and taller than most Mexicans, with dark eyes and a smiling, windburned face. Beside him, laden with tools and scraps of lumber, a small gray burro stood patiently. Manuela was stroking its nose, glancing shyly at its owner. "You'd better explain," said the Mother Superior, "that the child can hear him, but she can't speak."

Good-byes were quick — the best kind when you leave a place you love. Southwest, then, along the dusty trail, the mountains purple with shadow, the Rio Grande a ribbon of green far off to the right. The pace was slow, but Mother Magdalene and Sister Mary Helen amused themselves by singing songs and telling Christmas stories as the sun marched up and down the sky. And their leathery driver listened and nodded.

Two days of this brought them to Santo Domingo Pueblo, where the sickness was not cholera after all, but measles, almost as deadly in an Indian village. And so they stayed, helping the harassed Father Sebastian, visiting the dark adobe hovels where feverish brown children tossed and fierce Indian dogs showed their teeth.

At night they were bone-weary, but sometimes Mother Magdalene found time to talk to Father Sebastian about her plans for the dedication of the new chapel. It was to be in April; the archbishop himself would be there. And it might have been dedicated sooner, were it not for this incredible business of a choir loft with no means of access — unless it were a ladder.

"I told the bishop," said Mother Magdalene, "that it would be a mistake to have the plans drawn in Paris. If something went wrong, what could we do? But he wanted our chapel in Santa Fe patterned after the Sainte Chapelle in Paris, and who am I to argue with Bishop Lamy? So the talented Monsieur Mouly designs a beautiful choir loft high up under the rose window, and no way to get to it."

"Perhaps," sighed Father Sebastian, "he had in mind a heavenly choir. The kind with wings."

"It's not funny," said Mother Magdalene a bit sharply. "I've prayed and prayed, but apparently there's no solution at all. There just isn't room on the chapel floor for the supports such a staircase needs."

The days passed, and with each passing day Christmas drew closer. Twice, horsemen on their way from Santa Fe to Albuquerque brought letters from Sister Francis Louise. All was well at the convent, but Mother Magdalene frowned over certain paragraphs. "The children are getting ready for Christmas," Sister Francis Louise wrote in her first letter. "Our little Manuela and the carpenter have become great friends. It's amazing how much he seems to know about us all. . . . "

And what, thought Mother Magdalene, is the carpenter still doing there?

The second letter also mentioned the carpenter. "Early every morning he comes with another load of lumber, and every night he goes away. When we ask him by what authority he does these things, he smiles and says nothing. We have tried to pay him for his work, but he will accept no pay...."

Work? What work? Mother Magdalene wrinkled up her nose in exasperation. Had that softhearted Sister Francis Louise given the man permission to putter around in the new chapel? With firm and disapproving hand, the Mother Superior wrote a note ordering an end to all such unauthorized activities. She gave it to an Indian pottery-maker on his way to Santa Fe.

But that night the first snow fell, so thick and heavy that the Indian turned back. Next day at noon the sun shone again on a world glittering with diamonds. But Mother Magdalene knew that another snowfall might make it impossible for her to be home for Christmas. By now the sickness at Santo Domingo was subsiding. And so that afternoon they began the long ride back.

The snow did come again, making their slow progress even slower. It was late on Christmas Eve, close to midnight, when the tired horses plodded up to the convent door. But the lamps still burned. Manuela flew down the steps, Sister Francis Louise close behind her. And chilled and weary though she was, Mother Magdalene sensed instantly an excitement, an electricity in the air that she could not understand.

Nor did she understand it when they led her, still in her heavy wraps, down the corridor, into the new, as-yet-unused chapel where a few candles burned. "Look, Reverend Mother," breathed Sister Francis Louise. "Look!"

Like a curl of smoke the staircase rose before them, as insubstantial as a dream. Its base was on the chapel floor; its top rested against the choir loft. Nothing else supported it; it seemed to float on air. There were no banisters. Two complete spirals it made, the polished wood gleaming softly in the candlelight. "Thirty-three steps," whispered Sister Francis Louise. "One for each year in the life of our Lord."

Mother Magdalene moved forward like a woman in a trance. She put her foot on the first step, then the second, then the third. There was not a tremor. She looked down, bewildered, at Manuela's ecstatic, upturned face. "But it's impossible! There wasn't time!"

"He finished yesterday," the sister said. "He didn't come today. No one has seen him anywhere in Santa Fe. He's gone."

"But who was he? Don't you even know his name?"

The sister shook her head, but now Manuela pushed forward, nodding emphatically. Her mouth opened; she took a deep, shuddering breath; she made a sound that was like a gasp in the stillness. The nuns stared at her, transfixed. She tried again. This time it was a syllable, followed by another. "Jo-se." She clutched the Mother Superior's arm and repeated the first word she had ever spoken. "Jose!"

Sister Francis Louise blessed herself. Mother Magdalene felt her heart contract. Jose — the Spanish word for *Joseph*. Joseph the Carpenter. Joseph the Master Wood-worker of....

"Jose!" Manuela's dark eyes were full of tears. "Jose!"

Silence, then, in the shadowy chapel. No one moved. Far away across the snow-silvered town Mother Magdalene heard a bell tolling midnight. She came down the stairs and took Manuela's hand. She felt uplifted by a great surge of wonder and gratitude and compassion and love. And she knew what it was. It was the spirit of Christmas. And it was upon them all.

Just a legend? Of course. But all good legends contain a grain of truth, and in this case the irrefutable fact at the heart of the legend is the inexplicable staircase itself.

You may see it yourself in Santa Fe today. It stands just as it stood when the chapel was dedicated almost a century ago — except the banister, which was added later. Tourists stare and marvel. Architects shake their heads and murmur, "Impossible." No one

knows the identity of the designer-builder. All the sisters know is that the problem existed, a stranger came, solved it, and left.

The thirty-three steps make two complete turns without central support. There are no nails in the staircase; only wooden pegs. The curved stringers are put together with exquisite precision, spliced in seven places on the inside and nine on the outside. The wood is said to be a hard-fir variety, nonexistent in New Mexico. School records show that no payment for the staircase was ever made.

Who is real and who is imaginary in this version of the story? Mother Mary Magdalene was indeed the first Mother Superior; she came to Santa Fe by riverboat and covered wagon in 1852. Bishop J. B. Lamy was indeed her bishop. And Monsieur Projectus Mouly of Paris was indeed the absentminded architect.

Sister Francis Louise? Well, there must have been someone like her. And Manuela, the Indian girl, came out of nowhere to help with the embroidery.

The carpenter himself? Ah, who can say?

God Is at the Anvil

LEW SARETT

God is at the anvil, beating out the sun:
Where the molten metal spills,
At his forge among the hills,
He has hammered out the glory of a day
    that's done.

God is at the anvil, welding golden bars:
In the scarlet streaming flame,
He is fashioning a frame
For the shimmering silver beauty of the
    evening stars.

Hope is wishing for a thing to come true; faith is believing that it will come true.

Norman Vincent Peale

Loyalty

HIS NAME IS MR. JOHNNIE WILSON, and my friend, Joyce Blackburn, and I have been blessed to have him look after us, our big yard and our house for almost a decade.

Mr. Johnnie, after more than twenty years in responsible positions in New York, returned to his native St. Simons Island not long before we moved into our new house in the woods. He was on Social Security, but could work as much as we required, considering the simplicity of our daily lives, and it was more than enough to spoil us forever! We retained him in the first place to care for the yard and to do the heavy work in the house. We hit if off, the three of us, from the first meeting. He brought his equally charming wife, Ruby, for a little visit during our first Christmas of sharing our lives, and we have been Ruby-fans, too, ever since.

For a few months, Johnnie did the agreed amount of work for us with enormous care and judgment and sensitivity to our peculiar needs as writers. Then, before either Joyce or I realized it, *he* was adding things. Things such as building two new beautiful bird feeders for our brick wall out back. Next, he surprised us with three wooden bins built to fit into the corner of our big wood box on the back porch — one smaller bin for sunflower seeds and two larger ones for cracked corn and wild bird seed. Before we realized it, Johnnie had begun to keep check on the contents of each bin and, finding them low, would stop at the grocery where we deal to keep the bins replenished. If we happened to be already at work when he got here in the morning, we knew the birds would be fed with the same tender, loving care we try to give them — even to doughnuts for our temperamental mocker, crumbled on top of a certain post feeder, cracked corn in a particular place in the road that winds around our house, and just the right amount of suet cake in the right locations for the woodpeckers and catbirds. One day we discovered that Ruby, Mr. Johnnie's wife, would not mind keeping our shirts and blouses in order, so for years all we've had to do is put a bundle on a wicker table on the porch and in a couple of days, Johnnie comes smiling, swinging hangers filled with clean, beautifully ironed shirts.

Perhaps the strongest bond of all among Johnnie, Joyce, Ruby and me is our mutual dependence on Jesus Christ. Johnnie and Ruby are people of enormous childlike faith and trust. More than once, Johnnie has reminded me of the lilies of the field when I've worried over a deadline or a deluge of mail to be answered.

One Sunday afternoon, as we sat relaxing on our back porch, we heard Johnnie's car drive up the lane. He strode in, dressed to the nines, that melting smile lighting his handsome face, and then quite casually he told us that Dr. Ben "wants to do a little snipping in my throat to see if there's any reason I keep having trouble with hiccups and swallowing."

Of course, as people do, we talked all around the subject of a biopsy and tried to be gay and cheerful and hopeful, but Joyce and I were stunned to the depths of our beings. Johnnie told us two or three funny stories, checked on the bird seed, the Clorox and salt supply for our water conditioner, and left us with a wave and a smile.

He had known for a week that he was entering the hospital the next day. He had seen no reason to worry us!

After an endless day or two, Dr. Ben's terrifying report to us meant long cobalt treatments to shrink the malignant growth in Johnnie's esophagus. Through more than three anxious weeks of daily cobalt treatments at the Brunswick Hospital on the mainland — except for two days when he felt ill by the time he had driven himself back across the marshes — Johnnie came to "work" *smiling*.

Then, just before Christmas, when we were in deep conflict over leaving him to spend the holidays with our parents, he said, with that twinkle in his brown eyes: "Why do you ladies think I set the surgery for now? You've both been through enough worry over this thing. I'm not going to put you through that, too! Go on to your nice parents and don't worry about me. You're the ones always telling me that God is in charge — how about if I tell you the same thing right now? And don't give me any backtalk either!"

As soon as I returned from the holidays, I visited Johnnie in the intensive care unit at the hospital. In the long days and nights of his violent suffering, he managed to show that same giving love and patience to the nurses and doctors. Three times he almost slipped into the "life after life." He will some day, as we all will. But his selfless love toward us has made us so aware of the intensive love of God that I'm finding less and less resistance within myself to all of life's prickly problems. I hear myself complaining less, adjusting more — almost without effort.

I'll never forget the smile and the encouragement on the warm,

brown face of a man who concerned himself about others while facing the distinct possibility of his own death. If Johnnie's loving concern has so changed me, how can we be amazed at the changing power of the love of God?

And, as Mr. Johnnie reminded me, God is the one who's in charge. Always.

EUGENIA PRICE

Always There

HELEN LOWRIE MARSHALL

Bless those folks who are "always there,"
   Steadfast, loyal and true,
Standing by and happy to share
   Your joys and your cares with you.

Those who stand on the side and cheer
   The runners in life's race,
Whose faith supplies the needed boost
   To keep that winning pace.

Bless those backstage people,
   Whose art no plaudits rouse,
But who provide the background
   For those who take the bows.

Bless them all — those quiet ones,
   Steady and staunch and square,
The little matches that light the stars —
   The folks who are "always there."

By friendship you mean the greatest love, the greatest usefulness, the most open communication, the noblest sufferings, the severest truth, the heartiest counsel, and the greatest union of minds of which brave men and women are capable.

Jeremy Taylor

What sweetness is left in life, if you take away friendship? Robbing life of friendship is like robbing the world of the sun. Cicero

Remember

AUTHOR UNKNOWN

Whenever you know a desolate hour
And are steeped in misery,
Remember Christ was lonely too,
In bleak Gethsemane;
Whenever you feel that all of the world
Has turned its back on you,
Remember that Christ knew what it was
To feel abandoned too.

Whenever you feel that your burden
Is greater than you can bear,
Remember He too heartbreakingly knew
A moment of dark despair;
And remembering these things just bear
　　in mind
His victory was finally won
When He bowed His head and humbly
　　said,
"But Thy will, not Mine, be done!"

In the Eye of God

ANNE MORROW LINDBERGH

…I want first of all…to be at peace with myself. I want a singleness of eye, a purity of intention, a central core to my life…. I want, in fact — to borrow from the language of the saints — to live "in grace" as much of the time as possible. I am not using this term in a strictly theological sense. By grace I mean an inner harmony, essentially spiritual, which can be translated into outward harmony…. I would like to achieve a state of inner spiritual grace from which I could function and give as I was meant to in the eye of God.

The Secret

RALPH SPAULDING CUSHMAN

I met God in the morning
　　When my day was at its best,
And His presence came like sunrise,
　　Like a glory in my breast.

All day long the Presence lingered,
　　All day long He stayed with me,
And we sailed in perfect calmness
　　O'er a very troubled sea.

Other ships were blown and battered,
　　Other ships were sore distressed,
But the winds that seemed to drive them
　　Brought to us a peace and rest.

Then I thought of other mornings,
　　With a keen remorse of mind,
When I too had loosed the moorings,
　　With the Presence left behind.

So I think I know the secret,
　　Learned from many a troubled way:
You must seek Him in the morning
　　If you want Him through the day!

A Salute to Trees
HENRY VAN DYKE

Many a tree is found in the wood,
And every tree for its use is good.
Some for the strength of the gnarled root,
Some for the sweetness of flower or fruit,
Some for shelter against the storm,
And some to keep the hearthstone warm.
Some for the roof, and some for the beam,
And some for a boat to breast the storm.
In the wealth of the wood since the world
    began,
The trees have offered their gifts to man.

I have camped in the whispering forest of
    pines,
I have slept in the shadow of olives and
    vines;
In the knees of an oak, at the foot of a palm,
I have found good rest and slumber's balm.
And now, when the morning gilds the
    boughs
Of the vaulted elm at the door of my house,
I open the window and make a salute:
"God bless thy branches and feed thy root!
Thou hast lived before, live after me,
Thou ancient, friendly, faithful tree!"

From *Sheer Joy*
RALPH SPAULDING CUSHMAN

Oh the sheer joy of it!
    Walking with Thee,
Out on the hilltop,
    Down by the sea,
Life is so wonderful,
    Life is so free.

Oh the sheer joy of it!
    Working with God,
Running His errands,
    Waiting His nod.
Building His heaven,
    On common sod.

Hope
AMY CARMICHAEL

Great God of Hope, how green Thy trees,
    How calm each several star.
Renew us; make us fresh as these,
    Calm as those are.

For what can dim his hope who sees,
    Though faintly and afar,
The power that kindles green in trees,
    And light in star?

The Bridge Builder
WILL ALLEN DROMGOOLE

An old man going a lone highway
Came at the evening, cold and gray,
To a chasm vast and wide and steep,
With waters rolling cold and deep.
The old man crossed in the twilight dim,
The sullen stream had no fears for him;
But he turned when safe on the other side,
And built a bridge to span the tide.

"Old man," said a fellow pilgrim near,
"You are wasting your strength with
    building here.
Your journey will end with the ending day,
You never again will pass this way.
You've crossed the chasm, deep and wide,
Why build you this bridge at eventide?"

The builder lifted his old gray head.
"Good friend, in the path I have come,"
    he said,
"There followeth after me today
A youth whose feet must pass this way.
The chasm that was as nought to me
To that fair-haired youth may a pitfall be;
He, too, must cross in the twilight dim —
Good friend, I am building this bridge for
    him."

At Daybreak

AUTHOR UNKNOWN

Every morning lean thine arms awhile
Upon the window sill of heaven
And gaze upon thy Lord.
Then, with the vision in thy heart,
Turn strong to meet thy day.

Abide with Me

HENRY FRANCIS LYTE

Abide with me; fast falls the eventide;
The darkness deepens; Lord, with me
    abide;
When other helpers fail, and comforts flee,
Help of the helpless, oh abide with me.

Hold thou Thy cross before my closing
    eyes;
Shine through the gloom, and point me to
    the skies;
Heaven's morning breaks, and earth's vain
    shadows flee;
In life, in death, O Lord, abide with me.

A Blessing

ST. FRANCIS OF ASSISI

Blessed is the servant who loves his brother
as much when he is sick and useless as when
he is well and can be of service to him. And
blessed is he who loves his brother as well
when he is afar off as when he is by his side,
and who would say nothing behind his back
he might not, in love, say before his face.

You Can Touch Stars

ESTHER BALDWIN YORK

Stars have too long been symbols of the
    unattainable. They should not be so. For
    although our physical hands cannot
    reach them, we can touch them in other
    ways.
Let stars stand for those things which are
    ideal and radiant in life; if we seek
    sincerely and strive hard enough, it is not
    impossible to reach them, even though
    the goals seem distant at the onset.
And how often do we touch stars when we
    find them close by in the shining lives of
    great souls, in the sparkling universe of
    humanity around us!

Take Time

EDGAR A. GUEST

Take time for friendship when you can.
The hours fly swiftly, and the need
That presses on your fellowman
May fade away at equal speed
And you may sigh before the end
That you have failed to play the friend.

Not all life's pride is born of fame;
Not all the joy from work is won.
Too late we hang our heads in shame,
Remembering good we could have done;
Too late we wish that we had stayed
To comfort those who called for aid.

Take time to do the little things
Which leave the satisfactory thought,
When other joys have taken wings,
That we have labored as we ought;
That in a world where all contend,
We often stopped to be a friend.

The glory of friendship is not the outstretched hand, nor the kindly smile nor the joy of companionship; it is the spiritual inspiration that comes to one when he discovers that someone else believes in him and is willing to trust him.

Ralph Waldo Emerson

Thou shalt love thy neighbor as thyself.

Leviticus 19:18

The Unexpected

MARJORIE HOLMES

Thank you, Lord, for these unexpected moments of love.

For the times in life when suddenly we feel your nearness uniting us with other people.

I felt it so keenly yesterday. In a small group of people — not family, not even close friends. Actually, I had never felt any real attachment for any of them, and some I thought rather dull.

But suddenly, sitting around the fire, they became dear — very dear. Qualities I hadn't noticed before became manifest. Kindness, tenderness, gaiety, goodness.

You were suddenly with us, uniting us, your children. Revealing us to each other in a new dimension. Giving us understanding.

I felt my antagonism toward one of them melting, giving way to joy. A new awareness of another came to me; I saw a charm, a loveliness unsensed before.

And as my new-sensed love flowed out to them I felt their love encompassing me. We were brothers and sisters all, needing and wanting each other.

We were your children together around the hearthfire of life. We were your family.

A Ray of Light

FULTON J. SHEEN

Imagine a large circle and in the center of it rays of light that spread out to the circumference. The light in the center is God; each of us is a ray. The closer the rays are to the center, the closer the rays are to one another. The closer we live to God, the closer we are bound to our neighbor.

It was neither preaching nor praying that made a better man of me, but one or two people who believed in me better than I deserved, and I hated to disappoint them. Owen Wister

The Father and His Sons

AESOP

A father had a family of sons who were perpetually quarreling among themselves. When he failed to heal their disputes by his exhortations, he determined to give them a practical illustration of the evils of disunion; and for this purpose he one day told them to bring him a bundle of sticks. When they had done so, he placed the faggot into the hands of each of them in succession, and ordered them to break it in pieces. They tried with all their strength, and were not able to do it. He next opened the faggot, took the sticks separately, one by one, and again put them into his sons' hands, upon which they broke them easily. He then addressed them in these words: "My sons, if you are of one mind, and unite to assist each other, you will be as this faggot, uninjured by all the attempts of your enemies; but if you are divided among yourselves, you will be broken as easily as these sticks."

A friend is one to whom one may pour out all the contents of one's heart, chaff and grain together, knowing that the gentlest of hands will take and sift it, keep what is worth keeping, and with a breath of kindness blow the rest away.

Arabian Proverb

Two at a Fireside

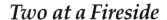

EDWIN MARKHAM

I built a chimney for a comrade old;
    I did the service not for hope or hire:
And then I traveled on in winter's cold,
    Yet all the day I glowed before the fire.

True friendship between two people is infinite and immortal.   Plato

We Have Lived and Loved Together

CHARLES JEFFERYS

We have lived and loved together
    Through many changing years;
We have shared each other's gladness
    And wept each other's tears;
I have known ne'er a sorrow
    That was long unsoothed by thee;
For thy smiles can make a summer
    Where darkness else would be.

Like the leaves that fall around us
    In autumn's fading hours.
Are the traitor's smiles, that darken
    When the cloud of sorrow lowers;
And though many such we've known,
     love.
    Too prone, alas, to range.
We both can speak of one love
    Which time can never change.

We have lived and loved together
    Through many changing years,
We have shared each other's gladness
    and wept each other's tears.
And let us hope the future,
    As the past has been will be:
I will share with thee my sorrows.
    And thou thy joys with me.

I'm going your way, so let us go hand in hand. You help me and I'll help you. We shall not be here very long, for soon death, the kind old nurse, will come back and rock us all to sleep. Let us help one another while we may.   William Morris

Thank You

ROBERT H. SCHULLER

Thank you, Lord:
You are the Light that never goes out.
You are the Eye that never closes,
You are the Ear that is never shut,
You are the Mind that never gives up,
You are the Heart that never grows cold,
    and
You are the Hand that never stops reaching.
Amen.

Devotion

YEARS AGO, when one of our children was away from the Lord and I had reached the point of desperation, the Lord seemed to say to me, "You take care of the possible — and trust me for the impossible."

I had been trying with all my might to do God's work for Him: to convict of sin, create a hunger and thirst for righteousness — in short, to convert. And God was showing me that such things were miracles, and miracles are not in my department. As a mother, my job was to take care of the possible: loving, caring, praying, ministering to, providing for, encouraging. Constantly affirming and encouraging. Yes, these were things I could do.

But still I was concerned. And then the Lord said to me (not audibly, of course), "Get your eyes off the problems, and begin studying the promises."

So I opened my Bible, and there I found:

For I will give you abundant water for your thirst and for your parched fields. And I will pour out my Spirit and my blessings on your children (Isaiah 44:3)

...I will fight those who fight you, and I will save your children (Isaiah 49:25)

The Lord has made the heavens his throne; from there he rules over everything there is (Psalm 103:19)

And all your citizens shall be taught by me, and their prosperity shall be great (Isaiah 54:13)

As I read these promises, I could feel the load lifting from my spiritual shoulders. There was no need for me to worry, because God was in charge and my children were safe in His care. And as I thanked God for trusting me with each one of our children — particularly the one for whom I had been so concerned — I understood that worship and worry cannot dwell together in the same heart. They are mutually exclusive.

RUTH GRAHAM

If You Meet God in the Morning, He'll Go with You Through the Day

HELEN STEINER RICE

"The earth is the Lord's
    and the fullness thereof" —
It speaks of His greatness,
    it sings of His love,
And each day at dawning
    I lift up my heart high
And raise up my eyes
    to the infinite sky…
I watch the night vanish
    as a new day is born,
And I hear the birds sing
    on the wings of the morn,
I see the dew glisten
    in crystal-like splendor
While God, with a touch
    that is gentle and tender,
Wraps up the night
    and softly tucks it away
And hangs out the sun
    to herald a new day…
And so I give thanks
    and my heart kneels to pray —
"God, keep me and guide me
    and go with me today."

Honestly…

COLLEEN TOWNSEND EVANS

Everybody gets angry at times, and when we're all stirred up it's pretty hard to pray — unless we are able to pray honestly, pouring out our hearts before our God. Unless we are able to say, "Lord, I'm angry. You know it. I know it. Is it okay to feel this way? I mean, would the cause of my anger also anger you? Or am I all wound up in myself, acting on my own, instead of letting you guide my feelings?"

Sometimes we just aren't in the mood to pray. We may be depressed, we may be preoccupied, or we may not feel that "glow" we like to feel when we are in God's pres-

ence. Well, as someone very wise said, "When you cannot pray as you would, pray as you can."

God's Will

ELIZA M. HICKOK

I know not by what methods rare,
But this I know: God answers prayer.
I know not if the blessing sought
Will come in just the guise I thought.
I leave my prayer to Him alone
Whose will is wiser than my own.

The good man walks along in the ever brightening light of God's favor; the dawn gives way to morning splendor.   Proverbs 4:18, Living Bible

For Courage

ROBERT H. SCHULLER

I have it!

My fears are going, going, gone!

I feel a mysterious,
calm,
quiet,
tranquil
assurance rising deep within my being.

This remarkable spirit of courage is
    overpowering me.

It is the very presence of God
working peace
at the core of my invisible soul.

Thank you, Lord.

All my fears are gone.

What a relief!
Amen.

When and Where to Pray

C.S. LEWIS

No one in his senses, if he has any power of ordering his own day, would reserve his chief prayers for bedtime — obviously the worst possible hour for any action which needs concentration. The trouble is that thousands of unfortunate people can hardly find any other.... My own plan, when hard pressed, is to seize any time, and place, however unsuitable, in preference to the last waking moment. On a day of traveling — with, perhaps, some ghastly meeting at the end of it — I'd rather pray sitting in a crowded train than put it off till midnight when one reaches a hotel bedroom with aching head and dry throat and one's mind partly in a stupor and partly in a whirl. On other, and slightly less crowded, days a bench in a park, or a back street where one can pace up and down, will do.

From *Sheer Joy*

RALPH SPAULDING CUSHMAN

Oh the sheer joy of it!
    Living with Thee,
God of the universe,
    Lord of a tree,
Maker of mountains,
    Lover of me!

Oh the sheer joy of it!
    Breathing thy air;
Morning is dawning,
    Gone every care,
All the world's singing,
    "God's everywhere."

The Secret Place

JOHN OXENHAM

Each soul has its secret place,
Where none may enter in
Save it and God — to them alone
What goeth on therein is known —
To it and God alone.

Praise Ye the Lord!

ANNE MORROW LINDBERGH

How wonderful are islands! Islands in space, like this one I have come to, ringed about by miles of water, linked by no bridges, no cables, no telephones.... The past and the future are cut off; only the present remains.... One lives like a child or a saint in the immediacy of here and now....

We are all, in the last analysis, alone. And this basic state of solitude is not something we have any choice about....

Naturally. How one hates to think of oneself as alone. How one avoids it. It seems to imply rejection or unpopularity. An early wallflower panic still clings to the word. One will be left, one fears, sitting in a straight-backed chair *alone*, while the popular girls are already chosen and spinning around the dance floor with their hot-palmed partners. We seem so frightened today of being alone that we never let it happen. Even if family, friends, and movies should fail, there is still the radio or television to fill up the void. Women, who used to complain of loneliness, need never be alone anymore. We can do our housework with soap-opera heroes at our side. Even day-dreaming was more creative than this; it demanded something of oneself and it fed the inner life. Now, instead of planting our solitude with our own dream blossoms, we choke the space with continuous music, chatter, and compan-

ionship to which we do not even listen. It is simply there to fill the vacuum. When the noise stops there is no inner music to take its place. We must re-learn to be alone.

It is a difficult lesson to learn today — to leave one's friends and family and deliberately practice the art of solitude for an hour or a day or a week. For me, the break is the most difficult. Parting is inevitably painful, even for a short time.... And yet, once it is done, I find there is a quality to being alone that is incredibly precious. Life rushes back into the void, richer, more vivid, fuller than before....

For a full day and two nights I have been alone. I lay on the beach under the stars at night alone. I made my breakfast alone. Alone I watched the gulls at the end of the pier, dip and wheel and dive for the scraps I threw them. A morning's work at my desk, and then, a late picnic lunch alone on the beach. And it seemed to me, separated from my own species, that I was nearer to others: the shy willet, nesting in the ragged tide-wash behind me; the sand piper, running in little unfrightened steps down the shining beach rim ahead of me; the slowly flapping pelicans over my head, coasting down wind; the old gull, hunched up, grouchy, surveying the horizon. I felt a kind of impersonal kinship with them and a joy in that kinship. Beauty of earth and sea and air meant more to me. I was in harmony with it, melted into the universe, lost in it, as one is lost in a canticle of praise, swelling from an unknown crowd in a cathedral. "Praise ye the Lord, all ye fishes of the sea — all ye birds of the air — all ye children of men — Praise ye the Lord!"

I come here to find myself
It is so easy to get lost
in the world.　　　　Author Unknown

From *Sanctuary*

JOHN OXENHAM

'Mid all the traffic of the ways,
Turmoils without, within,
Make in my heart a quiet place,
And come and dwell therein.

A little shrine of quietness,
All sacred to Thyself,
Where Thou shalt all my soul possess,
And I may find myself.

A little place of mystic grace,
Of self and sin swept bare,
Where I may look into Thy face,
And talk with Thee in prayer.

Prayer is the mortar that holds our house together.
St. Teresa

On a Church Plaque

AUTHOR UNKNOWN

Enter this door
As if the floor
Within were gold;
And every wall
Of jewels all
Of wealth untold;
As if a choir
In robes of fire
Were singing here;
Nor shout nor rush
But hush...
For God is here.

Noah and the Ark

EUGENIA PRICE

Noah was an upright man who walked with God. And with Noah, God began to talk about His plan to give the earth a new start.

Realizing that the people who knew Noah would think he was crazy, God was careful to give him exact instructions so the jeers and criticisms of his friends wouldn't throw him off the course God had set for him. After all, God did ask Noah to build a boat on a vast stretch of dry land with no water in sight! People were bound to laugh. They laughed, too, at Noah's earnest warnings about the events to come. God did not act without warning, but the people turned deaf ears to His message.

Explaining to Noah that the whole earth would be washed clean by a mighty flood, He gave the one man who obeyed Him detailed dimensions and plans for the building of a great boat or ark into which Noah would take his wife, his three sons and their families, and two of every living thing on the earth — one male and one female. God told Noah how much food to take into the ark, so that he and all those with him could stay alive and well during the flood that would come.

Noah carried out God's orders to the letter, and with his wife, his sons and his sons' wives, a male and female of each of the living things on earth, he boarded the ark just ahead of the flood-waters.

That very day all the fountains of the great deep broke through and all the sluices of the heavens were opened up; the rains gushed down upon the earth for forty days and forty nights. But Noah and those he took with him were safe. God Himself had sealed the door behind them from the outside.

For forty days the flooding continued on the earth. The waters mounted and lifted the ark so that it rose from the ground, and still the waters kept rising on the earth with overwhelming volume, while the ark floated on top of the waters. Higher and higher the waters rose until all the high mountains under heaven were covered, and every living creature that moved on earth. Only Noah and those with him in the ark remained alive. For one hundred and fifty days the waters dominated the earth.

But God kept Noah and his family in mind, as well as all the animals and all the livestock with him in the ark.

Then a great wind began to blow over the water-covered mountains and valleys of the earth, and the rain stopped. Steadily the waters moved back from the mountains first and then moved back still more from the low hills and the edges of the valleys, and the ark was grounded at last on a mountain range called Ararat, in Armenia.

Realizing that the rains must have stopped, Noah decided to try an experiment. But to be sure, he waited another forty days and then opened one small window in the ark. Picking up one of the two ravens with him, Noah held the ugly black bird at the open window and watched it stretch its cramped wings and soar first in circles near the ark and then farther and farther out until the dark speck it made in the sky was gone.

Ravens thrive on dead and rotting things and so the raven did not come back at all. The water-logged land and trees and the dead bodies floating in the remaining flood-waters made the raven feel right at home.

Next Noah released a dove from the little window in the ark. Knowing that the dove would not put her dainty foot down on any unclean thing, Noah could tell when the dove came back that the waters were not yet drained from the earth. He put out his hand and caught the dove and brought her back into the safety of the ark.

After seven more days, he again sent the dove out over the silent earth outside, and about twilight Noah had his answer. Back came the dove with a freshly plucked olive leaf in her beak!

All the people in the ark were restless to get outside again, as were the animals and birds, but Noah thought it wise to wait another seven days, and when once more he released the dove she did not return at all.

Noah removed the covering from the ark, looked out, and saw that the empty earth was dry at last.

After they had all left the big boat, safe and healthy, Noah built an altar to the Lord and gave thanks. And they all breathed deeply of the fresh, sweet, rain-washed air.

God blessed Noah and his sons and told them, "Be fruitful, multiply and populate the earth.... Every living, moving thing shall be yours for food; I have given it all to you like the vegetables."

God was talking once again with one family about a fresh start on the earth.

"Take note! I Myself am establishing My covenant with you, with your descendants and with every living creature — of all that left the ark. I covenant with you that never shall all flesh again be eliminated by the waters of a flood, nor shall there be another deluge to destroy the earth."

Here God was making a binding covenant with man. Noah and his family were not one with God as Adam and Eve had been. They were the descendants of Adam and Eve, and the downpull of sin was still strong upon them. God had not yet sent His promised offspring of woman to redeem them. But Noah had done his best to obey God, and so God had made another great gesture of love toward all human nature.

"This is the sign of the covenant I am making between Me and you.... I will set My bow in the clouds; it shall be for a token of a covenant between Me and the earth. When I collect My clouds above the earth, then the bow shall appear in the clouds and I will remember My covenant that exists between Me and you and every living creature...."

As a token of His love and to remind us of His faithfulness to us, God put a rainbow in the sky that day.

And when He collects His clouds still, there stretches across the sky the sign of the love of God, arched and glowing above those who love Him and above those who do not.

A Mile with Me

HENRY VAN DYKE

One who will walk a mile with me
    Along life's merry way.
A comrade blithe and full of glee,
Who dares to laugh out loud and free,
And let his frolic fancy play,
Like a happy child, through the flowers gay
That fill the field and fringe the way
    Where he walks a mile with me.

And who will walk a mile with me
    Along life's weary way?
A friend whose heart has eyes to see
The stars shine out o'er the darkening lea,
And the quiet rest at the end o' the day, —
A friend who knows, and dares to say,
The brave, sweet words that cheer the way
    Where he walks a mile with me.

With such a comrade, such a friend,
    I fain would walk till journey's end,
Through summer sunshine, winter rain,
    And then? — Farewell, we shall meet
    again!

...in him we live, and move, and have our being.
Acts 17:28, King James Version

February Twilight

SARA TEASDALE

I stood beside a hill
    Smooth with new-laid snow,
A single star looked out
    From the cold evening glow.

There was no other creature
    That saw what I could see —
I stood and watched the evening star
    As long as it watched me.

Rain in the Night

AMELIA JOSEPHINE BURR

Raining, raining,
All night long;
Sometimes loud, sometimes soft,
Just like a song.

There'll be rivers in the gutters
And lakes along the street.
It will make our lazy kitty
Wash his little dirty feet.

The roses will wear diamonds
Like kings and queens at court;
But the pansies all get muddy
Because they are so short.

I'll sail my boat to-morrow
In wonderful places,
But first I'll take my watering-pot
And wash the pansies' faces.

The Pasture

ROBERT FROST

I'm going out to clean the pasture spring;
I'll only stop to rake the leaves away
(And wait to watch the water clear, I may):
I sha'n't be gone long. — You come too.

I'm going out to fetch the little calf
That's standing by the mother. It's so young
It totters when she licks it with her tongue.
I sha'n't be gone long. — You come too.

The light shed by any good relationship illuminates all relationships. Anne Morrow Lindbergh

As I love nature, as I love singing birds, and gleaming stubble, and flowing rivers, and morning and evening, and summer and winter, I love thee my friend. Henry David Thoreau

To Love Another

SIR HUGH WALPOLE

The most wonderful of all things in life, I believe, is the discovery of another human being with whom one's relationship has a glowing depth, beauty, and joy as the years increase. This inner progressiveness of love between two human beings is a most marvelous thing, it cannot be found by looking for it or by passionately wishing for it. It is a sort of Divine accident.

From *I Love You*

ROY CROFT

I love you
For the part of me
That you bring out;
I love you
For putting your hand
Into my heaped-up heart
And passing over
All the foolish, weak things
That you can't help
Dimly seeing there,
And for drawing out
Into the light
All the beautiful belongings
That no one else had looked
Quite far enough to find.

Marriage

ROBERT H. SCHULLER

O God, look down upon us as we begin
our married life on our knees. Jesus
Christ, we pray that your Holy Spirit
will come to make our hearts your home.
So may you be the head of our house.
May you be the unseen guest at every
meal.
The silent listener to every word that
is spoken.
The friend that never slumbers or sleeps.
The one who can bring peace in times of
tension and restore joy after sorrow.
Father, our path may take us through
difficult years ahead.
So be with us through our laughter and
tears,
through our labor and leisure, through our
lying down and our rising up.
Always remind us that our Lord is forever
within our reach, keeping watch over his
own.
You have brought us together, a young man
and a young woman to become one in
marriage.
O God, our life's plan is unfolding as it
should. Now we stand, hand in hand,
husband and wife. This is our golden
moment,
our happy hour.
May all the love we hope for and all the
joy we pray for come true. And may our
highest expectations be realized and our
most beautiful dreams find full blossom
in the years that are ahead. This is our
prayer. In the name of Christ our Savior,
we pray!
Amen.

In Love is all the law we need,
In Christ is all the God we know.

Edwin Markham

What I Live For

GEORGE LINNAEUS BANKS

I live for those who love me, for those
who know me true;
For the heaven that smiles above me, and
awaits my spirit too;
For the cause that lacks assistance, for the
wrong that needs resistance,
For the future in the distance, and the good
that I can do.

So long as we love, we serve. So long as we are
loved by others, I should say that we are almost
indispensable; and no man is useless while he has
a friend. Robert Louis Stevenson

A Prayer

FRANK DEMPSTER SHERMAN

It is my joy in life to find
At every turning of the road
The strong arm of a comrade kind
To help me onward with my load.

And since I have no gold to give,
And love alone must make amends,
My only prayer is, while I live —
God make me worthy of my friends.

The World Is My Classroom

CORRIE TEN BOOM

The school of life offers some difficult courses, but it is in the difficult class that one learns the most — especially when your teacher is the Lord Jesus Himself.

The hardest lessons for me were in a cell with four walls. The cell in the prison of Scheveningen, Holland, was six paces in length, two paces in breadth, with a door that could be opened only from the outside. Later there were four barbed-wire fences, charged with electricity, enclosing a concentration camp in Germany. The gates were manned by guards with loaded machine guns. It was there in Ravensbruck that more than ninety-six thousand women died.

After that time in prison, the entire world became my classroom. Since World War II, I have traveled around it twice, speaking in more than sixty countries on all continents. During these three decades I have become familiar with airports, bus stations, and passport offices. Under me have been wheels of every description: wheels of automobiles, trains, jinrikishas, horse-drawn wagons, and the landing gear of airplanes. Wheels, wheels, wheels! Even the wheels of wheelchairs.

I have enjoyed hospitality in a great number of homes and have slept in many times more than a thousand beds. Sometimes I have slept in comfortable beds with foam rubber mattresses in the United States, and sometimes on straw mats on dirt floors in India. There have been clean rooms and dirty rooms.

One bathroom in Hollywood had a view of exotic plants and flowers from the sunken Roman bathtub; while a bathroom in Borneo was simply a mud hut equipped with nothing but a barrel of cold water. Once, while staying with a group of young Jewish girls in Israel, I had to climb over a mountain of building materials, and walk through a junk-filled field to make my way to a tiny outhouse which was nothing more than a hole in the ground. Such a place would have been impossible to find at night.

Always in my travels, even now that I am in my ninth decade of life, I have carried in my hand and in my heart the Bible — the very Word of Life which is almost bursting with Good News. And there has been plenty for everyone. I often feel as the disciples must have felt as they fed more than five thousand with five loaves and two fishes. The secret was that they had received it from the blessed hand of the Master. There was abundance for all and twelve basketfuls of fragments left over.

There has been plenty for the dying ones in the concentration camps — plenty for the thousands gathered in universities in town halls, and in churches all over the world. Sometimes I have spoken to a few men in prison who stood behind bars and listened hungrily. Once to a group of six missionaries in Japan who offered me hospitality during a twenty-eight-hour rainstorm in which more than a thousand persons perished around us. Groups of hundreds and crowds of thousands have listened under pandals in India and in theaters in South America. I have spoken to tens of thousands at one time in the giant stadiums of America and retreated to the mountains of North Carolina to spend time with a small group of girls in a summer camp.

"God so loved the world..." (John 3:16) Jesus said. And that is why I keep going, even into my eightieth years, because we've a story to tell to the nations, a story of love and light.

God has plans — not problems — for our lives. Before she died in the concentration camp in Ravensbruck, my sister Betsie said to me, "Corrie, your whole life has been a training for the work you are doing here in prison — and for the work you will do afterward."

...Looking back across the years of my life, I can see the working of a divine pattern which is the way of God with His children. When I was in a prison camp in Holland

during the war, I often prayed, "Lord, never let the enemy put me in a German concentration camp." God answered *no* to that prayer. Yet in the German camp, with all its horror, I found many prisoners who had never heard of Jesus Christ. If God had not used my sister Betsie and me to bring them to Him, they would never have heard of Him. Many died, or were killed, but many died with the name of Jesus on their lips. They were well worth all our suffering. Faith is like radar which sees through the fog — the reality of things at a distance that the human eye cannot see.

From *The Prophet*
KAHLIL GIBRAN

Love gives naught but itself and takes naught but from itself.

Love possesses not nor would it be possessed;

For love is sufficient unto love.

When you love you should not say, "God is in my heart," but rather, "I am in the heart of God."

And think not you can direct the course of love, for love, if it finds you worthy, directs your course.

Love has no other desire but to fulfill itself.

But if you love and must needs have desires, let these be your desires:

To melt and be like a running brook that sings its melody to the night.

To know the pain of too much tenderness.

To be wounded by your own understanding of love;

And to bleed willingly and joyfully.

The Sacred Day
GRACE NOLL CROWELL

Whatever else be lost, throughout a
    lifetime,
Let us keep Christmas sacred in the heart.
The passing years may strive to rob our
    treasures,
But let us hold this special day apart
As a time to set the waxen candles burning
Upon our sills to cheer the passersby;
Let us have faith in Christmas and its
    meaning;
Let us move forward facing the starlit sky.

What could be purer than the dear Christ
    Child?
What could be surer than His blessed birth?
What could be lovelier than a great star
    spreading
Its silver glory on a waiting earth?
The Christ once said: "Except ye become as
    children...."
May we be childlike for a while tonight,
With hope in our hearts, our clear eyes
    filled with rapture,
And the whole wide world agleam with
    silver light.

Blessing for Light
OLD IRISH BLESSING

Blessed art Thou,
O Lord our God,
King of the Universe,
Who has sanctified us
By Thy commandments
And commanded us
To kindle the Sabbath light.

At Sunrise

HENRY VAN DYKE

Flowers rejoice when night is done,
Lift their heads to greet the sun;
Sweetest looks and odours raise,
In a silent hymn of praise.

So my heart would turn away
From the darkness to the day;
Lying open in God's sight
Like a flower in the light.

The Radiant Company

MARJORIE HOLMES

The Lord has led me into the radiant company of his people. Praise the Lord.

The Lord has given me the fellowship of others on the selfsame journey to find him.

He has given me a spiritual family. He has given me sisters in the dearest sense of the word. He has given me brothers.

We worship together, work together, pray together. And are as richly rewarded in the praying as those we pray for.

I can worship the Lord alone. I can pray alone.

I can know him fully and completely in total solitude. And this is good. For most of our lives we are alone. Despite the presence of many people, we are alone.

But to pray and worship the Lord with others who earnestly, honestly seek him, is to add new dimensions of strength and joy.

Praise the Lord for this gift of fellowship and friendship. For the miracles of work and happiness and healing that burst like stars and change the course of lives when people come together who truly love the Lord.

Blessed are they that have not seen, and yet have believed. John 20:29, King James Version

Heaven's Glories

EMILY BRONTË

No coward soul is mine,
  No trembler in the world's
    storm-troubled sphere;
I see heaven's glories shine,
  And faith shines equal, arming me
    from fear.

Dawn

FRANK DEMPSTER SHERMAN

Out of the scabbard of the night
  By God's hand drawn,
Flashes his shining sword of light,
  And lo — the dawn!

I Am

JOHN CLARE

…I long for scenes where man has never
    trod;
  A place where woman never smiled or
    wept;
There to abide with my Creator, God,
  And sleep as I in childhood sweetly
    slept;
Untroubling and untroubled where I lie;
The grass below — above the vaulted sky.

A Lesson from Grandma

NORMAN VINCENT PEALE

I learned a great deal about prayer from my grandmother. She lived in a little town in the Midwest, in an old-fashioned house, typical of that region. There was a romance about the old-fashioned house. My grandmother's heating plant was a wood-burning stove. One side of you was warm and the other side freezing. Never in her lifetime did she have modern refrigeration. Her butter and eggs were placed in a crock outside the door. She was a strong, simple, old-fashioned woman.

My brother and I used to spend our summers with her. She took us over from our parents. After supper (dinner was the noonday meal in those days) she would read to us by a kerosene lamp. Her concave lenses sat rather far down on her nose as she read stories to us.

Then she would take us upstairs to bed. It was a great high-poster bed laid with handmade quilts, and had an old-fashioned featherbed mattress in which we would sink so far that only our ears protruded. She would put the lamp on a stand and kneel by our bed. On her knees she would talk to the Lord, as to one with whom she was well acquainted and — as I see it now — to reassure us.

"O Lord," so her prayer ran, "I hate to put these two little fellows away off here in this bedroom. When I take this light away it is going to be very dark, and they are so little. They may be scared, but they do not need to be, because You are here, and You are going to watch over them all through the night. You will watch over them all their life long too, if they are good boys. Now, Lord, I ask You to watch over the pillows of these little fellows this night."

Then she would take the lamp, the glow fading upon the wall as she passed from the room. Her soft footfalls died away as she passed down the steps. On stormy nights, especially when the wind would howl around the house, my brother and I would huddle together in that big bed. I used to look up in the darkness and in imagination see a great, kindly face looking down on my pillow. I have always thought there was something magnificent about that prayer, "Look down upon the pillows of these little fellows."

My grandmother said, "Remember, God is not some Oriental potentate sitting upon a throne; He is your friend; He is right by your side. Talk to Him in simple, plain language, telling Him what is on your heart, and He will listen to you."

Sunrise

MARGARET E. SANGSTER

Though the midnight found us weary,
    The morning brings us cheer;
Thank God for every sunrise
    In the circuit of the year.

To God with Love

ALICE JOYCE DAVIDSON

Dear God,

This is the first time ever that I've written you a letter...but I just had to thank you, now that everything is better.

I came to you a while back so troubled and distressed, I didn't know what course to take, what action would be best.... I told you all my troubles, and I felt your presence near...and as I talked the clouds broke up and seemed to disappear.

So, thank you, God, for listening, for keeping me from harm, for wiping tears and holding me within your loving arms.

Compassion

SOON AFTER MIDNIGHT I rose from the tiny, sleepless cot in my husband's hospital room. He lay terribly sick. Beyond the window no moon shone. Not even a street lamp pierced the darkness that churned against the pane. It seemed the night conspired with the darkness in my soul...with the churning anguish I felt over my husband's precarious condition.

As my fears blackened, I pulled on my shoes and fled out into the hospital corridor where dim artificial light laced the wall with shadows. Tears trembled on my face...a sob crowded my throat. A few feet away I saw the visitor's elevator, its doors open. I ducked inside and fumbled with the buttons. As it swept me up, my sobs gave way, echoing anonymously along the elevator's silent pathway. I do not know how many times I rode up and down while my despair poured out. But it was the middle of the night, and who would notice?

Suddenly I heard a soft ping. The elevator stopped. The doors opened. Inside stepped an elderly man with thinning white hair and eyes that searched the tears streaming down my face. He pushed a button, then dug into his pocket. As we lurched upward, he handed me a neatly folded handkerchief. I wiped my eyes, staring into his kind, steady gaze. And his compassion reached my heart like the first fingers of morning sun dispelling the night. God was strangely present in the little elevator, as if He were there in the old man's face.

The doors swished open. I thanked the stranger and handed back his handkerchief, damp and soiled with my anguish. Then he nodded me a gentle smile and slipped away.

As I returned to my husband's room, I was quite sure...God does not fail us in our distress. His compassion is everywhere. And the tenderest promise in the Bible is true — God shall wipe away every tear from their eyes.

And He shall...one way or another.

SUE MONK KIDD

The House with Nobody in It

JOYCE KILMER

Whenever I walk to Suffern along the Erie
    track
I go by a poor old farmhouse with its
    shingles broken
    and black.
I suppose I've passed it a hundred times,
    but I always stop
    for a minute
And look at the house, the tragic house, the
    house with
    nobody in it.

I never have seen a haunted house, but I
    hear there are
    such things;
That they hold the talk of spirits, their mirth
    and
    sorrowings.
I know this house isn't haunted, and I wish
    it were, I do;
For it wouldn't be so lonely if it had a ghost
    or two.

This house on the road to Suffern needs a
    dozen
    panes of glass,
And somebody ought to weed the walk and
    take a scythe to
    the grass.
It needs new paint and shingles, and the
    vines should
    be trimmed and tied;
But what it needs the most of all is some
    people living inside.

If I had a lot of money and all my debts
    were paid
I'd put a gang of men to work with brush
    and saw and spade.
I'd buy that place and fix it up the way it
    used to be

And I'd find some people who wanted a
    home and give
    it to them free.

Now, a new house standing empty, with
    staring window
    and door,
Looks idle, perhaps, and foolish, like a hat
    on its block
    in the store.
But there's nothing mournful about it; it
    cannot be sad
    and lone
For the lack of something within it that it
    has never known.

But a house that has done what a house
    should do, a house
    that has sheltered life,
That has put its living wooden arms around
    a man
    and his wife,
A house that has echoed a baby's laugh and
    held up his
    stumbling feet,
Is the saddest sight, when it's left alone,
    that ever your eyes
    could meet.

So whenever I go to Suffern along the Erie
    track
I never go by the empty house without
    stopping and
    looking back,
Yet it hurts me to look at the crumbling roof
    and the shutters
    fallen apart.
For I can't help thinking the poor old house
    is a house with
    a broken heart.

*Lord, lift thou up the light of thy countenance
upon us.*   Psalm 4:6, King James Version

Prayer

GEORGIA HARKNESS

Give me, O God, the understanding
    heart —
The quick discernment of the soul to see
Another's inner wish, the hidden part
Of him that, wordless, speaks for
    sympathy.

Folks Need a Lot of Loving

STRICKLAND GILLILAN

Folks need a lot of loving in the morning;
    The day is all ahead, with cares
        beset —
The cares we know, and those that give no
    warning;
    For love is God's own antidote for fret.

Folks need a heap of loving at the
    noontime —
    The battle lull, the moment snatched
        from strife —
Halfway between the waking and the
    croontime,
    When bickering and worriment
        are rife.

Folks hunger so for loving at the nighttime,
    When wearily they take them home
        to rest —
At slumber song and turning-out-the-light
    time.
    Of all the times for loving, that's the
        best.

Folks want a lot of loving every minute —
    The sympathy of others and their
        smile!
Till life's end, from the moment they
    begin it,
    Folks need a lot of loving all the while.

The Enchanted Doll

PAUL GALLICO

…I remember just how it was that day: the first hint of spring wafted across the East River, mingling with the soft-coal smoke from the factories and the street smells of the poor neighborhood. The wagon of an itinerant flower seller at the curb was all gay with tulips, hyacinths, and boxes of pansies, and nearby a hurdy-gurdy was playing "Some Enchanted Evening."

As I turned the corner and came abreast of Sheftel's, I was made once more aware of the poor collection of toys in the dusty window, and I remembered the approaching birthday of a small niece of mine in Cleveland, to whom I was in the habit of despatching modest gifts.

…And thus it was my eyes eventually came to rest upon the doll tucked away in one corner.

…I could not wholly make her out, due to the shadows and the film through which I was looking, but I was aware that a tremendous impression had been made upon me, that somehow a contact had been established between her and myself, almost as though she had called to me.…

I laid her on the counter. "What's the price, Abe?"

"Fifteen dollars."

It was my turn to look astonished. Abe said "…I don't need to make no profit on you, Doc. You can have it for fourteen. Uptown in some a them big stores she gets as much as twenny and twenny-fi dollars for 'em."

"Who is 'she'?"

"Some woman over on Thirteenth Street who makes 'em.… She's a big, flashy, red-haired dame, but hard.… Not your type, Doc."

…"I'll take her," I said. It was more than I could afford, for my practice is among the poor, where one goes really to learn medicine. Yet I could not leave her lying there on the counter amidst the boxes of chewing gum, matches, punchboards, and magazines, for she was a creation, and something, some part of a human soul, had gone into the making of her....

It was three months or so later that my telephone rang and a woman's voice said, "Dr. Amony?"

"Yes?"

"I passed by your place once and saw your sign. Are you expensive? Do you cost a lot for a visit?"

I was repelled by the quality of the voice and the calculation in it. Nevertheless I replied, "I charge a dollar. If you are really ill and cannot afford to pay, I charge nothing."

"Okay, I could pay a dollar. But no more. You can come over...."

When I pushed the button under the name plate at that address,...I felt I was being subjected to scrutiny. Then the unpleasant voice said, "Dr. Amony? You can come in. I'm Rose Callamit."

I was startled by her. She was almost six feet tall, with brick, henna-dyed hair and an overpowering smell of cheap perfume.... There was a horrible vitality and flashy beauty about her....

The deepest shock, however, I sustained when I entered the room, which was one of those front parlor-bedrooms of the old-fashioned brownstone houses.... But hanging from the wall, lying about on the bed, or tossed carelessly onto the top of an old trunk were a dozen or so rag dolls, all of them different, yet, even at first glance, filled with the same indescribable appeal and charm as that of the similar little creature that had made such a profound impression upon me....

I asked, "Do you make these dolls?"

"Yup. Why?"

I was filled with a sense of desolation. I mumbled, "I bought one once, for a niece...."

She laughed. "Bet you paid plenty for it. They're the rage. Okay, come on."

She led me through a connecting bath and washroom into the smaller room at the back and opened the door partly, shouting,

"Essie, it's the doctor!" Then, before she pushed it wide to admit me, she cried loudly and brutally, "Don't be surprised, Doctor, she's a cripple!"

The pale girl, clad in a flannel peignoir, in the chair over by the window had a look of utter despair on her countenance....

She could not have been more than twenty-four or twenty-five. She seemed to be nothing but a pair of huge and misery-stricken eyes and what was shocking was how low the lamp of life appeared to be burning in them....

But I saw something else that astounded me and gave my heart a great lift. She was surrounded by small tables. On one of them were paints and brushes, on others, rag material, linen, stuffing threads and needles, the paraphernalia needed for the making of dolls....

I asked, "Can you walk, Essie?"

She nodded listlessly.

"Please walk to me."

"Oh don't," Essie said. "Don't make me."

The pleading in her voice touched me, but I had to be sure. I said, "I'm sorry, Essie. Please do as I ask."

She rose unsteadily from her chair and limped toward me, dragging her left leg.... "That's good," I said to her, smiled encouragingly, and held out my hands to her....

I asked, "How long have you been this way, Essie?"

Rose Callamit said, "Oh, Essie's been a cripple for years. I didn't call you for that. She's sick. I want to know what's the matter with her."

Oh yes, she was sick. Sick unto death perhaps....

When I had finished my examination I accompanied Rose into the front room. "Well?" she said.

I asked, "Did you know that her deformity could be cured? That with the proper treatment she could be walking normally in —"

"Shut up, you!" Her cry of rage struck like a blow against my ears. "Don't you ever dare mention that to her. I've had her looked at by people who know. I won't have any young idiot raising false hopes. If you ever do, you're through here. I want to know what's ailing her. She don't eat or sleep or work good anymore. What did you find out?"

"Nothing," I replied. "I don't know. There is nothing wrong organically. But there is something terribly wrong somewhere...."

"You'll keep your big mouth shut about curing her cripple, you understand? Otherwise I'll get another doctor."

...When I picked up my hat and bag to leave I said, "I thought you told me it was you who made those dolls."

She looked startled for a moment as though she had never expected the subject to come up again. "I do," she snapped. "I design 'em. I let the kid work at 'em sometimes to help take her mind off she's a cripple...."

But when I walked out into the bright, hot July day with the kids playing hopscotch on the sidewalk and handball against the old brewery wall and traffic grinding by, my heart told me that Rose Callamit had lied and that I had found the sweet spirit behind the enchanted doll....

Her name, I found out later, was Nolan, Essie Nolan, and she was slowly dying from no determinable cause....

After I had made a number of visits, Rose did not even bother to keep up the pretense that it was she herself who made the dolls, and I was able to piece together something of the picture.

When Essie was fifteen, her parents had been killed in an accident which also resulted in her injury. A court had awarded her in guardianship to her only relative, the cousin, Rose Callamit.... Through the years of their association, the older woman had made her deeply sensitive to and ashamed of her lameness....

Essie was completely under the domination of Rose and was afraid of her, but it was not that which was killing her. It was something else, and I could not find out what....

I did not mention my belief in the possibility of cure for Essie's lameness. It was more important to discover immediately what it was that was killing her. Rose would not let her be moved to a hospital. She would not spare the money.

For ten days I thought I had arrested the process that was destroying Essie before my eyes. I stopped her work on the dolls. I brought her some books to read.... When I returned for my next visit, she smiled at me for the first time, and the tremulousness, longing, hunger, the womanliness and despair of the smile would have broken a heart of stone....

It was shortly after this that I became ill myself....

I began to look shocking; my skin was losing its tone, my cheekbones were beginning to show, and I was hollow-eyed from loss of sleep. I did not like the look in my eyes, or the expression about my mouth. Sometimes my nights and my dreams were filled with fever and in them I saw Essie struggling to reach me while Rose Callamit held her imprisoned in her ugly, shapeless arms. I had never been free from worry over failure to diagnose Essie's case.

My whole faith in myself as a doctor was badly shaken. A desperately stricken human being had called upon me for help and I had failed. I could not even help myself. What right had I to call myself a doctor? All through one awful night of remorse and reproach the phrase burned through my brain as though written in fire:

"Physician, heal thyself!"

Yes, heal myself before I was fit to heal others....

And as morning grayed my back-yard window and the elevated trains thundered by in increasing tempo, I knew my disease. I was in love with Essie Nolan....

It had always been Essie....

For now, as the scales fell from my eyes and my powers were released again through the acknowledging and freeing inside of me of the hunger, love, and compassion I had for her, I knew the sickness of Essie Nolan in full, to its last pitiful detail, and what I must do....

It took me no more than a minute or two to run the few blocks to the brownstone house where Essie lived and press the buzzer under another name plate. When the door clicked open I went upstairs, two steps at a time. If the door was locked I would have to get the landlady. But I was in luck. Rose had expected to be gone only a few moments, apparently, and it was open. I hurried through the connecting bath and entering the back room, found Essie.

There was so little of her left....

She looked up when I came in, startled out of her lethargy. She had expected it to be Rose. Her hand went to her breast and she said my name. Not "Dr. Amony," but my given one — "Samuel!"

I cried, "Essie! Thank God I'm in time. I came to help you. I know what it is that has been...making you ill...."

...A change came over her. She closed her eyes for an instant and murmured, "No. Don't, please. Let me go. I don't want to know. It will be over soon."

...I sat down and took her hand.

"Essie. Please listen. Give me your mind. When a body is undernourished we give it food; when it is anemic, we supply blood; when it lacks iron or hormones we give it tonic. But you have had a different kind of leakage. You have been drained dry of something else without which the soul and body cannot be held together."

Her eyes opened and I saw they were filled with horror and a glazing fear. She seemed about to lose consciousness as she begged, "No! Don't say it!"

I thought perhaps she might die then and there. But the only hope for her, for us both, was to go on.

"Essie! My brave, dear girl. It is nothing so terrible. You need not be afraid. It is only that you have been drained of love. Look at me, Essie!"

...I could not be sure that she still heard me. "It was Rose Callamit," I continued.

"She took away your every hope of life, love, and fulfillment. But what she did later to you was a much blacker crime. For she took away *your children!*"

There, it was out! Had I killed her? Had it been I who loved her beyond words who had administered the death blow? And yet I thought I saw a flicker of life in those poor, stricken eyes, and even perhaps the faintest reflection of relief.

"Oh yes, they were your children, Essie, those enchanted creatures you created.... You created them with love; you loved them like your own children and then each one was taken from you at birth by that money-hungry monster and nothing was given to you to replace them. And so you continued to take them from your heart, your tissue, and your blood until your life was being drained away from you. Persons can die from lack of love."

Essie stirred. Her head beneath the flaxen hair moved ever so slightly....

I cried, "But you won't, Essie, because...I love you.... Do you hear me, Essie? I am not your doctor. I am a man telling you that I love you and cannot live without you."

I caught her incredulous whisper. "Love me? But I am a cripple."

"If you were a thousand times a cripple, I would only love you a thousand times more. But it isn't true. Rose Callamit lied to you. You can be cured. In a year I will have you walking like any other girl."

...A door slammed. Another crashed open. Rose Callamit stormed into the room.... There was nothing she could do anymore, and she knew it. There was not even a word spoken as I walked past her then and there carrying my burden held closely to me and went out the door and down into the street.

August had come to New York. Heat was shimmering from the melting pavements; no air stirred; water from the hydrants was flushing the streets and kids were bathing in the flow, screaming and shouting, as I carried Essie home.

That was three years ago and I am writing this on an anniversary. Essie is busy with our son and is preparing to welcome our second-to-be-born. She does not make dolls now. There is no need....

...when I sit in darkness, the Lord shall be a light unto me. Micah 7:8, King James Version

It's a Wonderful World
HELEN STEINER RICE

In spite of the fact
    we complain and lament
And view this old world
    with much discontent,
Deploring conditions
    and grumbling because
There's so much injustice
    and so many flaws,
It's a wonderful world
    and it's people like you
Who make it that way
    by the things that they do —
For a warm, ready smile
    or a kind, thoughtful deed,
Or a hand outstretched
    in an hour of need
Can change our whole outlook
    and make the world bright
Where a minute before
    just nothing seemed right —
It's a WONDERFUL WORLD
    and it always will be
If we keep our eyes open
    and focused to see
The WONDERFUL THINGS
    man is capable of
When he opens his heart
    to GOD and HIS LOVE.

Three Things to Remember
WILLIAM BLAKE

A Robin Redbreast in a cage
Puts all Heaven in a rage.
A Skylark wounded on the wing
Doth make a cherub cease to sing.
He who shall hurt the little Wren
Shall never be beloved by men.

Fringed Gentians
AMY LOWELL

Near where I live there is a lake
As blue as blue can be; winds make
It dance as they go blowing by.
I think it curtsies to the sky.

It's just a lake of lovely flowers,
And my Mamma says they are ours;
But they are not like those we grow
To be our very own, you know.

We have a splendid garden, there
Are lots of flowers everywhere;
Roses, and pinks, and four-o'clocks,
And hollyhocks, and evening stocks.

Mamma lets us pick them, but never
Must we pick any gentians — ever!
For if we carried them away
They'd die of homesickness that day.

What Does Love Look Like?
ST. AUGUSTINE

It has hands to help others.
It has feet to hasten to the poor and needy.
It has eyes to see misery and want.
It has ears to hear the sighs and sorrows
    of men.
That is what love looks like.

The Touch of the Master's Hand

MYRA BROOKS WELCH

'Twas battered and scarred, and the
    auctioneer
Thought it scarcely worth his while
To waste much time on the old violin,
But held it up with a smile.
"What am I bidden, good folks," he cried,
"Who will start bidding for me?
A dollar, a dollar" — then, "Two!" "Only
    two?
Two dollars, and who'll make it three?
Three dollars, once; three dollars, twice;
Going for three —" But no,
From the room, far back, a gray-haired man
Came forward and picked up the bow;
Then, wiping the dust from the old violin,
And tightening the loose strings,
He played a melody pure and sweet
As sweet as a caroling angel sings.

The music ceased, and the auctioneer,
With a voice that was quiet and low,
Said, "What am I bidden for the old violin?
And he held it up with the bow.
"A thousand dollars, and who'll make it
    two?

Two thousand! And who'll make it three?
Three thousand, once; three thousand,
    twice;
And going, and gone!" said he.
The people cheered, but some of them
    cried,
"We do not quite understand
What changed its worth?" Swift came the
    reply:
"The touch of the master's hand."

And many a man with life out of tune,
And battered and scattered with sin,
Is auctioned cheap to the thoughtless
    crowd,
Much like the old violin.
A "mess of pottage," a glass of wine;
A game — and he travels on.
He's "going" once, and "going" twice,
He's "going" and "almost gone."
But the Master comes, and the foolish
    crowd
Never can quite understand
The worth of a soul, and the change that's
    wrought
By the touch of the Master's hand.

Thanksgiving

ANGELA MORGAN

Thank Thee, O Giver of Life, O God!
For the force that flames in the winter sod;
For the breath in my nostrils, fiercely good,
The sweet of water, the taste of food;
The sun that silvers the pantry floor,
The step of a neighbor at my door;
For dusk that fondles the window-pane,
For the beautiful sound of falling rain.

Thank Thee for love and light and air,
For children's faces, keenly fair,
For the wonderful joy of perfect rest
When the sun's wick lowers within the West;
For huddling hills in gowns of snow
Warming themselves in the afterglow;
For Thy mighty wings that are never furled,
Bearing onward the rushing world.

God Is Beside Us

AUTHOR UNKNOWN

God is beside us each step
    of the way
If only we lean on His arm
    as we pray.
His love is eternal and help
    can be wrought
If faith is applied in each
    prayer and each thought.

Lazarus

EUGENIA PRICE

His disciples came within sight of the flat-roofed stone houses of Bethany. He made no effort to hide His return. That would have been futile, since Lazarus and his sisters were prominently known even in Jerusalem.

While they were still outside Bethany, word of His arrival reached the sisters by way of those who had come from the Holy City and its surrounding area to comfort the mourners.

Martha ran heavily toward them, already talking rapidly and bitterly.

"Lord, Lord, if You had been here, I know my brother would not have died! Why didn't You come? Why?"

Jesus gave her time to compose herself a little.

"You could have healed him," her voice softened. "And yet, even as I complain to You, Lord, now that I am face to face with You once more, I know that even now, whatever You ask of God, He will grant You."

Jesus said to her, "Martha, your brother will rise again."

For a minute she looked hopeful, and then covered her swollen, red eyes with her hands, realizing how long it might be before the promised resurrection of all the dead! Without any real hope but like one who wants to say what she knew was expected of her, Martha whispered:

"Yes — Yes, I know that he will rise again at the resurrection on the last day, but —"

Jesus lifted her head and forced her to look squarely at Him.

"Martha, I am the Resurrection and the Life."

She stepped back and stared at Him. Even the disciples had never heard Him say a thing like that!

"I am the Resurrection and the Life; the believer in Me will live even when he dies, and everyone who lives and believes in Me

shall never, never die! Do you believe this, Martha?"

"Yes, Lord, I have faith that You are the Christ, the Son of God, who was to come into the world."

The knot of people who followed Martha from her home stood staring at Jesus. Some had seen the attempts to stone Him in Jerusalem. Martha took advantage of their pre-occupation with the Master to slip away to tell Mary He was there, asking for her.

Jesus waited for Mary to come to Him outside the village.

Women customarily returned again and again, alone, to the tombs to weep. When those who had come to comfort her saw Mary rush from the house, they followed her, thinking she was returning to Lazarus' tomb.

Mary ran to Jesus instead, and fell at His feet weeping.

"Lord, had You been here, my brother would not have died!"

She didn't need to say any more to Him. He knew these words were said at the peak of Mary's faith. The same words from Martha meant a labored beginning. But a beginning just the same.

When He saw her great weeping, and that of the mourners with her, His spirit was indignant at death! A great stirring within Him to do battle with all that caused death in His Father's beloved world energized His weary body.

"Mary, where have you laid him?"

The mourners called, "Come and see!"

A storm of grief tore through Him. His soul trembled with the holy hatred of God for anything that caused suffering among His creatures. Jesus' shoulders shook with His own weeping as He walked toward the grave of His friend.

"Look," murmured one of the mourners, "look how He did love Lazarus."

Now, they had reached the cave-like tomb, dug out of the slanting side of the rocky garden hillside. A huge stone sealed its opening.

Jesus was in front now. He walked de-

liberately down the four stone steps leading to the grave's entrance and stood on the flagstones recently placed there.

Tears still wet His cheeks and beard, but He said in a clear, firm voice:

"Remove the stone!"

Martha's voice pierced the stunned silence of the crowd.

"Lord, by now there is an odor. It is four days!"

"Martha, did I not tell you if you will believe you will see the glory of God?"

They removed the stone, and Jesus began to talk to His Father quietly and naturally.

"Father, I thank You for having heard Me. I know You always do hear Me; but on account of the people standing here, I speak, so that they may believe that You have sent Me."

The spring breeze mingled the death and spice smells from the open grave with the garden flowers which Lazarus had tended and loved.

Jesus took a step back from the open grave and shouted:

"Lazarus, come out!"

Mary sobbed once.

Martha held her hand hard over her mouth and stared with the others at the dark, silent opening of the grave where they had laid the body of their beloved brother.

There was a scuffling sound, and a loose stone fell somewhere inside the tomb. The people gasped when their straining eyes caught the first glimpse of white. The body of Lazarus moved, sat up, and then hobbled out into the spring sun, bound hand and foot in the winding sheet, with the burial napkin still tied around his face.

Both sisters moved slowly toward their brother, who was trying now to get free of his grave clothes.

Jesus smiled exultantly, and said, "Untie him, and give him a chance to move!"

Many of the Jews visiting Bethany believed in Jesus from that moment on. Others hurried to Jerusalem to inform the Pharisees what He had done openly, not two miles from their stronghold in the Holy City!

Though a Thousand Branches...

SIR WALTER SCOTT

Though a thousand branches join their
     screen,
Yet the broken sunbeams glance between
And tip the leaves with lighter green,
     With brighter tints the flowers....

Joy and Peace in Believing

WILLIAM COWPER

Sometimes a light surprises
     The Christian while he sings;
It is the Lord who rises
     With healing in his wings:
When comforts are declining,
     He grants the soul again
A season of clear shining
     To cheer it after rain.

Wisdom and I

KAHLIL GIBRAN

In the silence of the night, Wisdom came into my chamber and stood by my bed. She gazed upon me like a loving mother, dried my tears, and said:

"I have heard the cries of your soul, and have come here to comfort you. Open your heart to me and I shall fill it with light. Ask, and I shall show you the path of Truth."

Eyes for Invisibles

HELEN KELLER

I have walked with people whose eyes are full of light but who see nothing in sea or sky, nothing in city streets, nothing in books. It were far better to sail forever in the night of blindness with sense, and feeling and mind, than to be content with the mere act of seeing. The only lightless dark is the night of darkness in ignorance and insensibility.

God's Children

JAMES J. METCALFE

Although God loves the whole wide world
    And blesses every part,
I think He has a special place
    For children in His heart.

I think He cherishes their smiles,
    Their eagerness and mirth,
And their appreciation of
    The wonders of His earth.

I think He listens closely to
    Whatever words they say;
I think He follows them to school
    And watches them at play.

And when they go to bed at night,
    He probably is there,
To see that they have happy dreams
    Beneath their tousled hair.

All children in a special way
    Belong to God above,
And I am sure He favors them
    With everlasting love.

The Pigeon That Went to Church on Christmas Eve

ELIZABETH YATES

Mary stopped in at the schoolhouse late in the afternoon of Christmas Eve. The room was empty and still. No echoes resounded of the gay party that had taken place the day before.

In one corner stood the tree — denuded of its presents but beautiful in itself, speaking of the forest in its green and fragrant branches, speaking of the season in the strands of bright cranberries that still festooned it.

So short a time ago the room had been filled with children — laughing, shouting, exchanging presents, singing carols. A quiet time had come when, just as twilight of the brief December day began to draw in, they had lit the Christmas candle.

"For the wayfaring man," Ruthie had said softly.

"For the Christ Child," Leonard had corrected her.

"For anyone," Nezar had murmured.

The candle stood on the window sill no longer. Nezar had begged to take it to the lonely shack in the Swamplands, which had been his and Renny's home before their mother had abandoned them and Mary had taken them under her wing.

"So many houses in Nearby will have candles in their windows," he had persuaded. "Just for tonight there should be one over there."

Mary had consented, and Nezar and Renny had gone off that afternoon with many promises that they would be back in time for the carols at the church and the supper in the vestry later.

It was that moment after the candle had been lit and while she was reading the Christmas story that Mary liked best to remember.

"This is what matters," she had thought to herself, "this is the moment that the gift-giving and the singing and the fun have all led up to. If they can remember this, then some light of Christmas will shine for them throughout their lives — however far they may go, however dark their paths may be." This was the time when wonder wrapped them all in it like a cloak.

She had told them, then, that they paid homage at that stable in Bethlehem whenever they cherished in their hearts a kindly thought, whenever they did a kindly deed.

"That is witnessing to love," she had said, "and love is the link that binds us together and will one day bind the world." Looking at their upturned faces she thought they understood and so she went on to say, "Christmas is a time for miracles because it is a time when we all love enough to do things for others."

An earnest of their feelings was the neat array in a corner of the schoolroom to be packed and sent to some part of the world where there was need. Early in December they had agreed that for every gift given to each other they would give one to an unknown child. Here were books and clothes and toys and cans of food and presents they had made themselves.

Even small Michael Morrison, whose parents had not been able to spare anything for him to give, felt happy. Someone had placed in the pile a pair of shoes without laces and he had promptly sat down, taken the laces from his own shoes, and run them into the gift ones.

"I can use string," he had said.

After the reading, they had another kind of giving. Satisfied with the gaiety behind them, made quiet by the Christmas story, and expansive by the spirit of the time, they all had said what they could give — not things now, but thoughts, for in them was real Christmas.

One led to another. When Andy said he could give more attention to his mother when she was speaking to him, Emily said she could give more smiles, and John said he would like to give more thanks for the beautiful things in the world. It was a curious assortment of things they thought to give, available to each and all in any quantity as if they were kept in some wonderful bank whose reserves were never depleted by using but rather grew.

Nezar said he would like to find and return the lost pigeon to Mr. Richard Alden Todd. Then they all started talking about the homing pigeon that had been missing for days. The whole countryside was on the lookout for it and its disappearance had even been announced on the radio, such a valuable and valiant bird it was.

Joyously, glibly, they had contributed ideas of what they would do for others. It seemed easy for them to think that way when they were all together and one with the security of the schoolroom but, Mary thought, remembering how they had raced from the room when dismissal came, would it be as easy for them to forget?

She opened a book on her desk, and, in the light that was almost gone, read again what she had read to the children just before they parted:

"Whosoever on ye nighte of ye nativity of ye young Lord Jesus, in ye great snows, shall fare forth bearing succulent bone for ye loste and lamenting hounde, a wisp of hay for ye shivering horse, a cloak of warm raiment for ye stranded wayfarer, a bundle of fagots for ye twittering crone,...a garland of bright berries for one who has worn chains...and divers lush sweetmeats for such babes' faces as peer from lonely windows — to him shall be proffered and returned gifts of such an astonishment as will rival the hues of the peacock and the harmonies of heaven, so that though he live to ye greate age when man goes stooping and querulous because of the nothing that is left in him, yet shall he walk upright and remembering as one whose heart shines like a great star in his breaste."

Silence had fallen on the schoolroom and what any of the children thought of the ancient words was locked in their hearts. Then bedlam broke out as Mary told them school was dismissed.

"Merry Christmas!" they had shouted, pulling on coats and slamming doors, racing down the street, or piling into the bus. And yet — and yet — they might all of them bear a great star in their breast for all that she might know.

She heard Dan's footsteps outside and looked quickly as he came in.

"It's cold in here," he said.

"I know. I'm not staying long. I just came to get some books and I was remembering the party yesterday, *wondering* how much of it they will remember."

Dan smiled. "You'll never hear from them how much, but you'll know it in the kind of lives they lead. Where's Nezar?"

"He and Renny have gone out to the Swamplands to put a candle in the window there."

"He thought there might be a wayfaring man going by?" Dan asked, amused.

"I don't know what he thought," Mary said.

"Perhaps a candle may be needed there more than in Nearby," Dan nodded. "Something must have told Nezar to go and so he went."

Mary's eyes widened.

Dan laughed outright. "Oh, my delicious Mary, why do you always look so surprised when you see your sowing bear fruit? You've been trying to teach them to listen, haven't you?" Then he looked at his watch. "Come on, let's drive out in the truck and fetch Nezar and Renny back or we'll all be late for the carols."

They closed the schoolhouse door behind them and got into the truck, driving over the rough road to the Swamplands in the dear silence Mary and Dan enjoyed as much as words.

It was so dark in the Swamplands that the light flickering from the window sill of the shack seemed very bright — lighting up the snow on the ground, making the ribbon of road darker than the night and the outline of trees fantastic, making the shack a place of warmth and shelter.

Mary and Dan drew up to the shack and got out, but no one came to the door to open it. Then they stepped across the snow and looked in the window.

There on the floor of the shack knelt Nezar and Renny and strutting between the two was the pigeon whose loss had given such concern to the countryside.

Nezar held out his palm with some grains of corn in it and the pigeon stepped daintily over and pecked them from his hand.

"So that's why he went to the henhouse before he left this afternoon," Mary whispered.

"He wanted to be ready for anything," Dan said.

The pigeon walked a little distance from the boys and hopped onto the rim of a wooden bucket they had filled with water. The long neck was pitched forward and the pigeon drank.

Then, as the head tilted back, the green of neck feathers melting into bronze glistened and shone. The gray body feathers lay soft as velvet. The red legs, both banded, were strong and slender. The heart-shaped marking on the beak looked like a fleck of snow. Used to airy regions, it was happy on the floor of a shack with two little boys, for it had safe shelter.

Mary and Dan went to the door and tapped lightly.

Nezar hurried to open it a crack, his smiling face pale with excitement.

"We've a visitor but you can come in too."

They slipped in the door quietly and the pigeon looked at them, sizing them up with his curious crimson eyes. Then he moved his head sideways and took a few steps toward Nezar and the hand that held out grain.

Renny spoke quickly. "Me and Nezar hadn't lit the candle very long when we heard a sort of thump at the window. When we went out we found the pigeon fluttering on the ground."

Nezar had the pigeon in his arms and was cuddling it to him, stroking the soft gray

feathers. "He's lost his bearings and was roosting in a tree. Then when he saw the light it drew him to the window." Nezar spoke as if the bird had confided in him.

Dan said, "It's almost time for the carol-singing at church. I brought the truck so we could all ride back."

"And the pigeon too?" Nezar asked.

"What better place for a pigeon than a church on Christmas Eve?"

"And then will you take us to Mr. Todd's?" Nezar demanded.

Dan smiled. "Well, it's a long way, but I guess we can get there."

So they blew the candle out and the Swamplands slid back into darkness while a truck drove off with Mary and Dan and the two boys, one of them holding tenderly to him a pigeon that had been lost and was found.

"And still you *wonder*," Dan said, looking at Mary in the shadowy darkness.

Awareness

MIRIAM TEICHNER

God — let me be aware.
Let me not stumble blindly down the ways,
Just getting somehow safely through the
       days,
Not even groping for another hand,
Not even wondering why it all was
       planned,
Eyes to the ground unseeking for the light,
Soul never aching for a wild-winged flight,
Please, keep me eager just to do my share.
God — let me be aware.

God — let me be aware.
Stab my soul fiercely with others' pain,
Let me walk seeing horror and stain.
Let my hands, groping, find other hands.
Give me the heart that divines,
       understands.

Give me the courage, wounded, to fight.
Flood me with knowledge, drench me in
       light.
Please, keep me eager just to do my share.
God — let me be aware.

Answer

CHARLES L. ALLEN

"Do you believe in prayer?" I really cannot explain why I asked my friend that question. He is a very successful man; we were talking about things in general when suddenly I felt an impulse to ask him about prayer. I think the question shocked him.

He waited a moment and then repeated the question: "Do I believe in prayer?" He said, "I am going to tell you a story I have never told another person." He told me of a fine promotion in his work he had received. He was working day and night. He so much wanted to make good.

One day he noticed his little boy was not well. He watched him several days until he was sure something was wrong. A doctor examined the boy and discovered he had a rheumatic heart, and no doubt would never be entirely well. Probably he could never play ball with the other boys. The young father was both worried and disappointed.

Another baby was to come in a few weeks, his wife was not getting along well, and the father thought it best not to tell her about the rheumatic heart until later. But his heart was heavier as he went to his work each day. When the baby came, there was some stomach trouble which kept her from digesting her food properly. With treatment the baby would be all right, but it would take time.

Because the young mother had complications at birth and needed rest, he would let her sleep downstairs with the older boy and carry the baby upstairs with him. Some nights the baby did not sleep at all. Other

nights she slept only half the hours. He would look after her as best he could, fixing the formulas and walking the floor.

The mother had to go back to the hospital and for a time she was in serious condition. Eventually she was restored to health as was the baby. But the older boy was still sick. Each morning he would have a high temperature. It would drop to normal during the day and rise again at night. It seemed nothing could be done for him.

Finally the young father just broke under the strain. They put him in a hospital for a few weeks and then ordered him to take a year's rest. It was a bitter disappointment. Not only did it mean losing his good promotion, but he had no money and no place to go. However, he took it graciously, borrowed a little money, got a light half-time job, and the couple did the best they could.

The older boy was in an Atlanta hospital but not getting any better. In fact, he was getting worse. He said, "What I am going to tell you now is the part I have never told another person." He and his wife left the hospital late one night. They had about reached the end of their rope. As they drove along, he felt an impulse to pull over to the curb and stop. He told his wife they had done all they could. He suggested they pray about it. This is the prayer he told me he prayed: "Lord, you know how much our boy means to us. We want so much for him to grow up to be a man. If we can keep him, we will be mighty thankful. But if he goes to Your House, we want You to know we will not be bitter. We want You to know we will be good children of Yours and do the best we can without him."

The next morning, when they went back to the hospital, they were astonished to find their boy had no temperature at all. The doctors were delighted with his condition, yet were amazed at the suddenness of his turn for the better. They carefully watched him but his high temperature did not return. That was three years ago.

My friend's face lighted up as he told me his wife is now well, their little girl lovely and sweet, the little boy is now strong. He himself has an even better job. And he said, "This coming Christmas is really going to be wonderful for me because I have figured out that by then I will have all my doctor and hospital bills paid, as well as the money I borrowed. I surely do believe in prayer."

Character

BY THE TIME I graduated from high school, the depression was daily dealing our town devastating blows: businesses failing, banks closing, bankruptcies, suicides, almost everyone living on credit. With our family's hand-to-mouth existence, how could there possibly be any money for college?

Already I had been accepted at Agnes Scott. Even though I had saved some money from debating prizes and had the promise of a work scholarship, we were still hundreds of dollars short of what was needed.

One evening Mother found me lying across my bed, face down, sobbing. She sat down beside me. "You and I are going to deal with this right now," she said quietly.

At this point Mother took me into the guest room, and together we knelt beside the old-fashioned, golden oak bed, the one that Mother and Father had bought for their first home. "Catherine, I know it's right for you to go to college," Mother said. "Every problem has a solution. Let's ask God to tell us how to bring this dream to reality."

As we knelt there together, instinctively I knew that this was an important moment, one to be recorded in heaven. We were about to meet God in a more intimate way than at bedtime prayers or during grace before a meal, or in family prayers together in Dad's study, or even as in most of the prayers in church. Mother was admitting me to the inner sanctum of her prayer closet.

In the silence, I quickly reviewed my relationship with this God with whom we were seeking an audience. At the age of nine I had given Him my life. Attendance at Sunday school and church had been regular ever since, little enough to do as the daughter of a preacher, I thought uneasily.

I had prayed many times since that encounter with Him years before, but how real had these prayers been? The truth then struck me — most had been for selfish purposes. I had given so little of myself to Him…. And with a sinking heart, I remembered all the times I had

seen members of the church coming up the front walk only to flee up the back stairs to my room where I could be alone to read and not have to give myself to others in the sharing of their problems.

Scene after scene flashed across my mind's eye of the times I had resented my brother and sister. Whenever they had interfered with what I wanted to do, I had scolded them, avoided them, rejected them. As I thought of the many occasions when my parents had gone without something they needed so that we children could have new clothing, piano lessons, books or sports equipment, I felt more unworthy than ever. And my going to college would call for yet more sacrifices from my parents.

I stole a look at Mother. She was praying intensely but soundlessly, with her lips moving. Then closing my eyes, silently I prayed the most honest prayer of my life to that point. "Lord, I've been selfish. I've taken everything from You, from Your Church and from my parents and given little of myself in return. Forgive me for this, Lord. Perhaps I don't deserve to go to a college like Agnes Scott."

A sob deep in my throat made me pause. I knew what I now had to do. "And Lord, I turn this dream over to You. I give it up. It's in Your hands. You decide." Now the tears did come!

Those quiet moments in the bedroom were the most honest I had ever spent with God up to that point. I was learning that the price of a relationship with Him is a dropping of all our masks and pretense. We must come to Him with stark honest "as we are" — or not at all. My honesty brought me relief; it washed away the guilt; it strengthened my faith.

❋

Several days later Dad and Mother decided that by faith, I should go ahead and make preparations for Agnes Scott. They felt strongly that this was right and that the Lord would soon confirm it. I was not so sure. God had convicted me of my selfishness. Perhaps He wanted me to give up college and serve Him in some other way.

Days passed, then weeks. Then one day Mother opened a letter and gave a whoop of joy. "Here it is! Here's the answer to our prayers."

The letter contained an offer from a special project of the federal government for Mother to write the history of the county. With what I already had, her salary would be more than enough for my college expenses.

…From those hours each day spent alone with Him had come her supreme confidence that He would always provide out of His limitless supply. How often she had told us children, "And don't forget, He will never, never let us outgive Him."

Out of this solid wealth, this certainty, Mother could always afford

to give to others, not just material things, but showering sparks of imagination, the gleam of hope, a thrust of courage — qualities that provided more substance than the coin of any realm and which opened the door for fulfillment in many a life she touched.

CATHERINE MARSHALL

Let your hope keep you joyful, be patient in your troubles, and pray at all times.
Romans 12:12, Good News for Modern Man

Always Finish

AUTHOR UNKNOWN

If a task is once begun
Never leave it till it's done.
Be the labor great or small,
Do it well or not at all.

This Is My Prayer

RABINDRANATH TAGORE

This is my prayer to thee, my lord — strike,
Strike at the root of penury in my heart.
Give me the strength lightly to bear my joys
    and sorrows.
Give me the strength to make my love
    fruitful in service.
Give me the strength never to disown the
    poor or bend my knees before
    insolent might.
Give me the strength to raise my mind high
    above daily trifles.
And give me the strength to surrender my
    strength to thy will with love.

If we build on a sure foundation in friendship, we must love our friends for their sakes rather than for our own.
Charlotte Brontë

Love must be completely sincere. Hate what is evil, hold on to what is good.
Romans 12:9, Good News for Modern Man

The Day Before April

MARY CAROLYN DAVIES

The day before April
    Alone, alone,
I walked in the woods
    And sat on a stone.

I sat on a broad stone
    And sang to the birds.
The tune was God's making
    But I made the words.

Moral Choices

C.S. LEWIS

People often think of Christian morality as a kind of bargain in which God says, "If you keep a lot of rules, I'll reward you, and if you don't I'll do the other thing." I do not think that is the best way of looking at it. I would much rather say that every time you make a choice you are turning the central part of you, the part of you that chooses, into something a little different from what it was before. And taking your life as a whole, with all your innumerable choices, all your life long you are slowly turning this central thing either into a Heaven creature or into a hellish creature: either into a creature that is in harmony with God, and with other creatures, and with itself, or else into one that is in a state of war and hatred with God, and with its fellow creatures, and with itself. To be the one kind of creature is Heaven: that is, it is joy, and peace, and knowledge, and power. To be the other means madness, horror, idiocy, rage, impotence, and eternal loneliness. Each of us at each moment is progressing to the one state or the other.

Better keep yourself clean and bright; you are the window through which you must see the world.

George Bernard Shaw

Myself

EDGAR A. GUEST

I have to live with myself, and so
I want to be fit for myself to know;
I want to be able as days go by
Always to look myself straight in the eye;
I don't want to stand with the setting sun
And hate myself for the things I've done.

I don't want to keep on a closet shelf
A lot of secrets about myself,
And fool myself as I come and go
Into thinking that nobody else will know
The kind of a man I really am;
I don't want to dress myself up in sham.

I want to go out with my head erect,
I want to deserve all men's respect;
But here in the struggle for fame and pelf,
I want to be able to like myself.
I don't want to think as I come and go
That I'm bluster and bluff and empty show.

I never can hide myself from me,
I see what others may never see,
I know what others may never know,
I never can fool myself — and so,
Whatever happens, I want to be
Self-respecting and conscience free.

Keep conscience clear, then never fear.

Benjamin Franklin

Work is love made visible.   Kahlil Gibran

Keep Me at It

MARJORIE HOLMES

God, give me due respect for the abilities you have given me.

Don't let me sell them short. Don't let me cheapen them. Don't let me bury my talents through indecision, cowardice, or laziness.

Plant in me the necessary determination. Keep me at it.

Rouse in me the fires of dedication. Keep me at it.

Give me the energy, strength, and will power to bring your gifts to their proper fruition. Keep me at it.

When I falter or fail lift me up and set me back on my destined path. Keep me at it.

Oh, God, when the way seems dark and there is no light there, plant at least one small signal fire at the end of the long black tunnel that I may keep plodding steadily forward toward it.

When friends laugh at me, keep me at it.

When people tempt me away from it, keep me at it.

When others scorn what I have produced, let me not be discouraged. Keep me at it.

When those who have tried and failed or who have never tried at all, those who are envious or indolent, when such people would hurt me by spiteful words or acts, let me not be bothered. Return me to my task. Keep me at it.

Let nothing really matter but these precious gifts you have entrusted to me. For their sake let me be willing and proud to make the sacrifice. Keep me at it.

Brighten the Corner Where You Are

HELEN STEINER RICE

We cannot all be famous
    or be listed in "WHO'S WHO,"
But every person great or small
    has important work to do,
For seldom do we realize
    the importance of small deeds
Or to what degree of greatness
    unnoticed kindness leads —
For it's not the big celebrity
    in a world of fame and praise,
But it's doing unpretentiously
    in undistinguished ways
The work that God assigned to us,
    unimportant as it seems,
That makes our task outstanding
    and brings reality to dreams —
So do not sit and idly wish
    for wider, new dimensions
Where you can put in practice
    your many "GOOD INTENTIONS" —
But at the spot God placed you
    begin at once to do
Little things to brighten up
    the lives surrounding you,
For if everybody brightened up
    the spot on which they're standing
By being more considerate
    and a little less demanding,
This dark old world would very soon
    eclipse the "Evening Star"
If everybody BRIGHTENED UP
    THE CORNER WHERE THEY ARE!

The Job That's Crying to Be Done

RUDYARD KIPLING

There's not a pair of legs so thin, there's not
    a head so thick,
There's not a hand so weak and white, nor
    yet a heart so sick,
But it can find some needful job that's
    crying to be done
For the glory of the Garden glorifieth
    every one.

My Work Is Best

HENRY VAN DYKE

Let me but do my work from day to day,
    In field or forest, at the desk or loom,
In roaring market-place or tranquil room;
Let me but find it in my heart to say,
When vagrant wishes beckon me astray,
    "This is my work; my blessing, not my
        doom:
Of all who live, I am the one by whom
    This work can best be done in the right
        way."

Then shall I see it not too great, nor small,
    To suit my spirit and to prove my
        powers;
Then shall I cheerful greet the laboring
    hours,
    And cheerful turn, when the long
        shadows fall
At eventide, to play and love and rest,
Because I know for me my work is best.

Prayer at Dawn

JULE CREASER

When morning breaks and I face the day,
This, dear Lord, is what I pray.
That when the same day fades to gray,
Some child of yours may happier be,
May find himself more close to Thee,
Because I lived this day.

I hope I shall always possess firmness and virtue enough to maintain what I consider the most enviable of all titles, the character of an "honest man."
George Washington

Welcome to the New Year

ELEANOR FARJEON

Hey, my lad, ho, my lad!
    Here's a New Broom.
Heaven's your housetop
    And Earth is your room.

Tuck up your shirtsleeves,
    There's plenty to do —
Look at the muddle
    That's waiting for you!

Dust in the corners
    And dirt on the floor,
Cobwebs still clinging
    To window and door.

Hey, my lad! ho, my lad!
    Nimble and keen —
Here's your New Broom, my lad!
    See you sweep clean.

Cranking the Ford

VANCE HAVNER

We kept the old Ford under "the shed" in those bygone days. Nobody out there in the hills ever dignified the shelter of the jalopy by calling it a "garage." Never will this scribe forget those winter mornings when father and I set about getting that Model T into operation.

We jacked up one rear wheel. We put a block behind the other to keep it from running backwards and another block in front to keep it from running over us. Self-preservation was not to be forgotten, for standing in front of one of those temperamental jitneys was as uncertain as standing behind a mule. Either could pack a vicious wallop, and the machine age had not as yet improved on our chances of survival in changing from mules to motors.

After we had the old gas-buggy all set we poured a kettle of boiling water on the carburetor, maybe several kettles. Then first one and then the other of us quarter-turned that crank, with a wary eye for a kick that might break an arm. If we felt unusually well that morning we worked up to where we could "spin it." Spinning the crank was a gauge of muscular might in those days. Weaklings had to content themselves with quarter-turns, but the local huskies vied in "spinning" until breath ran short, muscles almost broke through the skin, and apoplexy lurked nigh.

Success in starting that old Ford varied. Sometimes it seemed in good humor and "caught" with a willing spirit. On other mornings it was in a grouch and for no apparent reason was dead set to stay under the shed. Usually our untiring efforts were rewarded first with an occasional cough, then a few protracted coughs, until, finally, the miserable contraption got going, quivering for all the world like some aching mortal in the throes of a malarial chill. By then we were so exhausted we were half resolved to leave the thing under the shed and not go anywhere, after all.

The old Ford has gone, and so have father and the years, but oft in meditation on more profound matters those ordeals under the shed come to mind. Paul advised Timothy to stir up the gift of God within him. He had in mind, of course, not cranking Fords but re-kindling fires. But our sullen, rebellious hearts are not unlike those old jalopies, and to get our souls going these days often requires spiritual exertion not one whit less intense than the muscular effort of those Model T years.

There is the heavenly spark in all of us if we are sons of God. The Spirit indwells and there is some fire inside. We are not to furnish that ourselves, lest we fall into the sin of Nadab and Abihu or, as Isaiah put it, walk in the light of our own fire and in the sparks which we have kindled. But we do have to get the flame going, and we must apply the means of grace and provide those conditions under which the spark will break into flame and furnish power.

It takes prayer and the Word and definite application and effort. Sometimes it takes hot water on the carburetor! Isaiah lamented that there was no one who stirred himself up to take hold of God. Many of the saints today have hearts as cold and lifeless as ever that old Ford was. And until they take matters in hand and themselves by the back of the neck and make themselves meet the conditions of power, there will be no motion, they will never get anywhere. Prayer is hard work, as hard as cranking Fords, but it takes prayer and all that goes with it to get us out from under the shed.

Just for Today
VIRGINIA ELY

Just for today I will try to live through this day only, and not tackle my whole life problem at once....

Just for today I will be happy. This assumes to be true what Abraham Lincoln once said, that "Most folks are as happy as they make up their minds to be."

Just for today I will try to strengthen my mind.... I will not be a mental loafer. I will read something that requires effort, thought and concentration.

Just for today I will adjust myself to what is, and not try to adjust everything to my own desires. I will take my "luck" as it comes, and fit myself to it.

Just for today I will exercise my soul in three ways: I will do somebody a good turn, and not get found out. I will do at least two things I don't want to do — just for exercise. I will not show anyone that my feelings are hurt....

Just for today I will be agreeable. I will...not find fault with anything and not try to improve or regulate anybody except myself.

Just for today I will have a program.... I will save myself from two pests: worry and indecision.

Just for today I will have a quiet half hour all by myself, and relax.... I will try to get a better perspective of my life.

Just for today...I will not be afraid to enjoy what is beautiful, and to believe that as I give to the world, so the world will give to me.

We must always remember that God has given to every soul the responsibility of deciding what its character and destiny shall be.

Charles E. Jefferson

Prayer for Every Day
ANONYMOUS

Make me too brave to lie or be unkind.
Make me too understanding, too, to mind
The little hurts companions give, and friends,
The careless hurts that no one quite intends.
Make me too thoughtful to hurt others so.
Help me to know
The inmost hearts of those for whom I care,
Their secret wishes, all the loads they bear,
That I may add my courage to their own.
May I make lonely folks feel less alone,
And happier ones a little happier yet.
May I forget
What ought to be forgotten; and recall,
Unfailing, all
That ought to be recalled, each kindly thing,
Forgetting what might sting.
To all upon my way,
Day after day,
Let me be joy, be hope! Let my life sing!

Let Me Grow Lovely
KARLE WILSON BAKER

Let me grow lovely, growing old —
　So many fine things do:
Laces, and ivory, and gold,
　And silks need not be new;
And there is healing in old trees,
　Old streets a glamour hold;
Why may not I, as well as these,
　Grow lovely, growing old?

Face Lines

BOBBIE SOUTAR

If you haven't a few face lines then you
        haven't
really lived. Palm lines reveal what can be.
Face lines reveal what was. They begin like
        little
seedlings. Sunny days and rainy days make
them grow. Take for instance my face lines.

The one above, up near my brow, came
        from
twenty years of, "Why not mom," "Ah
        gee,"
"Why can't I go out" and "How mom how."
The little skinny ones, faint but there,
began to grow when my number one son
began to ignore the barber's chair.
This crooked one etched deep and hard,
seems to thrive on school report cards.
My huge bumpy one that connects
my eyes with one big lump
came from four rounds of measles,
chicken pox, strep throat and mumps.
The gay one that swirls in circles alike,
started to travel when Jr. started
to travel on his gold and white bike.
The others are happiness lines that you see,
when I think how lucky I am
that this family belongs to me.
So, don't waste your precious gift of
        laughter
and immunize yourself from strife.
Only a face made of plaster
is immobilized to life.
Oh no, face lines are a treasure.
Be proud when yours begin to show.
My goodness, what on earth good
is a lovely cover if
the inside could not show.

Living Truth

EDWARD LEIGH PELL

I would rather plant a single acorn that will make an oak of a century and a forest of a thousand years than sow a thousand morning glories that give joy for a day and are gone tomorrow. For the same reason, I would rather plant one living truth in the heart of a child that will multiply through the ages than scatter a thousand brilliant conceits before a great audience that will flash like sparks for an instant and like sparks disappear forever.

Do not follow where the path may lead. Go, instead, where there is no path and leave a trail.
Anonymous

Influence

JOSEPH NORRIS

Drop a pebble in the water,
And its ripples reach out far;
And the sunbeams dancing on them
May reflect them to a star.

Give a smile to someone passing,
Thereby making his morning glad;
It may greet you in the evening
When your own heart may be sad.

Do a deed of simple kindness;
Though its end you may not see,
It may reach, like widening ripples,
Down a long eternity.

To Be a Woman

ANNE MORROW LINDBERGH

...To be a woman is to have interests and duties, raying out in all directions from the central mothercore, like spokes from the hub of a wheel. The pattern of our lives is essentially circular. We must be open to all points of the compass; husband, children, friends, home, community; stretched out, exposed, sensitive like a spider's web to each breeze that blows, to each call that comes. How difficult for us, then, to achieve a balance in the midst of these contradictory tensions, and yet how necessary for the proper functioning of our lives....

There is no easy answer, no complete answer. I have only clues, shells from the sea. The bare beauty of the channelled whelk tells me that one answer, and perhaps a first step, is in simplification of life, in cutting out some of the distractions. But how? Total retirement is not possible. I cannot shed my responsibilities. I cannot permanently inhabit a desert island. I cannot be a nun in the midst of family life. I would not want to be. The solution for me, surely, is neither in total renunciation of the world, nor in total acceptance of it. I must find a balance somewhere, or an alternating rhythm between these two extremes; a swinging of the pendulum between solitude and communion, between retreat and return. In my periods of retreat, perhaps I can learn something to carry back into my worldly life....

One learns first of all in beach living the art of shedding; how little one can get along with, not how much. Physical shedding to begin with, which then mysteriously spreads into other fields. Clothes, first.... One does not need a closet-full, only a small suitcase-full. And what a relief it is! Less taking up and down of hems, less mending, and — best of all — less worry about what to wear. One finds one is shedding not only clothes — but vanity.

Next, shelter.... Here I live in a bare sea-shell of a cottage. No heat, no telephone, no plumbing to speak of, no hot water, a two-burner oil stove, no gadgets to go wrong. No rugs. There were some, but I rolled them up the first day; it is easier to sweep the sand off a bare floor. But I find I don't bustle about with unnecessary sweeping and cleaning here.... No curtains. I do not need them for privacy; the pines around my house are enough protection. I want the windows open all the time, and I don't want to worry about rain. I begin to shed my Martha-like anxiety about many things. Washable slip-covers, faded and old — I hardly see them; I don't worry about the impression they make on other people. I am shedding pride. As little furniture as possible; I shall not need much. I shall ask into my shell only those friends with whom I can be completely honest. I find I am shedding hypocrisy in human relationships. What a rest that will be! The most exhausting thing in life, I have discovered, is being insincere. That is why so much of social life is exhausting; one is wearing a mask. I have shed my mask....

Is it not rather ugly, one may ask? One collects material possessions not only for security, comfort or vanity, but for beauty as well. Is your sea-shell house not ugly and bare? No, it is beautiful, my house. It is bare, of course, but the wind, the sun, the smell of the pines blow through its bareness. The unfinished beams in the roof are veiled by cobwebs. They are lovely, I think, gazing up at them with new eyes; they soften the hard lines of the rafters as grey hairs soften the lines on a middle-aged face. I no longer pull out grey hairs or sweep down cobwebs. As for the walls, it is true they looked forbidding at first. I felt cramped and enclosed by their blank faces. I wanted to knock holes in them, to give them another dimension with pictures or windows. So I dragged home from the beach grey arms of driftwood, worn satin-smooth by wind and sand. I gathered trailing green vines with floppy red-tipped leaves. I picked up the whitened

skeletons of conchshells, their curious hollowed-out shapes faintly reminiscent of abstract sculpture. With these tacked to walls and propped up in corners, I am satisfied. I have a periscope out to the world....

I love my sea-shell of a house. I wish I could live in it always. I wish I could transport it home. But I cannot. It will not hold a husband, five children and the necessities and trappings of daily life. I can only carry back my little channelled whelk. It will sit on my desk in Connecticut, to remind me of the ideal of a simplified life, to encourage me in the game I played on the beach. To ask how little, not how much, can I get along with....

Simplification of outward life is not enough. It is merely the outside. But I am starting with the outside. I am looking at the outside of a shell, the outside of my life — the shell. The complete answer is not to be found on the outside, in an outward mode of living. This is only a technique, a road to grace. The final answer, I know, is always inside. But the outside can give a clue, can help one to find the inside answer. One is free, like the hermit crab, to change one's shell.

Do More

JOHN H. RHOADES

Do more than exist, live.
Do more than touch, feel.
Do more than look, observe.
Do more than read, absorb.
Do more than hear, listen.
Do more than listen, understand.

I Can Look Up

LOUISA MAY ALCOTT

Far away there in the sunshine are my highest aspirations. I may not reach them, but I can look up and see their beauty, believe in them, and try to follow where they lead.

Greatness

ZANE GREY

To bear up under loss;
To fight the bitterness of defeat and the
      weakness of grief;
To be victor over anger;
To smile when tears are close;
To resist disease and evil men and base
      instincts;
To hate hate and to love love;
To go on when it would seem good to die;
To look up with unquenchable faith in
      something ever more about to be.
That is what any man can do, and be great.

The Cross Roads

JOHN OXENHAM

Oft as we jog along life's winding way,
Occasion comes for every man to say —
"This road? — or That?" and as he chooses
      then,
So shall his journey end in Night or Day.

Warm Our Hearts with Thy Love

HELEN STEINER RICE

Oh, God, who made the summer
    and warmed the earth with beauty,
Warm our hearts with gratitude
    and devotion to our duty,
For in this age of violence,
    rebellion and defiance
We've forgotten the true meaning
    of "dependable reliance" —
We have lost our sense of duty
    and our sense of values, too,
And what was once unsanctioned,
    no longer is taboo,
Our standards have been lowered
    and we resist all discipline,
And our vision has been narrowed
    and blinded to all sin —
Oh, put the summer brightness
    in our closed, unseeing eyes
So in the careworn faces
    that we pass we'll recognize
The heartbreak and the loneliness,
    the trouble and despair
That a word of understanding
    would make easier to bear —
Oh, God, look down on our cold hearts
    and warm them with Your love,
And grant us Your forgiveness
    which we're so unworthy of.

From *The Secret*

RALPH SPAULDING CUSHMAN

I met God in the morning
    When my day was at its best,
And His presence came like sunrise,
    Like a glory in my breast.

All day long the Presence lingered,
    All day long He stayed with me,
And we sailed in perfect calmness
    O'er a very troubled sea.

So I think I know the secret,
    Learned from many a troubled way:
You must seek Him in the morning
    If you want Him through the day!

The Craftsman

GRACE NOLL CROWELL

I have admired any skillful craftsman
Whose mind retains the fabric of a dream,
Dreamed in his youth, of labor's high
    perfection
From which some new accomplishment
    might gleam:
New use of tools which others long had
    handled,
Their steel blades glittering beneath his
    hands
That bridges and high climbing walls be
    safer,
Because one skilled in labor understands.

The vision of some possible invention
To ease men's aching muscles and tense
    nerves,
Regardless of the hours of endeavor
Through which a dedicated workman
    serves.
The seeking always for a higher standard
Of the completed tasks throughout his
    days,
With ever for his aim, clean, honest
    service —
Truly this man deserves our heartfelt
    praise.

God's Post Office

VANCE HAVNER

Our post office is a dull and commonplace affair, viewed from without by the uninterested passer-by. One would hardly connect it with anything thrilling or romantic. Just a little wired cage, a few boxes, a desk and a table — can anything worth while come through that little window from such a plain and unpoetic corner of a country store?

Indeed there can! Through that little window have come messages that have sent me fairly skipping down the road, gleeful as a farm-boy on his first spring fishing trip. It has relayed to me letters which have fairly changed the course of my career. And from that very ordinary post office have come missives that have saddened my soul.

Really there are few places on earth more charged with human interest than a post office. Have you ever thought how packed with joy and sorrow, despair and delight, one ugly mail-bag may be? Have you reflected how one day's batch of letters may file out through that little window to prosper some and pauperize others, lead this man to marriage and that to murder, kill here and cure there? I've almost decided our little old post office is the most romantic place of all!

But the post office is not a source, it is only a medium. It does not create these potent messages, it only relays them from one creator to you. You and I are human post offices. We are daily giving out messages of some sort to the world. They do not come from us, but through us; we do not create, we convey. And they come either from hell or from heaven.

Men study how to make their lives more interesting. Take a lesson from the post office. It is interesting, not because of itself, but because of what it passes on to men. The world will make a beaten path to your door if you bring them news from heaven. What letters go through the window of your life? Letters of truth and hope, to cheer and console? Or do you hand out dirty trash, worthless drivel, black-edged missives of misery?

Every Christian is a postmaster for God. His duty is to pass out good news from above. If the postmaster kept all the mail and refused to give it out, he would soon be in trouble. No wonder some Christians are so miserable: they keep God's blessings within their own little lives, and soon there is congestion. God does not send us good things from the heavenly headquarters merely for our personal enjoyment. Some of them may be addressed to us, but most of them belong to our fellow-men, and we must pass them on.

He would be a poor postmaster who spent his time decorating the post office and failed to distribute the mail. For people do not come there to see the post office: they come for the mail. The Christian seriously misunderstands his work as God's postmaster if he spends his time decorating his place of business and neglects to deliver God's messages through him to men. To be sure, a clean and tidy post office is desirable, and so is a holy life: but it is easy for one to become so engrossed in introspection that he makes his goodness his business. Keeping our lives clean is only tidying up the office to carry on God's business. If it is an end in itself, nothing passes out to men.

How thrilling the plainest life can be when it becomes a function in God's great system and not a selfish enterprise! The tiniest post office can bear a letter that may wreck or bless a nation. And the simplest life can relay blessings that may rock a continent toward God.

If you are a believer, you are God's postmaster in the little nook where you live. Keep the office clean, but do not make that more important than delivering the messages. Men will soon learn to gather at the window and will bring you, in return, letters of their own to pass on to others.

The Goat and the Goatherd

AESOP

A Goatherd had sought to bring back a stray Goat to his flock. He whistled and sounded his horn in vain; the straggler paid no attention to the summons. At last the Goatherd threw a stone, and breaking its horn, begged the Goat not to tell his master. The Goat replied, "Why, you silly fellow, the horn will speak though I be silent."

Do not attempt to hide things which cannot be hid.

A Life Heroic

SARAH K. BOLTON

I like the man who faces what he must
    With step triumphant and a heart of
      cheer;
    Who fights the daily battle without
      fear;
Sees his hopes fail, yet keeps unfaltering
    trust
That God is God; that somehow, true and
    just
    His plans work out for mortals; not a
      tear
    Is shed when fortune, which the world
      holds dear,
Falls from his grasp; better, with love, a
    crust
Than living in dishonor; envies not
    Nor loses faith in man; but does his
      best
Nor ever mourns over his humbler lot,
    But with a smile and words of hope,
      gives zest
To every toiler; he alone is great
Who by a life heroic conquers fate.

Let Me Dare

ROBERT H. SCHULLER

Lord,
give me the
courage to
dare to love.
It's risky, I know,
for I might be
rejected, and that hurts.
Or love-starved people
will leap to respond
to this rare
offer of honest affection,
and they may expect
too much — too soon.
So give me the nerve to
live bravely and love
dangerously! I may lose
my freedom, but
at least I won't be lonely.
In the name of my Savior, Jesus Christ.
Amen.

Another Look

ALICE JOYCE DAVIDSON

A critic's job is easy,
It's not hard to criticize —
But when you're on the "taking" end,
That's where the trouble lies,
For it's often hard to see ourselves
In someone else's eyes....
So, when you are corrected,
Don't take it as a blow,
But take correction graciously,
For in your heart you know
The better person you become,
The closer to God you grow!

From *Little Women*

LOUISA MAY ALCOTT

"November is the most disagreeable month in the whole year," said Margaret, standing at the window one dull afternoon, looking out at the frost-bitten garden.

"That's the reason I was born in it," observed Jo, pensively, quite unconscious of the blot on her nose.

"If something very pleasant should happen now, we should think it a delightful month," said Beth, who took a hopeful view of everything, even November.

"I dare say; but nothing pleasant ever does happen in this family," said Meg, who was out of sorts. "We go grubbing along day after day, without a bit of change, and very little fun. We might as well be in a treadmill...."

Meg sighed, and turned to the frost-bitten garden again; Jo groaned, and leaned both elbows on the table, in a despondent attitude, but Amy patted away energetically; and Beth, who sat at the other window, said, smiling, "Two pleasant things are going to happen right away; Marmee is coming down the street, and Laurie is tramping through the garden as if he had something nice to tell."

In they both came, Mrs. March with her usual question, "Any letter from Father, girls?" and Laurie to say in his persuasive way, "Won't some of you come for a drive? I've been working away at mathematics till my head is in a muddle, and I'm going to freshen my wits by a brisk turn.... Come, Jo, you and Beth will go, won't you?"

"Of course we will."

"Much obliged, but I'm busy"; and Meg whisked out her workbasket, for she had agreed with her mother that it was best, for her at least, not to drive often with the young gentleman.

"We three will be ready in a minute," cried Amy, running away to wash her hands.

"Can I do anything for you, Madam Mother?" asked Laurie, leaning over Mrs. March's chair, with the affectionate look and tone he always gave her.

"No, thank you, except call at the office, if you'll be so kind, dear. It's our day for a letter, and the postman hasn't been. Father is as regular as the sun, but there's some delay on the way, perhaps."

A sharp ring interrupted her, and a minute after Hannah came in with a letter.

"It's one of them horrid telegraph things, mum," she said, handling it as if she was afraid it would explode and do some damage.

At the word "telegraph," Mrs. March snatched it, read the two lines it contained, and dropped back into her chair as white as if the little paper had sent a bullet to her heart. Laurie dashed downstairs for water, while Meg and Hannah supported her, and Jo read aloud, in a frightened voice:

"Mrs. March:
    Your husband is very ill. Come at once.
        S. Hale,
        Blank Hospital, Washington."

How still the room was as they listened breathlessly, how strangely the day darkened outside, and how suddenly the whole world seemed to change, as the girls gathered about their mother, feeling as if all the happiness and support of their lives was about to be taken from them. Mrs. March was herself again directly; read the message over, and stretched out her arms to her daughters, saying, in a tone they never forgot, "I shall go at once, but it may be too late. Oh, children, children, help me to bear it!"

For several minutes there was nothing but the sound of sobbing in the room, mingled with broken words of comfort, tender assurances of help, and hopeful whispers that died away in tears. Poor Hannah was the first to recover, and with unconscious wisdom she set all the rest a good example; for, with her, work was the panacea for most afflictions.

"The Lord keep the dear man! I won't

waste no time a cryin', but git your things ready right away, mum," she said, heartily, as she wiped her face on her apron, gave her mistress a warm shake of the hand with her own hard one, and went away, to work like three women in one.

"She's right; there's no time for tears now. Be calm, girls, and let me think."

They tried to be calm, poor things, as their mother sat up, looking pale, but steady, and put away her grief to think and plan for them.

"Where's Laurie?" she asked presently, when she had collected her thoughts, and decided on the first things to be done.

"Here, ma'am. Oh, let me do something!" cried the boy, hurrying from the next room, whither he had withdrawn, feeling that their first sorrow was too sacred for even his friendly eyes to see.

"Send a telegram saying I will come at once. The next train goes early in the morning. I'll take that."

"What else? The horses are ready; I can go anywhere, do anything," he said, looking ready to fly to the ends of the earth.

"Leave a note at Aunt March's. Jo, give me that pen and paper."

Tearing off the blank side of one of her newly-copied pages, Jo drew the table before her mother, well knowing that money for the long, sad journey must be borrowed, and feeling as if she could do anything to add a little to the sum for her father.

"Now go, dear; but don't kill yourself driving at a desperate pace; there is no need of that."

Mrs. March's warning was evidently thrown away; for five minutes later Laurie tore by the window on his own fleet horse, riding as if for his life....

Everything was arranged by the time Laurie returned with a note from Aunt March enclosing the desired sum, and a few lines repeating what she had often said before — that she had always told them it was absurd for March to go into the army, always predicted that no good would come of it,

and she hoped that they would take her advice next time. Mrs. March put the note in the fire, the money in her purse, and went on with her preparations, with her lips folded tightly, in a way which Jo would have understood if she had been there.

The short afternoon wore away; all the other errands were done, and Meg and her mother busy at some necessary needlework, while Beth and Amy got tea, and Hannah finished her ironing with what she called a "slap and a bang," but still Jo did not come. They began to get anxious; and Laurie went off to find her, for no one ever knew what freak Jo might take into her head. He missed her, however, and she came walking in with a very queer expression of countenance, for there was a mixture of fun and fear, satisfaction and regret in it, which puzzled the family as much as did the roll of bills she laid before her mother, saying, with a little choke in her voice, "That's my contribution towards making Father comfortable, and bringing him home!"

"My dear, where did you get it? Twenty-five dollars? Jo, I hope you haven't done anything rash?"

"No, it's mine honestly; I didn't beg, borrow, or steal it. I earned it; and I don't think you'll blame me, for I only sold what was my own."

As she spoke, Jo took off her bonnet, and a general outcry arose, for all her abundant hair was cut short.

"Your hair! Your beautiful hair!" "Oh, Jo, how could you? Your one beauty." "My dear girl, there was no need of this." "She doesn't look like my Jo anymore, but I love her dearly for it!"

As everyone exclaimed, and Beth hugged the cropped head tenderly, Jo assumed an indifferent air, which did not deceive anyone a particle, and said, rumpling up the brown bush, and trying to look as if she liked it, "It doesn't affect the fate of the nation, so don't wail, Beth. It will be good for my vanity; I was getting too proud of my wig. It will do my brains good to have that mop taken off; my head feels deliciously light and cool, and the barber said I could soon have a curly crop, which will be boyish, becoming, and easy to keep in order. I'm satisfied; so please take the money, and let's have supper."

"Tell me all about it, Jo. I am not quite satisfied, but I can't blame you, for I know how willingly you sacrificed your vanity, as you call it, to your love. But, my dear, it was not necessary, and I'm afraid you will regret it one of these days," said Mrs. March.

"No, I won't!" returned Jo, stoutly, feeling much relieved that her prank was not entirely condemned.

"What made you do it?" asked Amy, who would as soon have thought of cutting off her head as her pretty hair.

"Well, I was wild to do something for Father," replied Jo, as they gathered about the table, for healthy young people can eat even in the midst of trouble. "I hate to borrow as much as Mother does, and I knew Aunt March would croak; she always does, if you ask for a ninepence. Meg gave all her quarterly salary toward the rent, and I only got some clothes with mine, so I felt wicked, and was bound to have some money, if I sold the nose off my face to get it."

"You needn't feel wicked, my child; you had no winter things, and got the simplest with your own hard earnings," said Mrs. March, with a look that warmed Jo's heart.

"I hadn't the least idea of selling my hair at first, but as I went along I kept thinking what I could do, and feeling as if I'd like to dive into some of the rich stores and help myself. In a barber's window I saw tails of hair with the prices marked; and one black tail, not so thick as mine, was forty dollars. It came over me all of a sudden that I had one thing to make money out of, and without stopping to think, I walked in, asked if they bought hair, and what they would give for mine."

"I don't see how you dared to do it," said Beth, in a tone of awe.

"Oh, he was a little man who looked as if he merely lived to oil his hair. He rather stared, at first, as if he wasn't used to having girls bounce into his shop and ask him to buy their hair. He said he didn't care about mine, it wasn't the fashionable colour, and he never paid much for it in the first place; the work put into it made it dear, and so on. It was getting late, and I was afraid, if it wasn't done right away, that I shouldn't have it done at all, and you know when I start to do a thing, I hate to give it up; so I begged him to take it, and told him why I was in such a hurry. It was silly, I dare say, but it changed his mind, for I got rather excited, and told the story in my topsy-turvy way, and his wife heard, and said so kindly: 'Take it, Thomas, and oblige the young lady; I'd do as much for our Jimmy any day if I had a spire of hair worth selling.'"

"Who was Jimmy?" asked Amy, who liked to have things explained as they went along.

"Her son, she said, who was in the army. How friendly such things make strangers feel, don't they? She talked away all the time the man clipped, and diverted my mind nicely."

"Didn't you feel dreadfully when the first cut came?" asked Meg, with a shiver.

"I took a last look at my hair while the man got his things, and that was the end of it. I never snivel over trifles like that; I will confess, though, I felt queer when I saw the dear old hair laid out on the table, and felt only the short, rough ends on my head. It almost seemed as if I'd an arm or a leg off. The woman saw me look at it, and picked out a long lock for me to keep. I'll give it to you, Marmee, just to remember past glories by; for a crop is so comfortable I don't think I shall ever have a mane again."

Mrs. March folded the wavy chestnut lock, and laid it away with a short grey one in her desk. She only said, "Thank you, deary," but something in her face made the girls change the subject, and talk as cheerfully as they could about Mrs. Brooke's kindness, the prospect of a fine day tomorrow, and the happy time they would have when Father came home to be nursed.

No one wanted to go to bed, when, at ten

o'clock, Mrs. March put up the last finished job, and said, "Come girls." Beth went to the piano and played the father's favourite hymn; all began bravely, but broke down one by one, till Beth was left alone, singing with all her heart, for to her music was always a sweet consoler.

"Go to bed and don't talk, for we must be up early, and shall need all the sleep we can get. Good night, my darlings," said Mrs. March, as the hymn ended, for no one cared to try another.

They kissed her quietly, and went to bed as silently as if the dear invalid lay in the next room. Beth and Amy soon fell asleep in spite of the great trouble, but Meg lay awake, thinking the most serious thoughts she had ever known in her short life. Jo lay motionless, and her sister fancied that she was asleep, till a stifled sob made her exclaim, as she touched a wet cheek: "Jo, dear, what is it? Are you crying about Father?"

"No, not now."

"What then?"

"My — my hair!" burst out poor Jo, trying vainly to smother her emotion in the pillow.

It did not sound at all comical to Meg, who kissed and caressed the afflicted heroine in the tenderest manner.

"I'm not sorry," protested Jo, with a choke. "I'd do it again tomorrow, if I could. It's only the vain, selfish part of me that goes and cries in this silly way. Don't tell anyone, it's all over now. I thought you were asleep, so I just made a little private moan for my one beauty. How came you to be awake?"

"I can't sleep, I'm so anxious," said Meg.

"Think about something pleasant, and you'll soon drop off."

"I tried it, but felt wider awake than ever."

"What did you think of?"

"Handsome faces — eyes particularly," answered Meg, smiling to herself, in the dark.

"What colour do you like best?"

"Brown — that is, sometimes; blue are lovely."

Jo laughed, and Meg sharply ordered her not to talk, then amiably promised to make her hair curl, and fell asleep to dream of living in her castle in the air.

The clocks were striking midnight, and the rooms were very still, as a figure glided quietly from bed to bed, smoothing a coverlet here, settling a pillow there, and pausing to look long and tenderly at each unconscious face, to kiss each with lips that mutely blessed, and to pray the fervent prayers which only mothers utter. As she lifted the curtain to look out into the dreary night, the moon broke suddenly from behind the clouds, and shone upon her like a bright, benignant face, which seemed to whisper in the silence, "Be comforted, dear soul! There is always light behind the clouds."

A Prayer

EDWIN MARKHAM

Teach me, Father, how to be
Kind and patient as a tree.
Joyfully the crickets croon
Under shady oak at noon;
Beetle, on his mission bent,
Tarries in that cooling tent.
Let me, also, cheer a spot,
Hidden field or garden grot —
Place where passing souls can rest
On the way and be their best.

If I Had Three Wishes

MALCOLM SARGENT

I would not ask for health because unbroken health might rob me of experiences that come through sharing illness and suffering. My first wish would be for sympathy and understanding of others. My second wish would be for a sense of humor; and my third wish, a very firm one indeed, for the gift of faith, the Christian faith, because men and women get from such a faith strength to live, and, indeed, strength to die.

My Creed

EDGAR A. GUEST

To live as gently as I can;
To be, no matter where, a man;
To take what comes of good or ill
And cling to faith and honor still;
To do my best, and let that stand
The record of my brain and hand;
And then, should failure come to me,
Still work and hope for victory.

To have no secret place wherein
I stoop unseen to shame or sin;
To be the same when I'm alone
As when my every deed is known;
To live undaunted, unafraid
Of any step that I have made;
To be without pretense or sham
Exactly what men think I am.

To leave some simple mark behind
To keep my having lived in mind;
If enmity to aught I show,
To be an honest, generous foe,
To play my little part, nor whine
That greater honors are not mine.
This, I believe, is all I need
For my philosophy and creed.

Knowledge and understanding are life's faithful companions who will never prove untrue to you. For knowledge is your crown, and understanding your staff; and when they are with you, you can possess no greater treasures. Kahlil Gibran

The Falling Star

SARA TEASDALE

I saw a star slide down the sky,
Blinding the north as it went by,
Too burning and too quick to hold,
Too lovely to be bought or sold,
Good only to make wishes on
And then forever to be gone.

The Glimmer of God

IRENE PETTIT McKEEHAN

I have closed the door on doubt.
I will go by what light I can find,
And hold up my hands and reach them out
To the glimmer of God in the dark, and call,
"I am Thine. Though I grope and stumble
       and fall,
I serve, and Thy service is kind."

Understanding

ONE SUMMER NIGHT in a seaside cottage, a small boy felt himself lifted from bed. Dazed with sleep, he heard his mother murmur about the lateness of the hour, heard his father laugh. Then he was borne in his father's arms, with the swiftness of a dream, down the porch steps, out onto the beach.

Overhead the sky blazed with stars. "Watch!" his father said. And incredibly, as he spoke, one of the stars moved. In a streak of golden fire, it flashed across the astonished heavens. And before the wonder of this could fade, another star leaped from its place, and then another, plunging toward the restless sea. "What is it?" the child whispered. "Shooting stars," his father said. "They come every year on certain nights in August. I thought you'd like to see the show."

That was all: just an unexpected glimpse of something haunting and mysterious and beautiful. But, back in bed, the child stared for a long time into the dark, rapt with the knowledge that all around the quiet house the night was full of the silent music of the falling stars.

Decades have passed, but I remember that night still, because I was the fortunate seven-year-old whose father believed that a new experience was more important for a small boy than an unbroken night's sleep. No doubt in my childhood I had the usual quota of playthings, but these are forgotten now. What I remember is the night the stars fell....

ARTHUR GORDON

From *The Old Astronomer*

SARAH WILLIAMS

Though my soul may set in darkness, it will
    rise in perfect light,
I have loved the stars too fondly to be
    fearful of the night.

Little Boys in Church

ROBERT P. TRISTRAM COFFIN

Small boys in the church pews grow
Very fast, the first you know
Ones only halfway up are older
And at their father's cheek or shoulder.

One day they are only bright
Heads that in the high church light
Look as if they were washed in dew,
Their ears and hair are all so new.

This Sunday only heads that dance,
Next Sunday heads and coats and pants,
All the boys have sprung uphill,
Heads are erect, and ears stand still.

One week they are boys, and then
Next week they are slim young men
Standing very still and lean,
Perilously scrubbed and clean.

Enjoy each small boy while you can,
Tomorrow there will be a man
Standing taller than belief,
Little boys in church are brief.

The amen of Nature is always a flower.
                Oliver Wendell Holmes

There Are Blessings in Everything

HELEN STEINER RICE

Blessings come in many guises
    That God alone in love devises,
And sickness which we dread so much
    Can bring a very "healing touch" —
For often on the "wings of pain"
    The peace we sought before in vain
Will come to us with "sweet surprise"
    For God is merciful and wise —
And through long hours of tribulation
    God gives us time for meditation,
And no sickness can be counted loss
    That teaches us to "bear our cross."

Somewhere the Child

KATE DOUGLAS WIGGIN

Among the thousands of tiny things growing up all over the land, some of them under my very wing — watched and tended, unwatched and untended, loved, unloved, protected from danger, thrust into temptation — among them somewhere is the child who will write the novel that will stir men's hearts to nobler issues and incite them to better deeds.

There is the child who will paint the greatest picture or carve the greatest statue of the age, another who will deliver his country in an hour of peril; another who will give his life for a great principle; and another, born more of the spirit than of the flesh, who will live continually on the heights of moral being, and dying, draw men after him.

It may be that I shall preserve one of these children to the race. It is a peg big enough on which to hang a hope, for every child born into the world is a new incarnate thought of God, an ever fresh and radiant possibility.

The All-Embracing

FREDERICK W. FABER

If our love were but more simple,
    We should take Him at His word;
And our lives would be all sunshine
    In the sweetness of our Lord.

The most precious things of life are near at hand. Each of you has the whole wealth of the universe at your very door. All may be yours by stretching forth your hand and taking it.   John Burroughs

The Apprentice

DOROTHY CANFIELD

The day had been one of those unbearable ones, when every sound had set her teeth on edge like chalk creaking on a blackboard.... And of course it would happen, as the end to such a day, that just as the sun went down back of the mountain and the long twilight began, she noticed that Rollie was not around....

Perhaps he had sneaked upstairs to lie on her bed where he was not supposed to go — not that *she* would have minded! That rule was a part of Mother's fussiness, part too of Mother's bossiness. It was *her* bed, wasn't it? But was she allowed the say-so about it? Not on your life. They told her she could have things the way she wanted in her own room, now she was in her teens, but — her heart raged against unfairness as she took the stairs stormily, two steps at a time, her pigtails flopping up and down on her back. If Rollie was on her bed she was just going to

let him stay right there, and Mother could shake her head and frown all she wanted to.

But he was not there. The bedspread and pillow were crumpled but not from his weight. She had flung herself down to cry there that afternoon. And then she couldn't.... She could only lie there, her hands doubled up hard, furious that she had nothing to cry about. Not really. She was too big to cry just over Father's having said to her, severely, "I told you if I let you take the chess set you were to put it away when you got through with it. One of the pawns was on the floor of our bedroom this morning. I stepped on it. If I'd had my shoes on, I'd have broken it."

...She heard her mother coming down the hall, and hastily shut her door. She had a right to shut the door to her own room, hadn't she?

...But her mother did not open the door. Her feet went steadily on along the hall, and then, carefully, slowly, down the stairs.

...Up in her bedroom behind her closed door the thirteen-year-old stamped her foot in a rage, none the less savage and heart-shaking because it was mysterious to her.

But she had not located Rollie. Before she would let her father and mother know she had lost sight of him, forgotten about him, she would be cut into little pieces. They would not scold her, she knew. They would do worse. They would look at her. And in their silence she would hear droning on reproachfully what they had repeated and repeated when the sweet, woolly collie-puppy had first been in her arms and she had been begging to keep him for her own....

Even then, at the very minute when as a darling baby dog he was beginning to love her, her father and mother were saying, so cold, so reasonable — gosh! how she *hated* reasonableness! — "Now, Peg, remember that, living where we do, with sheep on the farms around us, it is a serious responsibility to have a collie dog. If you keep him, you've got to be the one to take care of him. You'll have to be the one to train him to stay at home. We're too busy with you children to start bringing up a puppy, too."

...All the time her parents kept hammering away: "If you want him, you can have him. But you must be responsible for him. If he gets to running sheep, he'll just have to be shot, you know that."

They had not said, aloud, "Like the Wilsons' collie." They never mentioned that awfulness — her racing unsuspectingly down across the fields just at the horrible moment when Mr. Wilson shot his collie caught in the very act of killing sheep. They probably thought that if they never spoke about it, she would forget it — *forget* the crack of that rifle, and the collapse of the great beautiful dog!...She hadn't forgotten. She never would. She knew as well as they did, how important it was to train a collie-puppy about sheep. They didn't need to rub it in like that....

And now, this afternoon, when he was six months old, tall, rangy, powerful, standing up far above her knee, nearly to her waist, she didn't know where he was.... She looked every room over carefully.

...But he did not answer. She stood still on the front porch to think.

Could he have gone up to their special place in the edge of the field where the three young pines, their branches growing close to the ground, made a triangular, walled-in space, completely hidden from the world?...

It didn't seem as though he would have gone alone there....

No, he was not there. She stood, irresolutely, in the roofless, green-walled triangular hide-out, wondering what to do next.

Then, before she knew what thought had come into her mind, its emotional impact knocked her down. At least her knees crumpled under her. Last Wednesday the Wilsons had brought their sheep down to the home farm from the upper pasture!...

She was off like a racer at the crack of the starting pistol, her long, strong legs stretched in great leaps, her pigtails flying.

She took the short cut down to the upper edge of the meadow, regardless of the brambles. Their thorn-spiked, wiry stems tore at her flesh, but she did not care. She welcomed the pain....

She was tearing through the pine woods now, rushing down the steep, stony path, tripping over roots, half-falling, catching herself just in time, not slackening her speed. She burst out on the open knoll above the river meadow, calling wildly, "Rollie, here, Rollie, here, boy! here! here!" She tried to whistle, but she was crying too hard to pucker her lips. She had not, till then, known she was crying....

Her breath had given out. For once in her life she had wept all the tears there were in her body. Her hands were so stiff with cold she could scarcely close them. How her nose was running! Simply streaming down her upper lip. And she had no handkerchief. She lifted her skirt, fumbled for her slip, stooped, blew her nose on it, wiped her eyes, drew a long quavering breath — and heard something! Far off in the distance, a faint sound, like a dog's muffled bark....

She began to run again, but now she was not sobbing.... She stopped short and leaned weakly against a tree.... For she could now not only hear that it was Rollie's bark. She could hear, in the dog language she knew as well as he, what he was saying in those excited yips — that he had run a woodchuck into a hole in the tumbled stone wall, that he almost had him, that the intoxicating wild-animal smell was as close to him — almost — as if he had his jaws on his quarry. Yip! Woof! Yip! Yip!... He was still only a puppy. Like all puppies, he got perfectly crazy over wild-animal smells. Probably he truly hadn't heard her calling and whistling.

All the same, all the same — she stood stock-still, staring intently into the twilight — you couldn't let a puppy grow up just as he wanted to. It wouldn't be safe — for *him*. Somehow she would have to make him understand that he mustn't go off this way, by himself. He must be trained to know how to do what a good dog does — not because *she* wanted it, but for his own sake....

When he heard his own special young god approaching, he...jumped up on her...and licked her face.

She pushed him away. Her face and voice were grave. "No, Rollie, *no!*" she said severely. "You're *bad.* You know you're not to go off in the woods without me! You are — a — *bad dog.*"

...The gladness went out of his eyes, the waving plume of his tail slowly lowered to slinking, guilty dejection....

With a shudder of misery he lay down, his tail stretched out limp on the ground, his head flat on his paws, his ears drooping — ears ringing with the doomsday awfulness of the voice he loved and revered....

As miserable as he, she sat down by him. "I don't *want* to scold you. But I have to! I have to bring you up right, or you'll get shot, Rollie. You mustn't go away from the house without me, do you hear, *never."*

...Hearing sternness, or something else he did not recognize, in the beloved voice, he shut his eyes tight in sorrow, and made a little whimpering lament in his throat.

...It was almost dark now. "We'll be late for supper, Rollie," she said, responsibly. Pushing him gently off she stood up. "Home, Rollie, home."

...When they came out into the open pasture, Rollie ran back to get her to play with him.... His high spirits were ridiculous. But infectious.... Following him, not noting in the dusk where she was going, she felt the grassy slope drop steeply.... She had rolled down that slope a million times — years and years before, when she was a kid herself, six or seven years ago. It was fun. She remembered well the whirling dizziness of the descent, all the world turning crazily over, and over. And the delicious giddy staggering when you first stood up, the earth still spinning under your feet.

"All right, Rollie, let's go," she cried, and flung herself down in the rolling position, her arms straight up over her head....

His wild frolicsome barking might have come from her own throat, so accurately did it sound the way she felt — crazy, foolish — like a little kid, no more than five years old, the age she had been when she had last rolled down that hill....

The living-room windows were just before them. How yellow the lighted windows looked when you were in the darkness going home....

Her mother could not see her. She did not need to. "For goodness' sakes, go and wash," she called.

In the long mirror across the room she saw herself, her hair hanging wild, her long bare legs scratched, her broadly smiling face dirt-streaked, her torn skirt dangling, her dog laughing up at her. Gosh, was it a relief to feel your own age, just exactly thirteen years old!

A Bundle of Possibilities

HARRY EMERSON FOSDICK

Rebellion against your handicaps gets you nowhere. Self-pity gets you nowhere. One must have the adventurous daring to accept oneself as a bundle of possibilities and undertake the most interesting game in the world — making the most of one's best.

We live in this world, that is true. But the point of living is: don't be subdued by it.   Billy Graham

The Nightingale and the Glowworm

WILLIAM COWPER

A Nightingale that all day long
Had cheer'd the village with his song,
Nor yet at eve his note suspended,
Nor yet when eventide was ended,
Began to feel, as well he might,
The keen demands of appetite;
When looking eagerly around,
He spied far off, upon the ground,
A something shining in the dark,
And knew the Glowworm by his spark;
So, stooping down from hawthorn top,
He thought to put him in his crop.
The worm, aware of his intent,
Harangued him thus, right eloquent:
"Did you admire my lamp," quoth he,
"As much as I your minstrelsy,
You would abhor to do me wrong,
As much as I to spoil your song:
For 'twas the self-same Power Divine
Taught you to sing, and me to shine;
That you with music, I with light,
Might beautify and cheer the night."
The songster heard this short oration,
And warbling out his approbation,
Released him, as my story tells,
And found a supper somewhere else.

God evidently does not intend us all to be rich, or powerful, or great, but He does intend us all to be friends.
                                                    Ralph Waldo Emerson

The Summer of Aunt Liz Noah

PEG BRACKEN

On a recent summer afternoon, looking out my kitchen window, I suddenly experienced an unexpected moment of mourning for all things brave and beautiful and funny that aren't around anymore, and especially for my Aunt Liz Noah.

Being Grandpa's younger sister, she was therefore my great-aunt, who'd painted pictures and illustrated books in New York's Greenwich Village, a cheerful spinster till age 35. But when she met John Noah, a splendid-looking actor, it was a swift, glorious, high-hearted romance. They honeymooned in Italy and resettled in the Village where she presently produced a beautiful baby daughter who wasn't quite three when the tragedy happened: both baby and husband died together in a theater fire.

It nearly killed Liz Noah, who was still in the hospital with a breakdown when both parents began their deaths back in Kansas. Suddenly regaining her equilibrium, she packed her grief, bags, and a trunkful of big-city hats to go back home and cope. (And coincidentally be there for me to visit and laugh with on our family vacations, for despite everything, she is the person I've laughed with most, more than with anyone.)

After they died, she stayed to construct — gradually — a workable life: reading, painting, teaching kids to paint, and riding Grandpa's amiable chestnut mare, old Kiwani Girl. To me, everything about Liz Noah was perfectly splendid: her strong aquiline nose and deep-set somber eyes, her leanness, her mane of silver-streaked dark hair, and her customary faded old riding pants and shirt.

Between her house and Grandpa's were eight well-populated blocks. You passed the Caramel Lady's house, 50 cents a pound, 60 cents with nuts. And the man-who'd-been-in-jail's house, which you walked past fast. And faster still past The Elms, the nursing home where old people in bathrobes shuffled around the yard on warm days. (I'd once asked Grandma if she'd end up there, and she'd said No, you only went there if you had neither chick nor child. It didn't occur to either of us, I'm sure, that Aunt Liz Noah had neither chick nor child.) And finally to Liz Noah's house, its blue front door opening into a quite different world.

In an ecru era, her bright-white walls were alive with paintings, lithographs, sketches, and the kitchen was her studio....

And everywhere were books. Which I read. I remember it was at Liz Noah's that I first encountered Anderson and Cather, Frost and Dickinson, Yeats and Henry James....

Then there were Liz Noah's hats, the trunkful she'd brought back from New York. She let me model them sometimes, and I'd look like a mushroom, for they were big, marvelous hats designed for a tall woman. I remember a lovely sea-green chiffon concoction, and a glorious red velvet, all tilt and feathers.

And we'd talk, swinging idly in the glider on the shady porch, and make rhymes, and she'd do funny spidery sketches for our growing collection of addled adages: *It's a wise child who spills his own milk. A rolling stone seldom bites.* (And if you think it impossible to depict a rolling stone in the very act of not biting, you just haven't seen Liz Noah's work.) And she'd talk about the family. I remember asking her once what heredity meant.

"Well—" and here she dropped one eyelid smooth as a rolled-down window shade while the other eye stayed stark-staring open, a remarkably droll wink she had — "It's like this," she explained. "If your grandma didn't have any children and your mother didn't either, then you probably inherit a tendency not to have any children yourself. That's heredity." Which made everything crystal-clear momentarily till it clouded up again.

And often we'd stroll down the drowsing summer street to the hotel soda fountain for an Osage Orange Soda, a luscious medley of rich vanilla ice cream, yellow as a four-egg custard, and fresh orange juice and lots of fizz.

Oh, we had good times, Aunt Liz Noah and I, and I know now that someone to laugh and wonder and speculate with is rare and to be valued. And I valued Aunt Liz Noah, though not enough. Or so I think now.

The trouble is that growing up is a full-time job. So often — busy with it — you shelve the elderly relatives you formerly found fascinating. Or think about them only when you're there, so they come alive only when you show up, the way the refrigerator light goes on when you open the door.

After McKinleyville High, Ganister moved to a far meadow of my mind. Busy growing up, I didn't realize that growing old takes time and attention too.

Two springs later, Mama wrote me that one afternoon a neighbor noticed milk curdling on the Noah back porch. So she pounded on the locked door, then forced open a window and found Liz Noah lying on the floor, in pajamas.

"What are you doing?" asked Mrs. Ostigsen.

"I like it down here," Aunt Liz Noah answered, with asperity. "I'm going to grow potatoes under the bed."

"She could've too," said Mrs. O, with relish, to anyone who'd listen. So Aunt Liz Noah went to the hospital with a broken hip, though it mended fast and she was soon back home.

Increasingly, though, she couldn't or wouldn't cope; wouldn't dust, swab out the sink, put butter away. Finally, after three months' virtual starvation on tea and toast, she developed on all-over skin rash the doctor called pellagra. He then wrote Mama. But Mama couldn't persuade Liz Noah to come home with her, and the only solution was The Elms.

She'd been there a year when I saw her again. My new husband and I were heading west in a secondhand car, and I asked him to disappear, briefly. I didn't want Mike to meet the Liz Noah I'd probably find here in this shabby, brown-linoleumed place with the ubiquitous handrailings and wheelchairs and bleak smells.

She was sitting by a window, wearing a crisp blue-and-pink housedress — Liz Noah, in a housedress! I hugged her, feeling her narrow delicate bones, fragile as matchsticks through the gingham, and I wanted to weep. She was lost in that atrocious dress. And her hair was a soiled-looking yellow-gray, cut in an institutional bob.

"I'm so glad to see you!" I said. Truth, but a lie too.

"It can't be much of a treat," she said, sounding like herself. But she was looking past me. "Where is — who is —" She stopped, frowning. "My words are all thumbs," she said, and tapped her wedding ring impatiently. She remembered my recent marriage but not my new name.

I told her, and felt clumsy saying I wanted Mike to meet her. Then why hadn't I brought him? But she dismissed that.

"I'm not dressed for it," she said. "How do you like this little number? Chanel, I think."

"It's awful," I said sincerely. "You're not really ready for old ladyhood yet." And I wondered then if anybody is; and now that I'm considerably closer to it myself, I still wonder. Because people assume you've turned into a nice old prudent somebody inside to match your white-hair-and-wrinkles costume, but ten to one you haven't. You don't *feel* different — everyone knows that. I understood Liz Noah when she lifted a scanty lock and said scornfully, "This isn't me. I've got thick, dark hair."

"I know," I said, and knew she valued my knowing....

"Yes, and furthermore," she said, "do you know you're actually *tested* to see if you've brains enough left to weave those ugly potholders? They ask you, Who's President? Where's straight up? What day's today?" She stopped.

"What day is today?" she asked slowly.

We just looked at each other. The tiny, busy ticking of a bedside clock was loud in the room.

It was growing late. Aunt Liz Noah walked me out to the glassed-in porch, humid with limp green things dangling from pots. There I left her, prisoner of her years as I, in another way, was prisoner of mine, my young husband waiting for me down the block. And I prayed then, *Get her out of there*, though I knew there was only one way she'd ever leave. But I didn't care; it was no place for Liz Noah, no place at all.

And so we left Ganister behind us, Mike and I, wanting to cover some distance before nightfall. The low winter sun was bothering our eyes, especially mine, because I was crying. And thinking how awkward and messy crying is — eyes flooding, nose filling. In the long evolutionary climb, why couldn't people have evolved something neater?...

And so I mourned, in concentrated fashion, for all lovable, warm, bright people who must grow old and die, especially my Aunt Liz Noah. I cried nearly all the way to Salina, where I had to stop crying to eat dinner. And at the old Victorian hotel there were down pillows and a nice old calico quilt on the nice old four-poster bed and my husband comforted me.

It was about three months later that my mother phoned me in Oregon from McKinleyville. Aunt Liz Noah had run away. Just like that. Or, anyway, walked out. One April day toward sundown, she'd packed an overnight bag, put on her old riding pants, shirt, and one of her three remaining fine old hats, and walked all the way down Main Street to move into the Grand Osage Hotel.

Kindly, the desk clerk accepted her registration, and wisely he called my mother, who drove over the next day. The sole drawback she could find, finally, was that no one had thought of it sooner.

Aunt Liz Noah was happier now; even sketching a little and sometimes holding court in the lobby, sitting tall. Financially it made sense too. Even with coffee-shop service and the occasional attentions of a practical nurse, it cost less than The Elms. And what happened was that about a year later she went to bed complaining mildly of a strawberry-shortcake stomachache. It was a heart attack, though, and next morning she was dead.

Camus wrote, somewhere, "In the midst of winter I finally learned that there was in me an invincible summer." I think of that lovely line now, whenever I think of my Aunt Liz Noah on her own personal independence day, that greening April afternoon. There she goes, the tall, frail stork of a lady, hair wispy under the gallant hat, walking purposefully down Main Street. I never heard which hat it was, but I always see her in the red velvet.

Things Enough
ROBERT P. TRISTRAM COFFIN

That man can thank his lucky stars
  Whose things to keep are few,
To which the rain and moth and rust
  Find little harm to do.

A faith to make his handshake warm
  And simple things most wise,
A wife to make each morning fine
  With morning-glory eyes.

A love to make him foot the roads
  That others motor on,
A garden small and kind enough
  To let him watch the dawn.

Pity for the hungry ones,
  The ragged, and ill-shod,
A tree that's tall and straight enough
  To make him think of God.

Humanity cannot forget its dreamers; it cannot let their ideals fade and die; it lives in them; it knows them as the realities which it shall one day see and know.
James Allen

Opportunity
ARCHIBALD RUTLEDGE

You should remember that though another may have more money, beauty, and brains than you, yet when it comes to the rarer spiritual values such as charity, self-sacrifice, honor, nobility of heart, you have an equal chance with everyone to be the most beloved and honored of all people.

Tomorrow
AUTHOR UNKNOWN

A way unknown, a book unread,
A tree with fruit unharvested,
A sea unsailed, a word unsaid,
A house with rooms untenanted,
A tale untold, a tear unshed,
A reel unrolled of colored thread,
A field untilled, a friend unfed,
A loaf unbaked of living bread,
A song unsung, a hill ahead,
A beauty spot unvisited,
A web unspun, a wing unspread,
A hope as yet unheralded,
A fight unfought, a fear unfled,
A conqueror with uncrowned head.

It Pays to Smile

RUTH STAFFORD PEALE

The thing I remember most vividly about that first job of mine was the department store customer who gave me such a hard time. She was a sharp-faced woman with bleached hair and a harsh voice, and I can see her now as she pawed through my neatly arranged merchandise at the ribbon counter, complaining, grumbling, criticizing, finding nothing that pleased her — and being quite rude in the process. When I applied for a summer job, I had been told that so far as salespeople were concerned, the customer was always right. It was hard to believe that such an impossible person as this could be right about anything. But I held my tongue. I needed the job, even if it paid only $11 per week. I was fourteen. I wouldn't be fifteen until September.

When the difficult customer finally moved on after a small purchase, I drew a sigh of relief. As I began sorting my tangled merchandise, I reviewed my performance and even felt a little smug. I had remained calm and polite; I had kept smiling — most of the time, anyway. And after all, I told myself, such people were the exception, not the rule.

I had gotten the job on my own, partly to earn a little spending money, partly to help out at home. My father, a minister, was a man of great kindliness and dignity, but I doubt if he ever earned more than $2,400 a year in his life. My mother, tiny and deeply devout, had a marked musical gift; she played the piano and sometimes gave music lessons that brought in a little extra cash. Both my brothers had paper routes; I remember very well that if one of them was sick, Mother and I would get up at five in the morning and walk the route for him, sometimes in freezing rain or deep snow, folding the papers as we went and tossing them onto porches of houses whose owners — fortunate souls — were still snug in bed. I didn't enjoy being a substitute papercarrier.

But delivering the papers was a family responsibility, and in our family that concept was never taken lightly.

My father, who had a strong sense of justice, thought that $11 per week was very little for the store to be paying me, even if I was only fourteen years old. He had advised me to ask for a raise, and (full of qualms) I had done so. The manager told me that he would think it over and let me know. At closing time that day — the day made memorable by the difficult customer — he called me in and told me that my request was granted. Henceforth I would be paid $13 per week. "And do you know why?" he said. "We sent one of our shoppers to your counter this morning, a lady we use to check on the performance of our salespeople. We told her to be as difficult as possible — and to observe how you reacted. I'm glad to say you passed the test very well indeed."

I don't think my feet touched the ground all the way home. I rushed in and threw my arms around my mother. "I got it! I got it!" I cried, breathless with excitement, and poured out my story. When I told it again at the supper table, my father smiled. "You see," he said, "it pays to be patient and kind, no matter how unfair life may seem to be at the time."

It was a lesson far more valuable than the extra two dollars a week.

When a man is gloomy, everything seems to go wrong; when he is cheerful, everything seems right!   Proverbs 15:15, Living Bible

Mellowness

LIN YUTANG

I like spring, but it is too young. I like summer, but it is too proud. So I like best of all autumn, because its leaves are a little yellow, its tone mellower, its colors richer, and it is tinged a little with sorrow. Its golden richness speaks not of the innocence of spring, nor of the power of summer, but of the mellowness and kindly wisdom of approaching age. It knows the limitations of life and is content.

It is magnificent to grow old, if one keeps young.
Harry Emerson Fosdick

This time, like all other times, is a very good one, if we but know what to do with it.
Ralph Waldo Emerson

Faith and Doubt

ANONYMOUS

Doubt sees the obstacles,
　　Faith sees the way;
Doubt sees the blackest night,
　　Faith sees the day;
Doubt dreads to take a step,
　　Faith soars on high;
Doubt questions, "Who believes?"
　　Faith answers, "I!"

Summer Shower

SELMA ROBINSON

Thundering, shimmering, silvery gray,
It's raining today,
Shining and slanting
Spears, such a shower as we've been
　　wanting.

Freesia and fuchsia and mignonette
And violet
And golden glow
And blue delphinium, row on row,

And morning glory and hollyhock
And four-o'clock
And sweet alyssum
And bachelor button and cucumber
　　blossom
And black-eyed susan and purple clover,
When the rain's over,
Will shake the shower
Out of each brimming, glistening flower.

And the sun will turn to a bright metal
Each bright petal;
When the rain's done
Each leaf and each petal will sparkle
　　in the sun.

You are like light for the whole world. A city built on a hill cannot be hid. Nobody lights a lamp to put it under a bowl; instead he puts it on the lamp-stand, where it gives light for everyone in the house. In the same way your light must shine before people, so that they will see the good things you do and give praise to your Father in heaven.
Matthew 5:14-16, Good News for Modern Man

I shall grow old, but never lose life's zest,
Because the road's last turn will be the best.

Henry van Dyke

Let us cherish and love old age; for it is full of pleasure, if one knows how to use it.   Seneca

From *The Christmas Star*

NANCY BYRD TURNER

Stars rise and set, that star shines on:
Songs fail, but still that music beats
Through all the ages come and gone,
In lane and field and city streets.
And we who catch the Christmas gleam,
Watching with children on the hill,
We know, we know it is no dream —
He stands among us still!

In everything you do, put God first, and he will direct you and crown your efforts with success.

Proverbs 3:6, Living Bible

A Night's Sleep

MARTIN LUTHER

What is our death but a night's sleep? For as through sleep all weariness and faintness pass away and cease, and the powers of the spirit come back again, so that in the morning we rise fresh and strong and joyous; so at the Last Day we shall rise again as if we had only slept a night, and shall be fresh and strong.

From *"Prospice"*

ROBERT BROWNING

Fear death? — to feel the fog in my throat,
    The mist in my face,
When the snows begin, and the blasts
        denote
    I am nearing the place,
The power of the night, the press of the
        storm,
    The post of the foe;
Where he stands, the Arch Fear in a visible
        form,
    Yet the strong man must go:
For the journey is done and the summit
        attained,
    And the barriers fall,
Though a battle's to fight ere the guerdon
        be gained,
    The reward of it all.
I was ever a fighter, so — one fight more,
    The best and the last!
I would hate that death bandaged my eyes,
        and forebore,
    And bade me creep past.
No! let me taste the whole of it, fare like my
        peers
    The heroes of old,
Bear the brunt, in a minute pay glad life's
        arrears
    Of pain, darkness and cold.
For sudden the worst turns the best to the
        brave
    The black minute's at end,
And the element's rage, the fiend-voices
        that rave,
    Shall dwindle, shall blend,
Shall change, shall become first a peace out
        of pain,
    Then a light, then thy breast,
O thou soul of my soul! I shall clasp thee
        again,
    And with God be the rest!

From *Start Loving*

COLLEEN TOWNSEND EVANS

…I remember one day several years ago when I attended a lecture by a speaker who asked an intriguing question: "Did you ever tell someone you love that he or she gives you joy?" I had to think about that. I wasn't sure I had — not in so many words, and the words, in this case, were what mattered. My husband and my children have always given me great joy, but I couldn't be sure that they knew it — because I hadn't told them. I told them I loved them — all the time — but *joy*…I wasn't sure I had ever mentioned that.

When I went home late that afternoon, my husband was in his study preparing his Sunday sermon. He was deep in concentration, but I simply had to interrupt him, if only for a moment. "Louie," I said, and when I had his attention, I went on, "I just wanted you to know that you give me real joy!" Hearing myself, I thought he might think I was a little silly — but no, he didn't. His face lit up.

"Thank you, Coke," he said. "That's special — it's wonderful to know that."

When our children came home from school, I told each one the same thing, and the delighted expressions on their faces made me choke up a bit. My daughter Andie hugged me and said, "Hey, Mom, that's great — because you bring us joy, too!" And then I knew how it felt to be *told* that I was loved, even though I had hoped it was true all along.

That day which you fear as being the end of all things is the birthday of your eternity. Seneca

Blessed are they who have the gift of making friends, for it is one of God's best gifts. It involves many things, but above all, the power of going out of one's self, and appreciating whatever is noble and loving in another. Thomas Hughes

I Heard a Bird Sing

OLIVER HERFORD

I heard a bird sing
    In the dark of December
A magical thing
    And sweet to remember.

"We are nearer to Spring
    Than we were in September,"
I heard a bird sing
    In the dark of December.

Each in His Own Tongue

WILLIAM HERBERT CARRUTH

A haze on the far horizon,
    The infinite, tender sky,
The ripe, rich tint of the cornfields,
    And the wild geese sailing high;
And all over upland and lowland
    The charm of the golden-rod, —
Some of us call it Autumn,
    And others call it God.

Tomorrow

JOHN FICO

Dear God,
The little plans I tried to carry through
Have failed.
I will not sorrow.
I'll pause a little while,
Dear God,
And try, again, tomorrow.

Trials & Triumphs

ONE NIGHT, almost three years ago, Louie and I were awakened from a deep sleep by the ringing of the telephone. I jumped out of bed and reached for the phone on my desk.

It was a long distance call for me. My stepfather — Jim Wilhelm, the wonderful man to whom my mother had been happily married for thirty years — was calling from California. His voice was choked with pain.

"Oh, God! — I can't believe it.
Stella's gone.
Your mother's dead."

Mother — gone?
No — no — she couldn't be!
I had just talked to her — yesterday.
She hadn't been feeling well — she was
in the hospital for tests.
But, gone?
No — God! — no!

Even at that moment, my suitcase lay open, half-packed, in our room. Louie and I had planned to fly west in a few days so the four of us — Mother, Jim, Louie and I — could be together for our son Dan's graduation the following week. Mother had looked forward to that so much — her first grandson's graduation from college. No — I just couldn't believe it.

"Heart attack," Jim said.

I felt a cold mass in my chest, and my whole body began to tremble. I heard words coming from my mouth — automatic, wooden.

"Jim — hold on.
I'll be there....
Just as soon as I can get a flight."

I was deeply aware of his need and wanted to comfort him, but my own pain and loss were overwhelming me.

Louie went to the kitchen to warm some milk, and I fell to my knees beside our bed. Waves of sorrow — too deep for words *or* tears

— washed over me as I thought of the woman who had been both mother and father to me as I grew up.... a mother so committed to me that I always felt secure in her love, and in the simple home she worked so hard to provide. She had been my friend — and such fun to be with — a wonderful mother. Even after Louie and I married — across time and distance — she and I remained close.

How I ached to hold my mother in my arms — or walk with her hand in mine as we used to do when we were together. I was devastated. Everything in me cried out, "God, help...*help!*"

I hardly knew what to ask Him for; I could only abandon myself to Him, trusting to His strength to fill my weakness.

As I knelt there — waiting — I was gradually aware of a change coming over me. It was a very gentle thing...a tiny shaft of light shining through the crack in the armor of darkness. A warm blanket of love enveloping me, very much like being wrapped in God. I felt His strength replacing my weakness, and then I knew — not only would I make it, but there would be strength to share with others.

On the flight to California, the much-needed tears began to flow. The shock of mourning had begun, and it was painful and deep. Even so, I marveled that while my heart could hurt so much, I could still feel such peace.

During the days and events that followed, the powerful Presence remained with me: choosing a coffin, clothes for the body, arrangements for the memorial service, greeting people, going through Mother's things...the "work" of death — painfully poignant reminders of the life she and I had shared, and, at the same time, therapeutic.

I felt a quality of strength I had never known before, and I knew it came from relying utterly on God. I had no alternative. There was no way I could make it without Him. I knew it — and He knew it. Leaning on Him every moment, I received His power and peace as a fruit of His spirit in me.

As I think back on that passage in my life, the words of the Indian poet, Rabindranath Tagore, come to me: "Death is not the extinguishing of the light — it is the putting out of the lamp because the dawn has come."

For Mother, the dawn —
for me, the light of God's presence
to see me through the dark night.

COLLEEN TOWNSEND EVANS

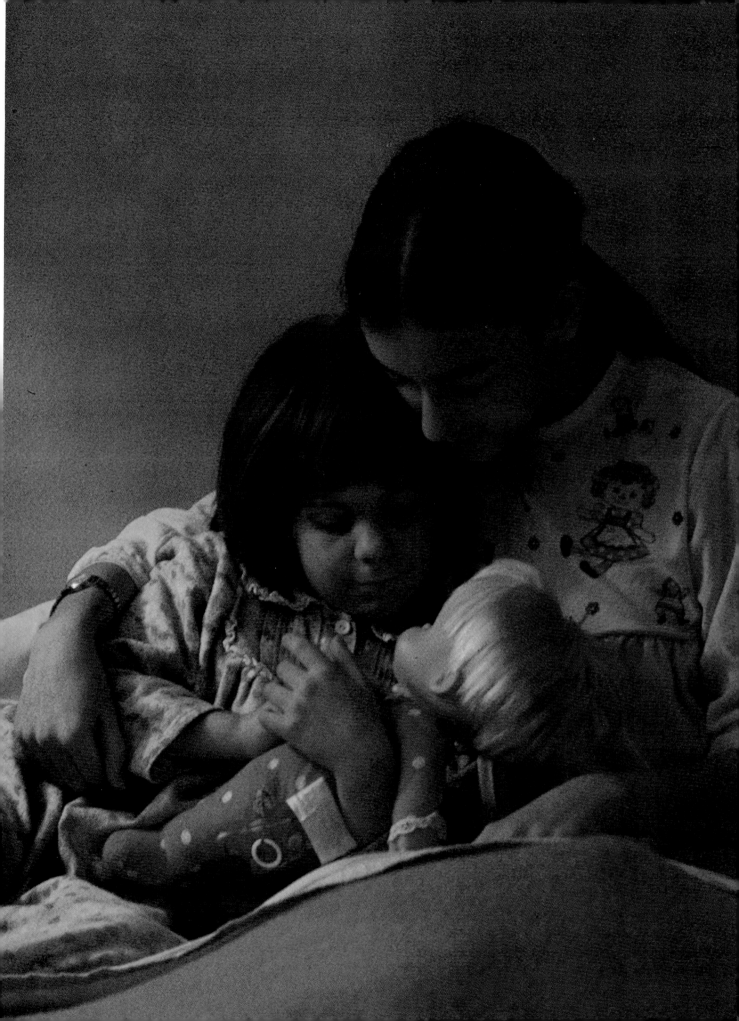

Be Like the Bird

VICTOR HUGO

Be like the bird, who
Halting in his flight
On limb too slight
Feels it give way beneath him,
Yet sings
Knowing he hath wings.

*I thank God for my handicaps, for, through them,
I have found myself, my work, and my God.*
Helen Keller

*I can do all things through Christ which strength-
eneth me.*   Philippians 4:13, King James Version

Shadows

ARTHUR J. PEEL

A dark, elusive shadow —
    Trailing my pleasant way
Through thronging street, and meadow
    All on a summer's day.

But what care I for shadows!
    Of substance, they have none;
And he who casts the shadows
    Is walking in the sun!

*For those who will fight bravely and not yield,
there is triumphant victory over all the dark
things of life.*   James Allen

The Ugly Duckling

HANS CHRISTIAN ANDERSEN

It was so beautiful out in the country. It was summer. The oats were still green, but the wheat was turning yellow. Down in the meadow the grass had been cut and made into haystacks; and there the storks walked on their long red legs talking Egyptian, because that was the language they had been taught by their mothers. The fields were enclosed by woods, and hidden among them were little lakes and pools. Yes, it certainly was lovely out there in the country!

The old castle, with its deep moat surrounding it, lay bathed in sunshine. Between the heavy walls and the edge of the moat there was a narrow strip of land covered by a whole forest of burdock plants. Their leaves were large and some of the stalks were so tall that a child could stand

God, Make Me Brave

AUTHOR UNKNOWN

God, make me brave for life: oh, braver
    than this.
Let me straighten after pain, as a tree
    straightens after the rain,
Shining and lovely again.
God make me brave for life; much braver
    than this.
As the blown grass lifts, let me rise
From sorrow with quiet eyes,
Knowing Thy way is wise.
God, make me brave, life brings
Such blinding things.
Help me to keep my sight;
Help me to see aright
That out of dark comes light.

upright under them and imagine that he was in the middle of the wild and lonesome woods. Here a duck had built her nest. While she sat waiting for the eggs to hatch, she felt a little sorry for herself because it was taking so long and hardly anybody came to visit her. The other ducks preferred swimming in the moat to sitting under a dock leaf and gossiping.

Finally the eggs began to crack. "Peep...Peep," they said one after another. The egg yolks had become alive and were sticking out their heads.

"Quack...Quack..." said their mother. "Look around you." And the ducklings did; they glanced at the green world about them, and that was what their mother wanted them to do, for green was good for their eyes.

"How big the world is!" piped the little ones, for they had much more space to move around in now than they had had inside the egg.

"Do you think that this is the whole world?" quacked their mother. "The world is much larger than this. It stretches as far as the minister's wheat fields, though I have not been there.... Are you all here?" The duck got up and turned around to look at her nest. "Oh no, the biggest egg hasn't hatched yet; and I'm so tired of sitting here! I wonder how long it will take?" she wailed, and sat down again.

"What's new?" asked an old duck who had come visiting.

"One of the eggs is taking so long," complained the mother duck. "It won't crack. But take a look at the others. They are the sweetest little ducklings you have ever seen; and every one of them looks exactly like their father. That scoundrel hasn't come to visit me once."

"Let me look at the egg that won't hatch," demanded the old duck. "I am sure that it's a turkey egg! I was fooled that way once. You can't imagine what it's like. Turkeys are afraid of the water. I couldn't get them to go into it. I quacked and I nipped them, but

nothing helped. Let me see that egg!...Yes, it's a turkey egg. Just let it lie there. You go and teach your young ones how to swim, that's my advice."

"I have sat on it so long that I guess I can sit a little longer, at least until they get the hay in," replied the mother duck.

"Suit yourself," said the older duck, and went on.

At last the big egg cracked too. "Peep ...Peep," said the young one, and tumbled out. He was big and very ugly.

The mother duck looked at him. "He's awfully big for his age," she said. "He doesn't look like any of the others. I wonder if he could be a turkey? Well, we shall soon see. Into the water he will go, even if I have to kick him to make him do it."

The next day the weather was gloriously beautiful. The sun shone on the forest of burdock plants. The mother duck took her whole brood to the moat. "Quack... Quack..." she ordered.

One after another, the little ducklings plunged into the water. For a moment their heads disappeared, but then they popped up again and the little ones floated like so many corks. Their legs knew what to do without being told. All of the new brood swam very nicely, even the ugly one.

"He is no turkey," mumbled the mother. "See how beautifully he uses his legs and how straight he holds his neck. He is my own child and, when you look closely at him, he's quite handsome.... Quack! Quack! Follow me and I'll take you to the henyard and introduce you to everyone. But stay close to me, so that no one steps on you, and look out for the cat."

They heard an awful noise when they arrived at the henyard. Two families of ducks had got into a fight over the head of an eel. Neither of them got it, for it was swiped by the cat.

...Other ducks gathered about them and said loudly, "What do we want that gang here for? Aren't there enough of us already? Pooh! Look how ugly one of them is! He's the last straw!" And one of the ducks flew over and bit the ugly duckling on the neck.

"Leave him alone!" shouted the mother. "He hasn't done anyone any harm."

"He's big and he doesn't look like everybody else!" replied the duck who had bitten him. "And that's reason enough to beat him."

…The poor little duckling, who had been the last to hatch and was so ugly, was bitten and pushed and made fun of both by the hens and by the other ducks. The turkey cock (who had been born with spurs on, and therefore thought he was an emperor) rustled his feathers as if he were a full-rigged ship under sail, and strutted up to the duckling. He gobbled so loudly at him that his own face got all red.

The poor little duckling did not know where to turn. How he grieved over his own ugliness, and how sad he was! The poor creature was mocked and laughed at by the whole henyard.

That was the first day; and each day that followed was worse than the one before. The poor duckling was chased and mistreated by everyone, even his own sisters and brothers, who quacked again and again, "If only the cat would get you, you ugly thing!"

Even his mother said, "I wish you were far away." The other ducks bit him and the hens pecked at him. The little girl who came to feed the fowls kicked him.

At last the duckling ran away. It flew over the tops of the bushes, frightening all the little birds so that they flew up into the air. "They, too, think I am ugly," thought the duckling, and closed his eyes — but he kept on running.

Finally he came to a great swamp where wild ducks lived; and here he stayed for the night, for he was too tired to go any farther.

He spent two days in the swamp; then two wild geese came — or rather, two wild ganders, for they were males. They had been hatched not long ago; therefore they were both frank and bold.

"Listen, comrade," they said. "You are so ugly that we like you. Do you want to migrate with us? Not far from here there is a marsh where some beautiful wild geese live. They are all lovely maidens, and you are so ugly that you may seek your fortune among them. Come along."

"Bang! Bang!" Two shots were heard and both the ganders fell down dead among the reeds, and the water turned red from their blood.

"Bang! Bang!" Again came the sound of shots, and a flock of wild geese flew up.

The whole swamp was surrounded by hunters; from every direction came the awful noise. Some of the hunters had hidden behind bushes or among the reeds but others, screened from sight by the leaves, sat on the long, low branches of the trees that stretched out over the swamp. The blue smoke from the guns lay like a fog over the water and among the trees. Dogs came splashing through the marsh, and they bent and broke the reeds.

The poor little duckling was terrified. He was about to tuck his head under his wing, in order to hide, when he saw a big dog peering at him through the reeds. The dog's tongue hung out of its mouth and its eyes glistened evilly. It bared its teeth. Splash! It turned away without touching the duckling.

"Oh,…" he sighed. "I am so ugly that even the dog doesn't want to bite me."

The little duckling lay as still as he could while the shots whistled through the reeds. Not until the middle of the afternoon did the shooting stop; but the poor little duckling was still so frightened that he waited several hours longer before taking his head out from under his wing. Then he ran as quickly as he could out of the swamp. Across the fields and the meadows he went, but a wind had come up and he found it hard to make his way against it.

Toward evening he came upon a poor little hut. It was so wretchedly crooked that it looked as if it couldn't make up its mind which way to fall and that was why it was still standing. The wind was blowing so hard that the poor little duckling had to sit down in order not to be blown away. Suddenly he noticed that the door was off its hinges, making a crack; and he squeezed himself through it and was inside.

An old woman lived in the hut with her cat and her hen. The cat was called Sonny and could both arch his back and purr. Oh yes, it could also make sparks if you rubbed its fur the wrong way. The hen had very short legs and that was why she was called Cluck Lowlegs. But she was good at laying eggs, and the old woman loved her as if she were her own child.

In the morning the hen and the cat discovered the duckling. The cat meowed and the hen clucked.

"What is going on?" asked the old woman, and looked around. She couldn't see very well, and when she found the duckling she thought it was a fat, full-grown duck. "What a fine catch!" she exclaimed. "Now we shall have duck eggs, unless it's a drake. We'll give it a try."

So the duckling was allowed to stay for three weeks on probation, but he laid no eggs. The cat was the master of the house and the hen the mistress. They always referred to themselves as "we and the world," for they thought that they were half the world — and the better half at that. The duckling thought that he should be allowed to have a different opinion, but the hen did not agree.

"Can you lay eggs?" she demanded.

"No," answered the duckling.

"Then keep your mouth shut."

And the cat asked, "Can you arch your back? Can you purr? Can you make sparks?"

"No."

"Well, in that case, you have no right to have an opinion when sensible people are talking."

…"I think I'll go out into the wide world," replied the duckling.

"Go right ahead!" said the hen.

And the duckling left. He found a lake where he could float in the water and dive to the bottom. There were other ducks, but they ignored him because he was so ugly.

Autumn came and the leaves turned yellow and brown, then they fell from the trees. The wind caught them and made them dance. The clouds were heavy with hail and snow. A raven sat on a fence and screeched, "Ach! Ach!" because it was so cold. When just thinking of how cold it was is enough to make one shiver, what a terrible time the duckling must have had.

One evening just as the sun was setting gloriously, a flock of beautiful birds came out from the rushes. Their feathers were so white that they glistened; and they had long, graceful necks. They were swans. They made a very loud cry, then they spread their powerful wings. They were flying south to a warmer climate, where the lakes were not frozen in the winter. Higher and higher they circled. The ugly duckling turned round and round in the water like a wheel and stretched his neck up toward the sky; he felt a strange longing. He screeched so piercingly that he frightened himself.

Oh, he would never forget those beautiful birds, those happy birds. When they were out of sight the duckling dove down under the water to the bottom of the lake; and when he came up again he was beside himself. He did not know the name of those birds or where they were going, and yet he felt that he loved them as he had never loved any other creatures. He did not envy them. It did not even occur to him to wish that he were so handsome himself. He would have been happy if the other ducks had let him stay in the henyard: that poor, ugly bird!

The weather grew colder and colder. The duckling had to swim round and round in the water, to keep just a little space for himself that wasn't frozen. Each night his hole became smaller and smaller. On all sides of him the ice creaked and groaned. The little duckling had to keep his feet constantly in motion so that the last bit of open water wouldn't become ice. At last he was too tired to swim anymore. He sat still. The ice closed in around him and he was frozen fast.

Early the next morning a farmer saw him

and with his clogs broke the ice to free the duckling. The man put the bird under his arm and took it home to his wife, who brought the duckling back to life.

The children wanted to play with him. But the duckling was afraid that they were going to hurt him, so he flapped his wings and flew right into the milk pail. From there he flew into a big bowl of butter and then into a barrel of flour. What a sight he was!

The farmer's wife yelled and chased him with a poker. The children laughed and almost fell on top of each other, trying to catch him; and how they screamed! Luckily for the duckling, the door was open. He got out of the house and found a hiding place beneath some bushes, in the newly fallen snow; and there he lay so still, as though there were hardly any life left in him.

It would be too horrible to tell of all the hardship and suffering the duckling experienced that long winter. It is enough to know that he did survive. When again the sun shone warmly and the larks began to sing, the duckling was lying among the reeds in the swamp. Spring had come!

He spread out his wings to fly. How strong and powerful they were! Before he knew it, he was far from the swamp and flying above a beautiful garden. The apple trees were blooming and the lilac bushes stretched their flower-covered branches over the water of a winding canal. Everything was so beautiful: so fresh and green. Out of a forest of rushes came three swans. They ruffled their feathers and floated so lightly on the water. The ugly duckling recognized the birds and felt again that strange sadness come over him.

"I shall fly over to them, those royal birds! And they can hack me to death because I, who am so ugly, dare to approach them! What difference does it make? It is better to be killed by them than to be bitten by the other ducks, and pecked by the hens, and kicked by the girl who tends the henyard; or to suffer through the winter."

And he lighted on the water and swam toward the magnificent swans. When they saw him they ruffled their feathers and started to swim in his direction. They were coming to meet him.

"Kill me," whispered the poor creature, and bent his head humbly while he waited for death. But what was that he saw in the water? It was his own reflection; and he was no longer an awkward, clumsy, gray bird, so ungainly and so ugly. He was a swan!

It does not matter that one has been born in the henyard as long as one has lain in a swan's egg.

He was thankful that he had known so much want, and gone through so much suffering, for it made him appreciate his present happiness and the loveliness of everything about him all the more. The swans made a circle around him and caressed him with their beaks.

Some children came out into the garden. They had brought bread with them to feed the swans. The youngest child shouted, "Look, there's a new one!" All the children joyfully clapped their hands, and they ran to tell their parents.

Cake and bread were cast on the water for the swans. Everyone agreed that the new swan was the most beautiful of them all. The older swans bowed toward him.

He felt so shy that he hid his head beneath his wing. He was too happy, but not proud, for a kind heart can never be proud. He thought of the time when he had been mocked and persecuted. And now everyone said that he was the most beautiful of the most beautiful birds. And the lilac bushes stretched their branches right down to the water for him. The sun shone so warm and brightly. He ruffled his feathers and raised his slender neck, while out of the joy in his heart, he thought, "Such happiness I did not dream of when I was the ugly duckling."

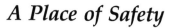

A Place of Safety

ELISABETH ELLIOT

I happened to arrive home alone from the airport one night in the middle of what newscasters like to call an "outage." I much prefer to call it a power failure. I could have unpacked my suitcase and found something to eat by candlelight — I lived for years with no other kind — but there was a show going on which I did not want to miss. I sat by the window and watched a storm over the ocean — driving rain and nearly continuous lightning, flashing in a hundred places along miles of horizon. Sometimes great billows of stormcloud were thrown into relief by a bright sheet of light from behind. Sometimes jagged bolts of lightning cracked the heavens, stabbing the skyline of Scituate and Cohasset to the southwest (our house faces south from Cape Ann over Massachusetts Bay). The rain swept the deck and blasted the windowpane while thunder, one of the many voices of God, rolled and crashed.

The signs God gives us of his power and glory (thunder and lightning, for example), to say nothing of the unimaginable forces which he puts into men's hands and allows them to harness for their own often evil purposes are in themselves fearsome.

As I watched God's storm that night I thought of his wonderful name, Father of Lights. Then as I saw the distant marine beacons sending their beams across the waves, they reminded me as they do every night of the Father's mercy. We live in a world created by his almighty power but corrupted by man's pride and selfishness. We need a place of safety.... There is one, but only one. It is the Father's arms. He will not — indeed, if he is to redeem and make us holy, he cannot — protect us from all suffering.

George MacDonald, in his novel *What's Mine's Mine*, wrote: "There are tender-hearted people who virtually object to the whole scheme of creation. They would neither have force used nor pain suffered; they talk as if kindness could do everything, even where it is not felt. Millions of human beings but for suffering would never develop an atom of affection. The man who would spare *due* suffering is not wise. Because a thing is unpleasant, it is folly to conclude it ought not to be. There are powers to be born, creations to be perfected, sinners to be redeemed, through the ministry of pain, to be born, perfected, redeemed, in no other way."

I am thankful that there are some earthly fathers who understand this. One of them wrote to me of a visit to the doctor with his three-year-old son who was limping as a result of a fall or a collision with a child in the church nursery.

"Walt was in the back seat as the two of us rode down to the doctor's. There, I told him to wait a minute while I checked to make sure the doctor was in his office. The receptionist told me I could catch him over at the hospital in the emergency room. I came out to the car and drove to the hospital.

"Walt III: 'Where we goin', Daddy?'

"'We're going to see if the doctor will check your foot out at the hospital. Won't that be neat?'

"A pause. 'Uh...Daddy, I think it'll be o.k. if we go on home. Yeah...I think it'd be better after while. Why'n't we just go home, 'kay?'

"'Son, we're going to go see if we can get the doctor to check and make sure everything is o.k.'

"(a tiny hint of a whine) 'Daddy, I'm sure it's go'n be better now, o.k.?'

"At the hospital: 'Walter, let's get out and go into the hospital. Everything is going to be all right. Just hold my hand.'

"In the emergency room he wanted to sit in my lap. The clerk asked the names and how we were going to pay, etc. Then the wait. We move to a row of chairs against the wall, and Walt III chooses to sit in my lap this time with more enthusiasm. His eyes are big and wide. He's very solemn, head moving around, taking it all in.

"'Daddy, we've been here before.'

"'Yes, Walt, we were here. Remember the time your leg was broken and Daddy put you in that green blanket and brought you here? The doctor looked at your leg and then they took you to take some pictures of your leg?'

"'Hunh.' (That means yes.) 'I 'member dat.'

"'Shall we pray together?' His head bows quickly.

"'Kay.'

"A prayer in which I asked for courage for both of us. And thanking the Lord that we could trust him. Walt III much more relieved, even calmed completely.

"A nurse calls his name, and we go into a room to be seen by the doctor. It was hard to keep from carrying him, but I wanted the doctor to see Walt's limp, and too, I kept saying to myself, 'Let's not smother him. Let's help him grow up and learn to lean on the Lord himself.'

"In the room we both sit on the table. I take off his shoe and sock (I was fearful that the original break was damaged again) and we hear a lady crying in the next room. Walt's eyes get wide and he says,

"'Daddy, what's the matter with that lady?'

"'She is hurting and she is scared. Are you afraid, son?'

"'No, Lord Jesus take care of me.'

"'Well, let's pray for her, o.k.?'

"'Kay.'

"A prayer. And sure enough, the lady seems to calm down. And the doctor's there now, asking Walt where it hurts. Then, off to X-ray. A nurse comes to talk to Walt.

"'Now listen — if we hurt you then you can cry. But if we don't hurt you, you are not to cry, o.k.?'

"'Kay.' She picks him up (he holds tightly to her, eyes very wide) and just before she takes him off he says to me, 'Daddy, we've been here before. Where you gon' be? In this room waiting for me?' (The X-ray process had terrified him when the nurse took him from us a year ago.)

"'Yes, son, I'll be right here, waiting for you.' Fifteen minutes later the nurse brought him back to me, raving about what a neat kid he was. Apparently he had kept talking to them the entire time.

"No bones broken. We go back to the doctor; I tell Walt to be sure and thank the doctor as we leave. Walt goes about 20 feet out of his way from the exit to say, 'Thank you, doctor. We go'n to family night supper at the church.'

"Next night he happily sang to himself in the dark for about 30 minutes. I went to the bedroom to hug him and tell him,

"'Walt, I'm proud of you for three reasons. One, you were very sweet in the tub when Mom washed your hair. Two, you make me happy singing so nicely to yourself in the dark. Three,...'

"'But Daddy — you making too much racket!' Then he grabs me and hugs me, giggling.

"Thank you, Lord, for that boy!"

And thank you, Lord, for that father, strong in his faith in you, strong enough in his love for the little child to lead him also to trust you.

I am sobered by the response of a tiny boy. With reason enough to fear, he resolved not to. How often my own faith deteriorates into a mere condition, shaped by circumstances, rather than a calm resolve, founded on one whose word I have come to trust. Perfect love casts out fear.

And what of the weeping woman in the next room? Was she calmed? Would she have believed, if told, that the God of Peace had laid his hands on her — in answer to the prayers of a little boy with a hurt foot? The God who rides stormclouds is also the God of Peace. The one who makes darkness his covering is also the Father of Lights.

The gem cannot be polished without friction, nor man perfected without trials.   Confucius

The Challenge of Resistance

HENRY VAN DYKE

No doubt a world in which matter never got out of place and became dirt, in which iron had no flaws and wood no cracks, in which gardens had no weeds, and food grew already cooked, in which clothes never wore out and washing was as easy as the soapmakers' advertisements describe it, in which rules had no exceptions and things never went wrong, would be a much easier place to live in. But for purposes of training and development it would be worth nothing at all.

It is the resistance that puts us on our mettle: it is the conquest of the reluctant stuff that educates the worker. I wish you enough difficulties to keep you well and make you strong and skillful!

Keep your face to the sunshine and you cannot see the shadow.   Helen Keller

Prayer

GAIL BROOK BURKET

I do not ask to walk smooth paths
Nor bear an easy load.
I pray for strength and fortitude
To climb the rock-strewn road.

Give me such courage I can scale
The hardest peaks alone,
And transform every stumbling block
Into a steppingstone.

Child in Trouble

MARJORIE HOLMES

My child is in trouble, deep trouble, God.

I come to you weak and limp from sheer alarm. I fall to my knees before you.

I am almost too dumb with disbelief to articulate this problem. You know the details all too well, and so I shall spare myself and you a wild recital.

But oh, dear God in heaven and upon this earth, please support me in this hour of trial. And support my child.

Lift us up, get us back on our feet. Don't abandon us; don't let us lose our common sense, or our faith in you.

What has happened can wreck many lives if we go to pieces and forget that you are standing by, ready to guide us if we will let you.

Ready to comfort us. Ready to help us through the difficult hours that lie ahead.

You, who are in the very breath and substance of each of us, including the tragedy of this child — let us feel your presence.

Fill us with your peace, your assurance of a right solution.

Let us feel that blessed presence now, and trust in your love, which will see us through this deep trouble with our child.

When life seems just a dreary grind,
And things seem fated to annoy,
Say something nice to someone else —
And watch the world light up with joy.
     Author Unknown

Faith Is Undefeatable

NORMAN VINCENT PEALE

When Almighty God created a human being He put a touch of greatness into his nature. A man is a mixture, that's for sure. But however weak, mixed up, however defeated he can be, there is still this element: Something in him entitles him to be called a child of God. No matter what happens to him in the way of difficulty and trouble, he still has what it takes to come out of it with dignity and power and get on top.

This fact was summed up quite well, I thought, by a taxi driver who took me into the city from Kennedy Airport one afternoon. I liked this taxi driver from the start. He flashed me a big smile. We drove along, chatting casually. Stopping for a red light, he looked around and asked, "What's your name?" When I gave it he said, "I thought so. Listen to you on radio. Thought I recognized your voice."

Then he continued. "I am glad to meet you, too. Funny, you getting into my cab at this time." The words came slowly, with effort. "You see, my wife died. The funeral was yesterday. We were married almost thirty years. You never saw a sweeter woman in your life. She was an angel. There was nothing but good in her. She loved everybody and everybody loved her. She was so good to me all those years...I can't imagine living without her."

As gently as I knew how, I said, "I don't believe you really will be without her. She will always be thinking of you. She will be with you in spirit. You will feel her love comforting you."

"Thanks. Thanks a lot," he said feelingly. "She was so wonderful. I wish you could have known her."

He was silent for a moment, then spoke again. "Life is full of trouble, isn't it? I've got five children. Four of them are real good, but one sure is a problem. He has taken to drugs and runs around with a bad crowd. He is full of hate and meanness. I am very worried about him. Can't seem to do a thing with him. It broke his poor mother's heart. Now I've got to be both mother and father to this kid."

I started to sympathize, but he interjected, "I know what you're going to say." And he assured me, "With the help of God I can handle it. Don't worry about me. I'm O.K."

Then he got off a tremendous statement; real truth is in it. He said, "You can be greater than anything that can happen to you." What a terrific fact!

This man was a strong personality who knew that a person with faith is undefeatable. And he was holding onto that. So even in the pain and sorrow of bereavement and his anxiety for a son seriously off the beam, he was able to say, "You can be greater than anything that can happen to you." There are some great human beings in this world and that man is one of them. Potentially we all have the quality of invincibility. You can if you think you can.

Out of Darkness

HELEN KELLER

Once I knew the depth where no hope was and darkness lay on the face of all things. Then love came and set my soul free. Once I fretted and beat myself against the wall that shut me in. My life was without a past or future, and death a consummation devoutly to be wished. But a little word from the fingers of another fell into my hands that clutched at emptiness, and my heart leaped up with the rapture of living. I do not know the meaning of the darkness, but I have learned the overcoming of it.

What Might Have Been

HAZEL LEE

I held a moment in my hand,
    Brilliant as a star,
    Fragile as a flower,
    A shiny sliver out of one hour.
I dropped it carelessly.
    O God! I knew not
    I held opportunity.

Lonesome

RALPH SPAULDING CUSHMAN

Dear Master, I am lonesome;
    Dear Master, speak to me!
I've been longing here at twilight
    For the voices o'er the sea,
And it seems as if my heartache
    Would be hushed, less piercing be,
If Thou, Lord, wouldst come still closer —
    I am lonesome; speak to me!

I've been thinking in the stillness,
    As I've watched the sunset glow
Die out yonder on the hilltop,
    Leaving naught but cold and woe —
I've been thinking of the faces
    That have come a-trooping by,
Old-time faces, long-time vanished,
    Leaving me to wait and sigh.

And I'm lonesome, Lord, I'm lonesome;
    Come Thou closer; speak to me,
For I am listening here at twilight
    To the voices o'er the sea,
And it seems as if my heartache
    Would be hushed, less piercing be,
If Thou, Lord, wouldst come still closer —
    I am lonesome; speak to me!

Forgive me if too close I lean
My human heart on thee.

John Greenleaf Whittier

A New Day

RALPH WALDO EMERSON

Finish every day and be done with it. You have done what you could. Some blunders and absurdities no doubt crept in; forget them as soon as you can. Tomorrow is a new day; begin it well and serenely and with too high a spirit to be cumbered with your old nonsense. This day is all that is good and fair. It is too dear, with its hopes and invitations, to waste a moment on the yesterdays.

Ideals

ALBERT SCHWEITZER

The power of ideals is incalculable. We see no power in a drop of water. But let it get into a crack in the rock and be turned to ice, and it splits the rock; turned into steam, it drives the pistons of the most powerful engines. Something has happened to it which makes active and effective the power that is latent in it.

A tree that it takes both arms to encircle grew from a tiny rootlet. A many-storied pagoda is built by placing one brick upon another brick. A journey of three thousand miles is begun by a single step.

Lao-Tzu

A Bit of Heaven

CORRIE TEN BOOM

One of the first places I visited, after my release from the concentration camp, was the *Grote Kerk* in Haarlem. Since it was so close to where I had grown up in Beje, I counted it as much of an old friend as I did the watchmaker's shop.

"May I show you through?" the old usher said as he met me at the door.

"If it is all right," I said. "I would like to be alone."

He nodded, understandingly, and disappeared into the shadows of the sanctuary. I walked over the gravestones that formed the floor of the ancient building. My shoes made a strange, scraping sound that gave forth a hollow echo in the empty cathedral. I remembered the many times I had played here as a child.

My cousin Dot was my closest friend. She was the youngest daughter of my Uncle Arnold who was the previous usher — the caretaker — of the *Grote Kerk*.

Dot and I did everything together, but our favorite pastime was to play hide-and-seek in the big church. There were many wonderful places to hide: pews, old doors giving entrance to spiral staircases, and many closets. There was a world-famous pipe organ in the cathedral and sometimes when there was a concert, Uncle Arnold would allow members of his family to come into the church, sit on a wooden bench without a back and lean against the cold, moist stone wall to hear the magnificent music.

The cathedral was a symphony in gray tones during the day, both inside and outside. In the evening, when the gas lamps were lit on the side transepts, we could see the pillars and ceilings pointing upwards as the shadows danced about in a mysterious glow.

Only one place was absolutely "off limits" as we played hide-and-seek. That was the old pulpit. We never went there, but for the rest — what a playground that old church

was! When we shouted, the echo would ring from transept to transept and our laughter never, never seemed to be sacrilegious. Unlike some of the stern adults who sometimes frowned on our frolic, I had always thought that the laughter of little children in an empty cathedral was the most beautiful of all hymns of praise. And so we grew up, knowing only a God who enjoyed our presence as we skipped, ran, and played through this building which was built for His Glory.

One afternoon we played very late and before we knew it, the darkness of the cathedral swallowed us up. I looked around. Through the beautiful stained-glass windows I saw a little light coming in from the streets around. Only the silhouettes of the Gothic pillars stood out in the darkness as they reached upward and upward.

"Let's go home," whispered Dot. "I'm scared."

I was not. Slowly I went to the usher's door that opened out to where Uncle Arnold lived. There was a Presence that comforted me, a deep peace in my heart. Even in the darkness, smelling the dust and dampness of the church building, I knew that the "Light of the World" was present. Was the Lord preparing me for some time in the future when I would need to know that His light is victorious over darkness?

Forty-five years later Betsie and I walked to the square where roll call was being held in the concentration camp. It was still early, before dawn. The head of our barracks was so cruel that she had sent us out into the very cold outdoors a full hour too early.

Betsie's hand was in mine. We went to the square by a different way from the rest of our barracks-mates. We were three as we walked with the Lord and talked with Him. Betsie spoke. Then I talked. Then the Lord spoke. How? I do not know. But both of us understood. It was the same Presence I had felt years before in the old cathedral in Haarlem.

The brilliant early morning stars were our only light. The cold winter air was so clear.

We could faintly see the outlines of the barracks, the crematorium, the gas chamber, and the towers where the guards were standing with loaded machine guns.

"Isn't this a bit of heaven!" Betsie had said. "And, Lord, this is a small foretaste. One day we will see You face-to-face, but thank You that even now You are giving us the joy of walking and talking with You."

Heaven in the midst of hell. Light in the midst of darkness. What a security!

Dear Lord...

FLOYD W. TOMKINS

Dear Lord, grant me Your peace. I do not ask for earthly peace which removes trouble or dulls the senses, but for that holy calm which never fails by day or by night, in joy or in sorrow, but ever lifts the soul to rest upon You. You were so peaceful Yourself, dear Christ, in Your life! Haste and worry and anxiety were never Yours, but a blessed calm which told of mastery. May it not be mine also? Speak to me, Lord. Bid the waves, which seem sometimes so big and threatening, to show themselves as under Your loving control. Touch my wearied heart, that it sink not in despair. Make me glad and brave and joyous always in the knowledge that I am Yours. And in all my ways lead me by Your own hand, and keep me in perfect peace. Amen.

An Easter Carol

PHILLIPS BROOKS

Tomb, thou shalt not hold Him longer;
Death is strong, but Life is stronger;
Stronger than the dark, the light;
Stronger than the wrong, the right;
Faith and Hope triumphant say,
Christ will rise on Easter Day.

"The Beautiful Dawn!"

ARCHIBALD RUTLEDGE

As a personal experience, none of my own ever surpassed in moving power that beautiful and dramatic scene which, though it lies years back in the moonlit land of the past and of memory, is vividly alive to me now. It happened at sunrise, and it was of a sunrise.

One dearer to me than all else in life had, for days, lain helpless, speechless. Consciousness was gone. We knew that the mortal mists were fast gathering; that the irremediable river must soon be crossed. The last morning of our watching was misty; the day emerged so wanly that we hardly knew that it had come. Suddenly the one we loved so dearly sat up in bed, a strange light on her face of a happiness past all our mortal joy. She stretched abroad her arms, crying in the radiant abandon of spiritual certainty, "The Dawn! The beautiful Dawn!"

Those were her dying words — glad, triumphant. And for me they hold the eternal promise of the sunrise. They glow with immortality. In every sense, our mortal dawn that day was anything but beautiful; but she saw the beginning of an immortal day. Believing in a God of infinite love and of infinite power, I find it natural to believe that death is not a disastrous sundown but rather a spiritual sunrise, ushering in the unconjectured splendors of immortality.

Humility

AS A YOUNG NEWSPAPERMAN, I worked for the Paris edition of the *New York Herald-Tribune*.

That was a long way geographically and spiritually from my home in the Midwest. The cafes of the Left Bank and all the other delights of the French capital were lulling me into spiritual somnolence.

One day I was visited by a man who undoubtedly had been sent by my family. He invited me to dinner at his home in the suburbs. About the last thing on earth that interested me then was anything faintly connected with the religion of my parents. And Robert Hoy was a missionary.

I still blush today when I recall how rudely I dismissed Mr. Hoy's gracious offer. He left, all right, but he came back again — twice — to press his invitation. So I went out to the Hoys one Sunday. In spite of my misgivings, it proved to be a happy occasion.

In the afternoon the Hoys took me to a Christian foundling home in which they were interested. We arrived as the Sunday school was opening — just in time to hear a dozen adorable boys and girls singing the songs in French that I had sung in English as a child back home.

The experience took me back to my childhood, to my loving parents, and even to the One I had been neglecting.

Somehow I could not shake the effects of that visit. I could still feel the Christian love motivating the men and women in charge of the orphanage. And I knew I had to follow the One about whom the foundlings sang.

RUSSELL T. HITT

Humility

C.S. LEWIS

If anyone would like to acquire humility, I can, I think, tell him the first step. The first step is to realize that one is proud. And a biggish step, too. At least, nothing whatever can be done before it. If you think you are not conceited, it means you are very conceited indeed.

To Be Said After Success

DAVID A. REDDING

O God,
Let me be Your servant still
In success as in failure.
Let me feel as close
To You
In happiness
As in heartbreak,
Never to be satisfied
So long as there is sorrow
And something I can do
In the name
Of the King
Who took upon Himself
The form
Of a Servant.

Amen

Getting the "Child-Spirit"

HANNAH WHITALL SMITH

I had a friend once whose Christian life was a life of bondage. She worked for her salvation harder than any slave ever worked to purchase his freedom. Among other things, she never felt as if the day could go right for herself or any of her family unless she started it with a long season of wrestling, and agonizing, and conflict; "winding up her machine," I called it. One day we were talking about it together, and she was telling me of the hardness and bondage of her Christian life, and was wondering what the Bible *could* mean when it said Christ's yoke was easy and His burden light. I told her that I thought she must have got things wrong somehow, that the Bible always expressed the truth of our relationships with God by using figures that did not admit of any such wrestlings and agonizings as she described. "What would you think," I asked, "of children that had to wrestle and agonize with their parents every morning for their necessary food and clothing, or of sheep that had to wrestle with their shepherd before they could secure the necessary care?" "Of course I see that would be all wrong," she said; "but, then, why do I have such good times after I have gone through these conflicts?" This puzzled me for a moment, but then I asked, "What brings about those good times finally?" "Why, finally," she replied, "I come to the point of trusting the Lord." "Suppose you should come to that point to begin with?" I asked. "Oh," she replied, with a sudden illumination, "I never until this minute thought that I might!"

Christ says that except we "become as little children" we cannot enter into the kingdom of Heaven. But it is impossible to get the child-spirit until the servant-spirit has disappeared. Notice, I do not say the spirit of service, but the servant-spirit. Every good child is filled with the spirit of service, but ought not to have anything of the servant-spirit. The child serves from love; the servant works for wages.

Doing little things with a strong desire to please God makes them really great.

St. Francis De Sales

The bluebird carries the sky on his back.

Henry David Thoreau

Light for Darkness

FELIX ADLER

The hero is one who kindles a great light in the world, who sets up blazing torches in the dark streets of life for men to see by. The saint is the man who walks through the dark paths of the world, himself a light.

The Manger Mouse

RALPH W. SEAGER

He opened a window in the straw
And poked out his nose, two ears, and
     a paw,
And all of midnight filled the skies
Except where two dots were his eyes.

He saw the glow around the manger,
And knew that something so much
     stranger
Than he had ever seen before
Had come in at the stable door.

The Light spread out to darker places,
And fired the garnets in the faces
Of goats and sheep…and all the cows
Wore amber jewels at their brows.

He stared at eyes that watched from under
Horns and fleece, and gazed with wonder;
Unaware the Light had thrown
Starry diamonds into his own.

From *Little Women*

LOUISA MAY ALCOTT

Jo was the first to wake in the gray dawn of Christmas morning. No stockings hung at the fireplace, and for a moment she felt as much disappointed as she did long ago, when her little sock fell down because it was so crammed with goodies. Then she remembered her mother's promise and, slipping her hand under her pillow, drew out a little crimson-covered book. She knew it very well, for it was that beautiful old story of the best life ever lived, and Jo felt that it was a true guidebook for any pilgrim going the long journey. She woke Meg with a "Merry Christmas," and bade her see what was under her pillow. A green-covered book appeared, with the same picture inside, and a few words written by her mother, which made their one present very precious in their eyes. Presently Beth and Amy woke to rummage and find their little books also — one dove-colored, the other blue — and all sat looking at and talking about them, while the east grew rosy with the coming day.

In spite of her small vanities, Margaret had a sweet and pious nature, which unconsciously influenced her sisters, especially Jo, who loved her very tenderly, and obeyed her because her advice was so gently given.

"Girls," said Meg seriously, looking from the tumbled head beside her to the two little nightcapped ones in the room beyond, "Mother wants us to read and love and mind these books, and we must begin at once. We used to be faithful about it, but since Father went away and all this war troubled us, we have neglected many things. You can do as you please, but I shall keep my book on the table here and read a little every morning as soon as I wake, for I know it will do me good and help me through the day."

Then she opened her new book and began to read. Jo put her arm around her and, leaning cheek to cheek, read also, with the quiet expression so seldom seen on her restless face.

"How good Meg is! Come, Amy, let's do as they do. I'll help you with the hard words, and they'll explain things if we don't understand," whispered Beth, very much impressed by the pretty books and her sisters' example.

"I'm glad mine is blue," said Amy. And then the rooms were very still while the pages were softly turned, and the winter sunshine crept in to touch the bright heads and serious faces with a Christmas greeting.

"Where is mother?" asked Meg, as she and Jo ran down to thank her for their gifts, half an hour later.

"Goodness only knows. Some poor creeter come a-beggin', and you ma went straight off to see what was needed. There never was such a woman for givin' away vittles and drink, clothes and firin'," replied Hannah, who had lived with the family since Meg was born, and was considered by them all more as a friend than a servant.

"She will be back soon, I think, so fry your cakes, and have everything ready," said Meg, looking over the presents which were collected in a basket and kept under the sofa, ready to be produced at the proper time. "Why, where is Amy's bottle of cologne?" she added, as the little flask did not appear.

"She took it out a minute ago, and went off with it to put a ribbon on it, or some such notion," replied Jo, dancing about the room to take the first stiffness off the new army slippers.

"How nice my handkerchiefs look, don't they? Hannah washed and ironed them for me, and I marked them all myself," said Beth, looking proudly at the somewhat uneven letters which had cost her such labor.

"Bless the child! She's gone and put 'Mother' on them instead of 'M. March.' How funny!" cried Jo, taking up one.

"Isn't it right? I thought it was better to do it so, because Meg's initials are M.M., and I don't want anyone to use these but Marmee," said Beth, looking troubled.

"It's all right, dear, and a very pretty idea — quite sensible, too, for no one can ever mistake now. It will please her very much, I know," said Meg, with a frown for Jo and a smile for Beth.

"There's Mother. Hide the basket, quick!" cried Jo, as a door slammed and steps sounded in the hall.

Amy came in hastily, and looked rather abashed when she saw her sisters all waiting for her.

"Where have you been, and what are you hiding behind you?" asked Meg, surprised to see, by her hood and cloak, that lazy Amy had been out so early.

"Don't laugh at me, Jo! I didn't mean anyone should know till the time came. I only meant to change the little bottle for a big one, and I gave all my money to get it, and I'm truly trying not to be selfish anymore."

As she spoke, Amy showed the handsome flask which replaced the cheap one, and looked so earnest and humble in her little effort to forget herself that Meg hugged her on the spot, and Jo pronounced her "a trump," while Beth ran to the window, and picked her finest rose to ornament the stately bottle.

"You see I felt ashamed of my present, after reading and talking about being good this morning, so I ran round the corner and changed it the minute I was up: and I'm so glad, for mine is the handsomest now."

Another bang of the street door sent the basket under the sofa, and the girls to the table, eager for breakfast.

"Merry Christmas, Marmee! Many of them! Thank you for our books; we read some, and mean to everyday," they cried, in chorus.

"Merry Christmas, little daughters! I'm glad you began at once, and hope you will keep on. But I want to say one word before we sit down. Not far away from here lies a poor woman with a little newborn baby. Six children are huddled into one bed to keep from freezing, for they have no fire. There is nothing to eat over there, and the oldest boy came to tell me they were suffering hunger and cold. My girls, will you give them your breakfast as a Christmas present?"

They were all unusually hungry, having

waited nearly an hour, and for a minute no one spoke — only a minute, for Jo exclaimed impetuously, "I'm so glad you came before we began!"

"May I go and help carry the things to the poor little children?" asked Beth eagerly.

"I shall take the cream and the muffins," added Amy, heroically giving up the articles she most liked.

Meg was already covering the buckwheats, and piling the bread into one big plate.

"I thought you'd do it," said Mrs. March, smiling as if satisfied. "You shall all go and help me, and when we come back we will have bread and milk for breakfast, and make it up at dinnertime."

They were soon ready, and the procession set out. Fortunately it was early, and they went through back streets, so few people saw them, and no one laughed at the queer party.

A poor, bare, miserable room it was, with broken windows, no fire, ragged bedclothes, a sick mother, wailing baby, and a group of pale, hungry children cuddled under one old quilt trying to keep warm.

How the big eyes stared and the blue lips smiled as the girls went in!

"It is good angels come to us!" said the poor woman, crying for joy.

"Funny angels in hoods and mittens," said Jo, and set them laughing.

In a few minutes it really did seem as if kind spirits had been at work there. Hannah, who had carried wood, made a fire, and stopped up the broken panes with old hats and her own cloak. Mrs. March gave the mother tea and gruel, and comforted her with promises of help, while she dressed the little baby as tenderly as if it had been her own. The girls meantime spread the table, set the children around the fire, and fed them like so many hungry birds.

The girls had never been called angel children before, and thought it very agreeable. That was a very happy breakfast, though they didn't get any of it; and when they went away, leaving comfort behind, I think there were not in all the city four merrier people than the hungry little girls who gave away their breakfasts and contented themselves with bread and milk on Christmas morning.

So long as we love, we serve. So long as we are loved by others, I would almost say we are indispensable; and no man is useless while he has a friend.
Robert Louis Stevenson

The Lion and the Mouse

AESOP

A Lion was awakened from sleep by a Mouse running over his face. Rising up angrily, he caught him and was about to kill him, when the Mouse piteously entreated, saying: "If you would only spare my life, I would be sure to repay your kindness." The Lion laughed and let him go. It happened shortly after this that the Lion was caught by some hunters, who bound him by strong ropes to the ground. The Mouse, recognizing his roar, came up, gnawed the rope with his teeth, and set him free, exclaiming: "You ridiculed the idea of my ever being able to help you, not expecting to receive from me any repayment of your favor; but now you know that it is possible for even a Mouse to confer benefits on a Lion."

Kindness

ANONYMOUS

I have wept in the night
For the shortness of sight
That to somebody's need made me blind;
But I never have yet
Felt a tinge of regret
For being a little too kind.

A Man You Could Trust

CATHERINE MARSHALL

It wasn't that my father was eloquent in the pulpit. He was an average preacher with only a mild interest in theology. His forte was people. He loved them and enjoyed mixing with them, friends and strangers alike. He was easy to be with and had a knack for finding a just-right conversational meeting ground with all manner of folk.

One of my favorite stories is about how Dad went down into the railroad yards near our home in Keyser, West Virginia, to seek out a new member of his congregation. Although our town was close to coalmining territory, Keyser's only industry was the Baltimore and Ohio Railroad's roundhouse and shops. It was in one of the B & O's enormous roundhouses that the Reverend Wood found his man at work.

"Can't shake hands with you," said the man apologetically. "They're too grimy."

John Wood reached down to the ground and rubbed his hands in coal soot. "How about it now?" he said, offering an equalized hand.

My All

PRUDENCE TASKER OLSEN

Lord, let me give and sing and sow
    And do my best, though I
In years to come may never know
    What soul was helped thereby.

Content to feel that thou canst bless
    All things however small
To someone's lasting happiness
    So, Lord, accept my all.

There is no happiness in having or in getting, but only in giving.   Henry Drummond

The Boy with Five Barley Loaves

LOUIS G. MILLER, C.SS.R.

One of Jesus' disciples, Andrew,
Simon Peter's brother,
remarked to him:
"There is a lad here
who has five barley loaves
and a couple of dried fish,
but what good is that for so many?"
                    John 6:8-9

Nicholaus is my name,
a deacon in good repute.
At twelve years of age
I had a grownup's job.
I had my mother to take care of
after my father's death.
There wasn't much time for play
with other boys my age.
I was always on the lookout
for money to buy our bread.
We were very poor,
just the two of us;
we struggled to stay alive.
I saw a crowd one day
churning dust upon the road.
Many from our village
went out into the hill country
to hear a holy man preach.
"They will be looking for food,"
I said to myself.
"If only I could get hold of a few dozen
        loaves."
It wasn't very likely.
I had no money to buy bread.
My mother said to me:
"Let us follow the crowd."
We took our last two loaves,

I begged some bread from an aunt
who lived next door —
she always liked me —
and she gave me three loaves
and added two dried fish.
I put the food in a basket
and we followed the people
out into the hills.
That's when I first saw Jesus.
He was standing quietly
under a tree,
watching the people
as they gathered around him.
I got as close to him as I could;
something about him held me,
I don't know what it was,
something in his eyes....
He looked at me and smiled.
I said in my heart:
"This is the man I must follow."

We were there all that day
and the crowd continued to grow —
more than a thousand of them —
the largest crowd I ever saw.
We forgot all about eating
while he spoke to us.
He didn't seem to shout,
yet everybody was able to hear him.
There was no stirring in the crowd,
even when he paused and rested.
Everybody sat there thinking
or talking quietly to each other.
Before we knew it, it was evening.
I heard Jesus say
to some who were his helpers,
"Where can we find food to feed this
        crowd?"
But no one had brought anything.
I was standing close by.
A man named Andrew —
I heard them call him by that name —
looked at my basket and said:
"Here is a boy
with a few loaves and fish,
but that won't go very far."
Jesus took my basket —
I didn't even think

of asking any money for it —
and I saw him bless it.
Then suddenly the basket
was filled to the very top.
Andrew and some others
began to hand out the loaves;
and as fast as they emptied it,
the basket seemed to fill up again,
and the same with the fish.
I didn't know what to make of it.
After they all had finished eating,
there was still enough left
to fill my basket and ten others.
My mother didn't know what to say;
I never saw her like that.
Some of the men came to Jesus.
I heard them say to him:
"Master, be our leader,
be our conquering king."
But Jesus looked sad,
as if they didn't understand,
and he walked off by himself
down the hill toward the lake.
But before he departed
he smiled at me standing there
and put his hand on my head.
Then he took my hand
and put two shekels into it
(one of his helpers
had the money in a purse),
and he said to me:
"This is for the bread and the fish
that you provided for our meal."
I didn't know what to say;
I stood there speechless,
and so did my mother.
We watched him walk away,
but I said to myself:
"I will follow him until death."
Now I am old,
my mother is dead.
I have kept my word;
I followed him to Jerusalem,
and saw him die on a cross.
I never gave up hope,
and when Andrew told me
he had risen from the grave,
I knew it had to be.

I've never been a dreamer;
I'm a practical man.
They made me a deacon
here in Capernaum
to help with the serving,
to look after the needy.
All these years I have labored;
they know they can count on me.
I don't have any visions,
I have to be active;
I'm glad to be active
for Jesus my Savior.

Prayer

B. Y. WILLIAMS

Oh, not for more or longer days, dear Lord,
    My prayer shall be —
But rather teach me how to use the days
    Now given me.

I ask not more of pleasure or of joy
    For this brief while —
But rather let me for the joys I have
    Be glad and smile.

Giving

KAHLIL GIBRAN

You give but little when you give of your
possessions.
  It is when you give of yourself that you
truly give.

Freely ye have received, freely give.
        Matthew 10:8, King James Version

A Share of Sunshine

ZELDA DAVIS HOWARD

In this big wide world of ours,
God has made enough sunshine
For everyone to have a share,
Sometime…Somewhere.

Thank You, Lord

JOHN BAILLIE

A true Christian is a man who never for a
moment forgets what God has done for him
in Christ, and whose whole comportment
and whole activity have their root in the
sentiment of gratitude.

Let Us Be Thankful

GRACE NOLL CROWELL

Despite the ashes of a bitter drought;
Despite the old earth's parched and thirsty
        mouth
There has been food. God's gracious hand
        has spread
Our tables with His gift of daily bread,
There has been water, though the streams
        ran dry,
But the sun and moon and stars still
        climbed the sky,
And the promise held that blessed rain
        would fall
Upon the just and the unjust — men have
        all
Shown faith unconsciously who plowed the
        land
And planted seed. They trust an unseen
        hand
To work in power for the year ahead.
We have been blest — we have been wisely
        led,
So let us thank the Maker of all good;

Let us pause today in sincere gratitude
To give God thanks. His mercy reaches far,
May we strive to be more worthy than we
   are,
Oh, let us be most grateful for the care
With which we are surrounded
   everywhere!

The World's Most Beautiful Rose

HANS CHRISTIAN ANDERSEN

There once was a mighty queen in whose garden grew the most beautiful flowers. Every season there were some in bloom, and they had been collected in all the countries of the world. But roses she loved above all flowers, and in her garden were many kinds, from the wild hedge rose with green leaves that smell like apples to the loveliest rose of Provence. Roses grew up the walls of the castle, twined themselves around the marble columns, and even entered the halls and corridors of the castle, where their ramblers crept across the ceilings and filled the rooms with the fragrance of their flowers.

But inside the castle sorrow lived, for the queen was dying. The wisest of all the doctors who were attending her said, "There is only one remedy that can save her. Bring her the world's most beautiful rose, the one that symbolizes the highest and purest love, and when her eyes see that flower, then she will not die."

The young and the old brought their roses — the most beautiful ones that grew in their gardens — but it was not such a flower that could cure the queen. From love's garden the rose must be brought, but which flower would be the symbol of the highest and purest love?

The poets sang of the world's most beautiful rose, and each mentioned a different one. Word was sent to all, regardless of rank and class, whose hearts did beat for love.

"No one has as yet mentioned the right flower," said the wise man. "No one has pointed to that place where it grows, in all its glory and beauty. It is not the rose from Romeo's and Juliet's tomb or Valborg's grave, though those roses will always bloom and shed their fragrance in stories and poetry. Nor is it the rose that blooms on Winkelried's blood-covered lance. From the hero's blood, shed in defense of his native land, the reddest rose springs; and it is said that such a death is sweet, but it is not the most beautiful rose in the world. The magical wonderful rose, which can only be grown under constant care, through days and years and sleepless nights: the rose of science, it is not either."

"I know where it blooms," exclaimed a happy mother who, carrying her babe, had entered the queen's bedchamber. "I know where the world's most beautiful rose is to be found, the rose of the highest and purest love. It blooms on the cheeks of my child, when he wakes from his sleep and laughs up at me, with all his love."

"Yes, in truth, that rose is lovely, but there are those even more beautiful," said the wise man.

"Yes, far more beautiful," said one of the ladies in waiting. "I have seen it, and a more exalted, sacred rose than that does not exist. It is as pale as the petals of a tea rose and I have seen it on our queen's cheeks when, without her golden crown, she walked, carrying her sick child in her arms, back and forth across the room one whole long night. She kissed her babe and prayed to God as only a mother prays in her agony."

"Yes, wonderful and holy is the white rose of sorrow, but that is not the one."

"No, the world's most beautiful rose I saw before the altar of Our Lord," a pious old priest said. "I saw it shine on an angel's face. Among a group of young girls who had come to take communion, there was one who looked with such simple and innocent a love up toward her God that on her face bloomed the rose of the highest and purest love."

"Blessed is that rose too," said the wise man. "But none of you has yet mentioned the world's most beautiful rose."

At that moment into the room stepped a little boy, the queen's son. His eyes were filled with tears and he was carrying a big book with silver clasps and bound in vellum. The book was open.

"Mother!" said the little one. "Listen to what I have read." And the child sat down by his mother's bedside and read about Him who suffered death on the Cross in order to save humanity. "Greater love there cannot be."

The queen's pale cheeks took on a pinkish shade, and her eyes became big and clear, as from the pages of the book grew the world's most beautiful rose, the one that grew from Christ's blood on the Cross.

"I see it," she said. "And those who have seen that rose, the most beautiful in the world, shall never die."

High Flight

PILOT OFFICER JOHN GILLESPIE MAGEE, JR., R.C.A.F.

Oh! I have slipped the surly bonds of earth
    And danced the skies on
        laughter-silvered wings;
Sunward I've climbed, and joined the
        tumbling mirth
    Of sun-split clouds — and done a
        hundred things
You have not dreamed of — wheeled and
        soared and swung
    High in the sunlit silence. Hov'ring
        there,
I've chased the shouting wind along, and
        flung
    My eager craft through footless halls
        of air.

Up, up the long, delirious, burning blue
    I've topped the wind-swept heights
        with easy grace
Where never lark, or even eagle flew —
    And, while with silent lifting mind I've
        trod
The high untrespassed sanctity of space,
    Put out my hand and touched the face
        of God.

Bring Tomorrow's Dawning

ALICE JOYCE DAVIDSON

If I have failed to do a thoughtful deed,
Or turned my back on anyone in need,
If I've ignored the clouds in someone's
    skies,
Or missed the chance to wipe another's
    eyes,
If I have spoken words of bitterness,
If I have failed or faltered, more or less,
If I've forgotten the golden rule
    someway —
Lord, bring tomorrow's dawning, so I may
Make up for all I've left undone today!

From *Mister God, This Is Anna*

FYNN

It looked pretty certain that the war would come. Already the gas masks were making rude noises in the streets. The men with the Anderson shelters were dumping corrugated iron sheets in back gardens. Notices about the gas attacks, sirens, shelters, and what to do "if," were multiplying like the spots of some disease. The decay of war was spreading everywhere. The walls against which the kids played their ball games had become the notice boards of war. The rules of "four sticks" chalked up on the wall had been covered over with the regulations for the blackout. We were being instructed in the rules of a new game....

The infection of war was spreading through the kids. Balls were no longer things to bounce; balls had become bombs. Cricket bats were pressed into service as machine guns. Kids with outstretched arms gyrated through imaginary skies with a *rat-a-tat-tat*, shooting down enemy planes or shooting up enemy soldiers. A shriek of *wheeeeee, booooom* and a dozen kids died in feigned agony. "Bang, you're dead!"

Anna held tightly to my hand and pressed herself close to me. It wasn't the kind of game that she could play; the acting and the pretending belonged to something real, and it was this reality that Anna saw so clearly. She pulled at my hand and we went indoors and out into the garden. It wasn't much better there, for over the housetops a barrage balloon made mock of the skies. She turned a full circle looking at these intruders in the sky. She looked me full in the face as her hand stretched out for mine. A frown flickered over her face.

"Why, Fynn? Why?" she asked, searching my face for an answer.

I could give her no answers. Kneeling down, she gently touched the few wild flowers that grew in the backyard. Bossy arrived and rubbed his battered old head on her leg. Patch, lying full length, eyed her with concern. It must have been the best part of an hour that I stood there watching her touch and explore these few square yards of garden. Delicately and reverently her fingers moved from beetle to flower, from pebble to caterpillar. I was waiting for her to cry, expecting her at any moment to run to my arms, but she didn't. I wasn't at all sure what was going on in her mind. All I knew was that the hurt was deep, perhaps too deep for my comfort.

...I heard her say, so very quietly, "I'm sorry." She wasn't talking to me, she wasn't talking to Mister God. She was talking to the flowers, to the earth, to Bossy and to Patch and to the little bugs and beetles. Humanity asking the rest of the world for forgiveness.

I was intruding here so I went into the kitchen.... I don't know how long I sat there. It seemed forever. It was the horror of my own imagination that drove me into the garden again. My imagination had somehow provided me with a machine gun and I was busy killing off those who had caused Anna so much hurt. Confused and bewildered at my own violent thoughts, I went out into the backyard half afraid that in some mysterious way she had divined them.

She was sitting on the garden wall with Bossy on her lap. She grinned as I approached her, not one of those full-blooded grins, but full enough for me to slam the door on my own violence.

I went back into the kitchen and put on the kettle. Soon after we were both sitting on the wall drinking our cocoa. My mind was racing away with questions I wanted to ask but I managed not to. I wanted to be assured that she was all right, but I wasn't given that assurance. I knew that she wasn't all right. I knew that the horror of the impending war had struck deep down inside her. No, she wasn't all right, but she was managing very well. For Anna, this war creeping up on us was a deep sorrow of the soul. It was me that was anxious.

Later that evening.... I knew full well that I was concerned for her, that I was aware of her distress, and that I was ready to do anything to comfort her. It was only in the middle of the night that I realized how much I needed her assurance that she was all right, how much her sheer sanity protected me. For all her few years, I saw her then as I see her now, the sanest, the most uncluttered, and the most direct of beings....

"Fynn, I love you." When Anna said that, every word was shattered by the fullness of meaning she packed into it.... Her use of the word *love* was not sentimental or mushy; it was impelling and full of courage and encouragement. For Anna, *love* meant the recognition of perfectibility in another. Anna *saw* a person in every part. Anna *saw* a *you*. Now that is something to experience, to be seen as a *you*, clearly and definitely, with no parts hidden. Wonderful and frightening. I'd always understood that it was Mister God who saw you so clearly and in your entirety, but then all Anna's efforts were directed to being like Mister God, so perhaps the trick is catching if only you try hard enough.

By and large, I thought I could understand Anna's attitude to Mister God, but on one aspect I got stuck completely. Perhaps it was hidden in "Thou didst hide these things from the wise and understanding and didst reveal them unto babes." How she managed it, I truly don't know, but in some manner she had scaled the walls of God's majesty, his awe-inspiring nature, and was on the other side. Mister God was a "sweetie." Mister God was fun, Mister God was lovable. Mister God was for Anna pretty straightforward, not presenting her with any real problem in the understanding of his nature. The fact that he could, and often did, put a large monkey wrench in the works was neither here nor there. He was perfectly free to do so, and obviously it was for some good purpose, even though we were not able to see or understand that purpose.

Anna saw, recognized, admitted to, and submitted to, all those attributes of God so often discussed. Mister God was the author of all things, the creator of all things, omnipotent, omniscient, and at the very heart of all things — except.... It was this exception that Anna saw as the key to the whole thing....

You could, if you wished, deny that Mister God existed, but then any denial didn't alter the fact that Mister God was. No, Mister God was; he *was* the kingpin, the center, the very heart of things; ...This is the curious nature of Mister God: that even while he is at the center of all things, he waits outside us and knocks to come in. It is we who open the door. Mister God doesn't break it down and come in; no, he knocks and waits.

Now it takes a real super kind of God to work that one out, but that's just what he's done. As Anna said, "That's very funny, that is. It makes me very important, don't it? Fancy Mister God taking second place!" Anna never got involved in the problem of free will. I suppose she was too young, but she had got to the heart of the matter: Mister God took second place, ain't that something!

Journeys

IDA NORTON MUNSON

How restful are unhurried things! —
The spreading light of dawn's gray hour,
Slow, rhythmic motion of birds' wings,
The opening petals of a flower....

Dim shadows moving on a wall,
The moon's calm light above the bay,
Soft murmurings that rise and fall
Within the dusk that hushes day.

My journey, too, may bring content
To the still place of heart's desire;
There, tranquilly, to pitch my tent —
Watch flames scale heavenward from
    my fire.

I'd like to live
I'd like to be
I'd like to give
  all the giving in me.

Hoyt Axton

Steadfastness

FOR TWO YEARS the agony of the Atlanta Prison spilled out of its walls into grisly headlines, congressional hearings and TV specials. Death struck swiftly, often and with impunity. Guards recoiled at the prospect of walking cellblock corridors; visitors were banned.

A new warden, named in the middle of the carnage, responded to our offer of help by scheduling an in-prison seminar.

"Are we ready to tackle Atlanta?" I asked.

"That's where the Lord would go, isn't it?" one Prison Fellowship director replied.

Still, we didn't know what to expect from the inmates. Tension built as the seminar date approached. It was an especially hot summer, and the cellblocks, ventilated only by antique fans, were like furnaces. Most prison riots, we knew, erupt in the "dog days" of late summer. We had not only chosen the toughest prison, but also the worst time of year.

The warden and prison chaplains escorted us through the maze of gates into the center corridor, past hundreds of peering, curious eyes and into the chaplain's office. There we met with eight brothers, a small fellowship core. We sat in a circle and they began to speak: "We're sure glad you're here, Chuck. The betting was two to one you wouldn't show.... Things are bad, the men are tense.... You can't preach or talk about Jesus, the men won't take it.... They feel you're out to con them."

"I came to tell the men what Christ can do for them," I responded. But the fire was gone from my words.

We prayed together — prayers claiming God's promises — but the circle seemed a tiny spot of light in a vast sea of darkness. Then I asked them to leave me alone so I could make quick notes for a different speech — one on prison reform. Minutes later my mind was churning and my heart pounding as we headed toward the auditorium.

More than 800 inmates crowded the hall. The heat was unbearable. Tension was crackling in the air like static electricity. Sullen restlessness, mixed with polite applause, was the only response

to the preliminary comments, prayer and soloist. My own anxieties were climbing as fast as the room temperature. It seemed hot enough to ignite the notes in my hand.

I bowed my head to say one last pithy, crisis prayer. "Lord," I thought, "if I've ever needed Your help, it's now." Then I drew a deep breath and something the prison chaplain had said paraded across my mind. That was it! These men couldn't figure out why I was there.

"I know what you're thinking," I began. "What is Chuck Colson doing here? What's his game? Right?" Heads nodded. This wasn't what I had planned to say at all. "Well, let me tell you why. Because I've committed my life to Jesus Christ, and this is where He calls me to be." This was exactly what my friends feared would set the crowd off.

By now I had stuck the "prison reform" notes in my pocket. If I was sure of anything, it was that I would talk about Jesus Christ. The crowd seemed intent as I traced the history of Prison Fellowship. Then I told them about Jesus, a man without any wordly possessions, a man betrayed, sentenced to die and executed on the cross. I told them that Jesus lives today — for the sick, the imprisoned, the powerless, for all people, just as he did 2,000 years ago.

The heat in the room was overpowering. I'm sure I looked as if I'd just come in from the rain. This should have brought weakness, but instead came strength.

What happened can only be explained as an extraordinary outpouring of the Holy Spirit. By the end of the meeting men were not only standing throughout the hall, they were getting on chairs, clapping and shouting. The change in their faces was awesome. They were warm and smiling. There were tears in eyes where there had been only distrust and hate. Many put their trust in Christ.

The lesson was clear for me that night. God always meets us at our point of need. I discovered in the Atlanta Prison that in my weakness, Christ makes me strong.

CHARLES COLSON

Example

JOHANN WOLFGANG VON GOETHE

Like the star
Shining afar
Slowly now
And without rest,
Let each man turn, with steady sway,
Round the task that rules the day
And do his best.

I count this thing to be grandly true;
That a noble deed is a step toward God.

Josiah Gilbert Holland

A Day Is Born

THOMAS CARLYLE

Lo, here hath been dawning another blue
    day;
Think, wilt thou let it slip useless away?

Out of eternity this new day is born,
Into eternity at night will return.

Behold it aforetime no eye ever did;
So soon it forever from all eyes hid.

Here hath been dawning another blue day;
Think, wilt thou let it slip useless away?

The Lightship

JOSEPHINE JOHNSON

Out with the tide, beneath the morning
    sun,
Along the highways of the wide bright sea
The ships go forth in beauty — even the
    smallest one
Goes forward eagerly!

Only the lightship, lonely, still, and proud,
Swings at her anchor, while a great
    undertow
Of passionate longing fills her, throbbing
    through keel and shroud,
For ports she may not know....

Then the blue dusk drops down, and from
    afar
The ships return. Beggared or riding deep,
For each a welcoming haven inside the
    harbor bar,
Furled canvas, quiet sleep.

But sleepless must the lightship lie, and
    lone
By the sharp reef — no dreams of curious
    lands,
Great burning unknown stars, bright birds,
    fantastic bone
Bleaching on island sands —

Never the voyage! Never the spreading sail!
Never the swift prow cutting through the
    foam
Of fabulous silver shorelines — after the
    fiercest gale.
Never the hope of home!

Steadfast and strong above the gathering
    chill
Her light burns on. How shall the passing
    bark
Surmise this desperate hunger? Lonely and
    proud and still
Are beacons in the dark!

The Hare and the Tortoise

AESOP

A Hare one day ridiculed the short feet and slow pace of the Tortoise, who replied, laughing: "Though you be swift as the wind, I will beat you in a race." The Hare, believing her assertion to be simply impossible, assented to the proposal; and they agreed that the Fox should choose the course and fix the goal. On the day appointed for the race the two started together. The Tortoise never for a moment stopped, but went on with a slow but steady pace straight to the end of the course. The Hare, trusting to his native swiftness, cared little about the race, and lying down by the wayside, fell fast asleep. At last waking up, and moving as fast as he could, he saw the Tortoise had reached the goal, and was comfortably dozing after her fatigue.

Slow but steady wins the race.

Faith

ROBERT H. SCHULLER

Lord, I believe
In the sun, even when
it is behind the clouds;
In the seed, even when
it lies unsprouted under the ground;
In faith, even when I have been
betrayed;
In love, even when I have been
rejected;
In hope, even when I have been hurt;
In God, even when
you do not answer my prayers.
Amen.

Night Duty

MARJORIE HOLMES

Oh, Lord, I hear it again, that little voice in the night, crying, "Mommy!"

At least I think I hear it. It may be my imagination. It may be just the wind. Or if not, maybe it will stop in a minute, the child will go back to sleep....

(Oh, let it be just the wind. Or let him go back to sleep. I'm so tired. I've been up so many nights lately. I've got to get some sleep too.)

But if it's true, if it's one of them needing me and it isn't going to stop, if I must go — help me.

Lift me up, steady me on my feet. And make me equal to my duty.

If he's scared give me patience and compassion to drive the fears of night away.

If he's ill give me wisdom. Make me alert. Let me know what to do.

If he's wet the bed again, give me even more patience and wisdom and understanding (and let me find some clean sheets).

Thank you, Lord, for helping my weary footsteps down this hall.

Thank you for sustaining me too as I comfort and care for the child.

Thank you for my own sweet...sweet ...eventual sleep.

Work is love made visible.   Kahlil Gibran

Keep your fears to yourself, but share your courage with others.   Robert Louis Stevenson

Finding Your Personal Power

NORMAN VINCENT PEALE

A soldier came home from overseas minus a leg. The amputation following battle wounds shocked the boy's mind deeply. He lay on his bed neither smiling nor speaking — just staring at the ceiling. He would not cooperate in learning to wear an artificial limb, although others around him were doing so. Obviously his problem was not his physical body but was in his mind and spirit. So deep was his acquired inferiority that he had completely given way to defeat.

It was thought that a period of time at his own home might help bring him out of himself and assist in lifting his depression. He came of a well-to-do family, and at home he had every attention. In fact, his family overdid it. He was tenderly lifted into his bath, he was hovered over and coddled in every conceivable manner. This is understandable, for everybody wants to show love and appreciation for a boy who has sacrificed himself for his country.

However, the doctor realized that they were making a permanent invalid of the boy. Accordingly he placed him in a convalescent hospital. An effort was made to help him to help himself, and to give him a normal attitude toward the problem of himself but with no success. He continued to lie on his bed, indifferent and uncooperative.

One day the rather baffled and exasperated young doctor said, "I have got to be hard on the boy; I hate to do it, but somehow I must break through this wall around him. He must cast out this inferiority psychosis if he is to recover to normal living."

He said, "Soldier, we are not going to pamper you anymore, or carry you around. You have got to be awakened, boy. We can do nothing for you until you open that mind of yours. We all feel sorry about that leg, but other men have lost legs in battle and they have carried on with good spirit. Besides, a man can live and be happy and have a successful career without a leg or an arm or an eye." The doctor pointed out how people are able to adjust themselves, and how so many have done astounding things.

This talk did not move the boy in the slightest. Finally, after many days of attempting to open the closed mind of his patient the doctor quite unconsciously did a peculiar thing, something which amazed even himself.

The doctor was not a particularly religious person, and up to this point had seldom, if ever, mentioned religion in his practice. However, this day in sheer desperation the doctor literally shouted at the boy, "All right, all right; if you won't let any of us help you — if you are so stubborn that you won't even help yourself — then, then — why don't you let God help you? Get up and get that leg on; you know how to do it."

With this he left the room.

A few hours later it was reported that the boy was up, had on his artificial leg, and was moving around. The doctor said that one of the most thrilling moments in his medical experience came some days later when he saw this boy walking around the grounds with a girl friend.

Later when the soldier was discharged from the hospital he came in to see the doctor. The physician started to give him some suggestion, but the boy said, "It's all right, Doc; I remember the medicine you gave me that day. And I think with that prescription I can get along well enough."

"What prescription?" asked the doctor.

"Don't you remember the day you told me that if I could not do it myself, to let God help me? Well, that did something to me. I felt sort of different inside, and as I thought about it, it began to come over me that maybe I could do it — that maybe I wasn't finished after all."

As the physician related this story he sat tapping his desk with a pencil in a thoughtful manner. "Whatever happened to that boy I cannot explain; the process eludes my knowledge. But I do know that in some spiritual manner that boy was released. His mind changed from a state of inner defeat to one of personal power." He hesitated, then added, "There seems to be a very great power in religious faith when it is practiced."

And he is right. Use your religious faith and you do not need to be a defeated person. It will recondition your mind from negative to positive reactions. It makes possible what formerly seemed impossible. This is the mechanism which explains the Biblical statement, "With men things are impossible, but with God all things are possible." When you mentally live with thoughts of God, your inferiority changes to power, impossibility changes to possibility.

In fact, that brief statement of ten short words from the Bible which I have quoted several times can absolutely revolutionize your life. "If God be for us, who can be against us?" Strong, sturdy words these. With these ten words of power you can stand up against any human situation and not be defeated.

Perseverance is a great element of success. If you only knock long enough and loud enough at the gate, you are sure to wake up somebody.
Henry Wadsworth Longfellow

Heroism

LIZETTE WOODWORTH REESE

Whether we climb, whether we plod,
    Space for one task the scant years
        lend —
To choose some path that leads to God,
    And keep it to the end.

Live every day of your life as though you expected to live forever.
Douglas MacArthur

The Eagle

ALFRED, LORD TENNYSON

He clasps the crag with crooked hands;
Close to the sun in lonely lands,
Ringed with the azure world, he stands.
The wrinkled sea beneath him crawls;
He watches from his mountain walls,
And like a thunderbolt he falls.

Reaching the Goal

ELBERT HUBBARD

Genius is only the power of making continuous efforts. The line between failure and success is so fine that we scarcely know when we pass it: so fine that we are often on the line and do not know it. How many a man has thrown up his hands at a time when a little more effort, a little more patience, would have achieved success. As the tide goes clear out, so it comes clear in. In business, sometimes, prospects may seem darkest when really they are on the turn. A little more persistence, a little more effort, and what seemed hopeless failure may turn to glorious success. There is no failure except in no longer trying. There is no defeat except from within, no really insurmountable barrier save our own inherent weakness of purpose.

The Bedquilt

DOROTHY CANFIELD

Of all the Elwell family Aunt Mehetabel was certainly the most unimportant member. It was in the old-time New England days, when an unmarried woman was an old maid at twenty, at forty was everyone's servant, and at sixty had gone through so much discipline that she could need no more in the world. Aunt Mehetabel was sixty-eight.

She had never for a moment known the pleasure of being important to anyone. Not that she was useless in her brother's family; she was expected, as a matter of course, to take upon herself the most tedious and uninteresting part of the household labors....

The Elwells were not consciously unkind to their aunt; they were even in a vague way fond of her; but she was so insignificant a figure in their lives that she was almost invisible to them. Aunt Mehetabel did not resent this treatment; she took it quite as unconsciously as they gave it. It was to be expected when one was an old-maid dependent in a busy family....

Her sister-in-law, a big hearty housewife, who ruled indoors with as autocratic a sway as did her husband on the farm, was rather kind in an absent, offhand way to the shrunken little old woman, and it was through her that Mehetabel was able to enjoy the one pleasure of her life. Even as a girl she had been clever with her needle in the way of patching bedquilts....

She never knew how her great idea came to her. Sometimes she thought she must have dreamed it, sometimes she even wondered reverently, in the phraseology of the weekly prayer-meeting, if it had not been "sent" to her.... Even when she finished drawing the design with her own fingers, she gazed at it incredulously, not daring to believe that it could indeed be her handiwork. At first it seemed to her only like a lovely but unreal dream....

But as she dreamed, her nimble old fingers reached out longingly to turn her dream into reality.... Her very first stitches showed her that it was even better than she hoped. By some heaven-sent inspiration she had invented a pattern beyond which no patchwork quilt could go....

"Land's sakes!" cried her sister-in-law. "Why, Mehetabel Elwell, where did you git that pattern?"

"I made it up," said Mehetabel. She spoke quietly but she was trembling.

"No!" exclaimed Sophia. "Did you! Why, I never see such a pattern in my life. Girls, come here and see what your Aunt Mehetabel is doing...."

As she lay that night in her narrow hard bed, too proud, too excited to sleep, Mehetabel's heart swelled and tears of joy ran down from her old eyes.

The next day her sister-in-law astonished her by taking the huge pan of potatoes out of her lap and setting one of the younger children to peeling them. "Don't you want to go on with that quiltin' pattern?" she said....

By the end of the summer the family interest had risen so high that Mehetabel was given for herself a little round table in the sitting room, for *her*, where she could keep her pieces and use odd minutes for her work.... She went on faithfully with her monotonous housework, not neglecting a corner. But the atmosphere of her world was changed. Now things had a meaning....

A year went by and a quarter of the quilt was finished. A second year passed and half was done.... In September of the fifth year, the entire family gathered around her to watch eagerly, as Mehetabel quilted the last stitches. The girls held it up by the four corners and they all looked at it in hushed silence.

Then Mr. Elwell cried as one speaking with authority, "By ginger! That's goin' to the County Fair!"

Mehetabel blushed a deep red. She had thought of this herself, but never would have spoken aloud of it....

The Fair was to last a fortnight. At the beginning of the second week Mr. Elwell asked his sister how early she could get up in the morning.

"I dunno. Why?" she asked.

"Well, Thomas Ralston has got to drive to West Oldton to see a lawyer. That's four miles beyond the Fair. He says if you can git up so's to leave here at four in the morning he'll drive you to the Fair, leave you there for the day, and bring you back again at night." Mehetabel's face turned very white. Her eyes filled with tears. It was as though someone had offered her a ride in a golden chariot up to the gates of heaven....

The next morning all the family rose early to see her off.... The buggy drove up to the door, and she was helped in. The family ran to and fro with blankets, woolen tippet, a hot soapstone from the kitchen range. Her wraps were tucked about her. They all stood together and waved good-bye as she drove out of the yard. She waved back, but she scarcely saw them. On her return home that evening she was ashy pale, and so stiff that her brother had to lift her out bodily. But her lips were set in a blissful smile.... They gathered about her, eager for news of the great world, and Sophia said, "Now, come, Mehetabel, tell us all about it!"

Mehetabel drew a long breath. "It was just perfect!" she said....

Mr. Elwell asked, "What did you think of that big ox we've heard so much about?"

"I didn't look at the stock," returned his sister indifferently....

"How did Jed Burgess' bay horse place in the mile trot?" asked Thomas.

"I didn't see the races."

"How about the preserves?" asked Sophia.

"I didn't see the preserves," said Mehetabel calmly.

Seeing that they were gazing at her with astonished faces she went on to give them a reasonable explanation, "You see I went right to the room where the quilt was, and then I didn't want to leave it.... I ate my lunch right there too, and I'm glad as can be I did, too; for what do you think?" — she gazed about her with kindling eyes. "While I stood there with a sandwich in one hand, didn't the head of the hull concern come in and open the glass door and pin a big bow of blue ribbon right in the middle of the quilt with a label on it, 'First Prize.'"

...She fell into a reverie. As if it hung again before her eyes she saw the glory that shone around the creation of her hand and brain. She longed to make her listeners share the golden vision with her. She struggled for words.... Vague recollections of hymnbook phrases came into her mind. They were the only kind of poetic expression she knew. But they were dismissed as being sacrilegious to use for something in real life....

Finally, "I tell you it looked real *good*," she assured them and sat staring into the fire, on her tired old face the supreme content of an artist who has realized his ideal.

He who cherishes a beautiful ideal in his heart, will one day realize it.　　　　James Allen

From *Tales of a Wayside Inn*

HENRY WADSWORTH LONGFELLOW

The dawn is not distant,
Nor is the night starless;
Love is eternal!
God is still God, and
His faith shall not fail us;
Christ is eternal!

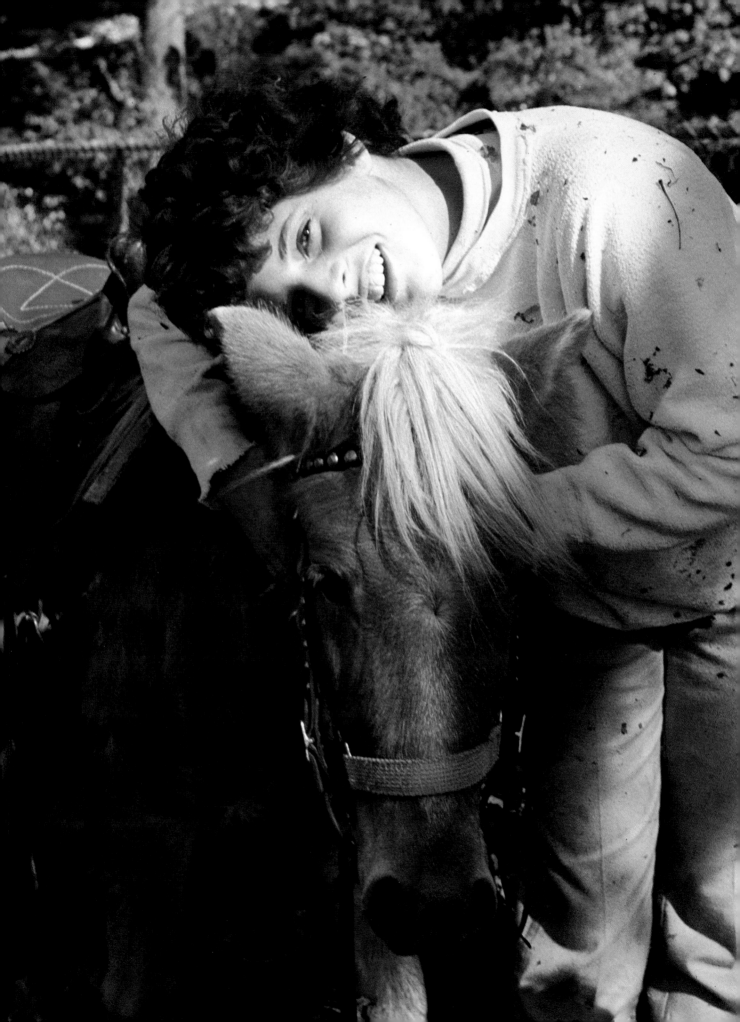

Before anything else existed, there was Christ, with God. He has always been alive and is himself God. He created everything there is — nothing exists that he didn't make. Eternal life is in him, and this life gives light to all mankind. His life is the light that shines through the darkness — and the darkness can never extinguish it.

John 1:1-4, Living Bible

The Dream

EDWIN MARKHAM

Ah, great it is to believe the dream
As we stand in youth by the stream;
But a greater thing is to fight life through,
And say at the end, "The dream is true!"

Promise Yourself

CHRISTIAN D. LARSON

Promise yourself to be so strong that nothing can disturb your peace of mind. To talk health, happiness and prosperity to every person you meet. To make all your friends feel that there is something in them. To look at the sunny side of everything and make your optimism come true. To think only of the best, to work only for the best and expect only the best. To be just as enthusiastic about the success of others as you are about your own. To forget the mistakes of the past and press on to the greater achievements of the future. To wear a cheerful countenance at all times and give every living creature you meet a smile. To give so much time to the improvement of yourself that you have no time to criticize others. To be too large for

worry, too noble for anger, too strong for fear and too happy to permit the presence of trouble.

Thought is what changes knowledge into energy.
Dorothy L. Sayers

If We Love

ANONYMOUS

If we love love, if we love friendliness, if we love helpfulness, if we love beauty, if we love health, if we love to create joy, if we love usefulness and are not self-seekers, the spirit which expresses itself in love and helpfulness and beauty will enter unto us and abide there. We become what we love.

The Way to a Happy New Year

ANONYMOUS

To leave the old with a burst of song;
To recall the right and forgive the wrong;
To forget the things that bind you fast
To the vain regrets of the year that's past;
To have the strength to let go your hold
Of the not worth while of the days
          grown old;
To dare go forth with a purpose true,
To the unknown task of the year that's new;
To help your brother along the road,
To do his work and lift his load;
To add your gift to the world's good cheer,
Is to have and to give a Happy New Year.

Forgiveness

A FEW YEARS AGO, in Pennsylvania, there was a sturdy farming family consisting of Jay Meck, his wife, Ruth, and three fine sons. The youngest son, Nelson, was a cheerful, freckle-faced schoolboy whose teachers called him "Sunshine" because of his lovable disposition and sunny smile. One day, when Jay and Ruth Meck were waiting for Nelson to come home from school, the school bus driver came running up the lane, frantic and white-faced. Nelson had been hit by a car as he was getting off the school bus. An ambulance had been summoned, but it was too late. Nelson was dead.

The driver of the car was an off-duty policeman from New York City. He and his wife had been driving through the tranquil Pennsylvania countryside. The school bus had stopped; its warning lights and stop sign were functioning, but somehow the driver of the car ignored them. He tried to pass the bus — and little Nelson was killed.

Jay and Ruth Meck were devastated. So were their other sons. Their neighbors were enraged and wanted the harshest penalties imposed. School authorities wanted to make an example of the guilty driver, an outsider, a big city stranger.

The days went by in a blur of grief and anguish. The insurance adjuster came to discuss settlements. Knowing the man had also been in touch with the policeman and his wife, something prompted Jay Meck to ask how they were.

"They seem broken up," the insurance man told him.

Broken up. The Mecks knew what those words meant; they meant the other couple was miserable too. The Mecks thought about it, talked about it, prayed about it. Finally they decided to ask the New York couple, whose names were Frank and Rose Ann, to come to their house for dinner. And the couple came.

It was awkward, of course. But the four grieving people sat down and broke bread together. The Mecks learned that Frank had been a policeman for eight years and had a spotless record. The accident, he said, might cost him his job. He and Rose Ann, like Ruth and Jay, had

three children. They had sent the children to Rose Ann's parents because they were afraid to face their neighbors. Both Frank and Rose Ann had dark circles under their eyes. They had lost a great deal of weight.

After the couple left, Ruth and Jay Meck sat down at the kitchen table and faced each other. They faced something else, too: the fact that Frank and Rose Ann were suffering almost as much as they were. They began to realize that only through compassion, only through applying the kind of love that their religion stood for, only through forgiveness offered and accepted could all of them find peace. And so, when the trial was held, Jay Meck decided not to press charges. Except for a traffic fine, Frank was free.

Forgiveness. What is it, really? Perhaps it is no more than the opportunity to try again, to do better, to be freed from the penalties and shackles of past mistakes. Whatever it is, it's something we all need and long for. That is why our hearts are touched and our eyes grow misty when we encounter truly great examples of it.

NORMAN VINCENT PEALE

Forgive

ALICE JOYCE DAVIDSON

God gave a tough assignment
For all of us to do —
To pray for all those who hurt us,
And to love our enemies, too…
So, when other people wrong you,
Instead of striking back,

Say a little prayer for them
For qualities they lack…
Ask the Lord to give them
An extra portion of
Insight and compassion —
And to bless them with His Love.

From *Start Living*

COLLEEN TOWNSEND EVANS

One of the great joys in life comes from watching a troubled person turn and go in a new—and better—direction. What causes such a thing to happen? A miracle? Sometimes. Forgiveness? Always!

Tom was a charming child, as most rascals are — but he was rebellious, a prankster, a rule breaker, a flaunter of authority. By the time he entered high school, his reputation had preceded him and he filled most of the teachers with dread. He took a special delight in disrupting classes and driving teachers to the limits of their patience. At home, he also was a problem. There were frequent confrontations between parents and child, each one seeking to prove he was more powerful than the other.

So many complaints were filed against Tom that the high school principal decided he would have to expel him — unless a teacher named Mrs. Warren agreed to take him into her class. Mrs. Warren was an exceptionally capable English teacher, but she also was a loving, endlessly patient woman who seemed to have a way with problem students. Yes, Mrs. Warren said, she would find a place for him in her eleven o'clock English Literature class, and also in her home room. She listened calmly as the principal read from a list of Tom's misdemeanors — a long list that had the principal shaking his head as he read. No, Mrs. Warren said, she wouldn't change her mind. She knew what she was getting into — she had heard about the boy.

When Tom was transferred to Mrs. Warren's class he behaved as he always did upon meeting a new teacher. He slouched in his seat in the last row and glared at her, daring her — by his attitude — to do something about him. At first Mrs. Warren ignored him. Then, as the class began to discuss the reading assignment, Tom whispered a joke to the boy in front of him, making the boy laugh. Mrs. Warren looked up.

Then she closed her book, stood and placed another chair at the desk, next to hers.

"Tom, come up here and sit with me for a while," she said — not as a reprimand, but as a friend. It was an invitation she was offering, and her manner was so sweet that Tom couldn't refuse. He sat next to her as she went on with the lesson. "Tom is new to our class and hasn't had time to read the assignment, so if you'll bear with me, I'll read it aloud to him."

With Tom next to her, sharing her book, Mrs. Warren began to read from *A Tale of Two Cities*. She was a fine reader and captured Dickens' sense of drama magnificently. Tom, for all his determination to be an obstruction, found himself following the text, losing himself in the unfolding of a great story, sharing the excitement of it with a woman who really seemed to care about his interest in the book. That evening he startled his parents by sitting down without any prodding — to do his homework — at least the assignment for Mrs. Warren's class.

That was only the beginning...Tom never missed a day of school after that first day in Mrs. Warren's class. Sometimes he cut other classes but never hers. He sat in the front row, participated in discussions, and seemed to enjoy reading aloud when he was called upon to do so. His appetite for reading suddenly became ravenous, and he asked Mrs. Warren to make up a list of books she thought he might enjoy in his free time. After school he stayed in the classroom when the other students went home and had long talks with Mrs. Warren about the things he had read and the ideas they stimulated.

Tom wasn't exactly an angel in other classes, but the effect of his behavior in Mrs. Warren's class began to rub off a little — for which the other teachers were most grateful.

Tom didn't finish high school. In his junior year, after an angry outburst at home, he defiantly joined the Navy. He didn't even say good-bye to Mrs. Warren, who was very sad to see him leave school, because she

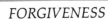

thought she had failed in her attempt to reach him.

Seven years later, when Mrs. Warren was closing up her desk one afternoon before leaving for home, a young man came to the doorway and stood there, smiling. He was much taller and more muscular now, but Mrs. Warren recognized him within seconds. It was Tom! He rushed to her and hugged her so hard her glasses slid down her nose.

"Where have you been?" she said, adjusting her glasses and looking at him intently. My — he was so clear-eyed, so happy and self-confident!

"In school," he said, laughing.

"But I thought —"

"Sure, you thought I was in the Navy.... Well, I was, for a while. I went to school there."

It was a long story he had to tell. Thanks to the Navy he was able to finish high school...and then he went on to college courses. When his enlistment was up he got a job and continued his education at night. During that time he met a lovely girl. By the time he graduated he was married and had a son. Then he went on to graduate school, also at night.

"Well, what are you doing with your fine education?" Mrs. Warren asked.

"I'm a teacher — I teach English... especially to kids who disrupt other classes."

Tom had never forgotten the feeling of acceptance he had had from that first day in Mrs. Warren's class. More than all the threats, all the arguments and confrontations he had known, her forgiving love got through to him. And now he was passing that love on to other young people. He had learned the give-and-take of forgiveness.

A Thought
MARGARET E. SANGSTER

He who died on Calvary,
Died to ransom you and me.

On the cross He bowed His head,
In the grave He made His bed.

Ever since, the lilies bloom
Round the portal of the tomb.

Ever since, o'er all our loss
Shines the glory of the cross.

I Thank Thee
CHRISTINE GRANT CURLESS

I Thank Thee, God, for these — the
    commonplace:
My home, my bed at night, a child's
    embrace;
A humble church where I may worship,
    too;
For rainy days, and little tasks to do.

I thank Thee, God, that such a lovely thing
As setting sun at end of day can bring
Me ecstasy; for loving friends who care;
I thank Thee for the privilege to share
Thy blessings; and assurance as I live —
I need but ask Thee, Lord, Thou wilt
    forgive!

Magdalene: Lament and Song

LOUIS G. MILLER, C.SS.R.

Jesus arose from the
dead early on the
first day of the week.
He first appeared to
Mary Magdalene, out
of whom he had cast
seven demons.
— Mark 16:9

Lord, I proclaim your greatness,
My soul overflows with your love.
They said of me in pity,
"The devil holds her fast."
I only knew that peace and love
were memories of the past.
My demons made me bitter,
hate was my daily bread.
I sneered at truth and goodness:
"It's all a lie," I said.
"No man on earth is honest;
I'll trust them when they're dead."

Lord, I proclaim your greatness,
My soul overflows with your love.

But when they dragged a woman
out on the city street,
and said she was a sinner
and thrust her at your feet,
their cruel eyes upon you,
confident of their prize,
you looked at her, Lord, with pity,
and love was in your eyes.
I watched you from a window,
my heart leaped in surprise.

Lord, I proclaim your greatness,
My soul overflows with your love.

Your way, Lord, was so gentle,
your charity so pure,
I knew within an instant
I also could be sure
you could command my demons
and take away my sin.

You had the power to do it,
to still the selfish din
within my soul and senses.
I said: I will begin.

Lord, I proclaim your greatness,
My soul overflows with your love.

I sought you out and found you
there in a noisy crowd.
The Pharisees were scornful:
"Is this to be allowed,"
they said, "that such a woman
should kiss the Master's feet?"
I paid no heed to hypocrites.
I wept for joy to meet
the kindness that you showed me,
your healing words so sweet.

Lord, I proclaim your greatness,
My soul overflows with your love.

I wept in joyful freedom
from chains that bound my life,
with all the sordid moments,
the bitterness and strife,
the seven cruel demons
within and at my side.
Your love, Lord, has redeemed me
and saved me from my pride.
You gave me strength and courage
in Calvary's dark hour
to share the tortured moments,
to mourn your fading power.

Lord, I proclaim your greatness,
My soul overflows with your love.

What joy on Easter morning
to find you risen and free
from death. There in the garden
your glorious face to see,
and hear your greeting,
"Mary!" What joy it was to me.
Lord, I long for your coming,
but I am content to wait,
and if this Magdalene's story
of one who was blind and lame

frees others from their demons
and lifts them from their shame
to a love that is true and lasting,
that is sufficient fame.
Blessed, Lord, be your name.

Lord, I proclaim your greatness,
My soul overflows with your love.

*Always remember to forget the things that made
you sad. But never forget to remember the things
that made you glad.*   Elbert Hubbard

"An Unforgettable Night"
(From *Born Again*)
CHARLES COLSON

It was eight P.M., a gray overcast evening,
when I turned off the country road connecting two of Boston's most affluent suburbs,
Wellesley and Weston. The towering gentle
pines brought sudden darkness and quiet to
the narrow macadam street. Another turn a
few hundred yards later brought me into a
long driveway leading to the Phillipses' big
white clapboard Colonial home. As I parked
the car I felt a touch of guilt at not telling
Patty the truth when I had left her alone with
my mother and dad in nearby Dover.

"Just business, honey," had been my explanation. Patty was used to my working at
odd times, even on this Sunday night at the
start of a week's vacation.

The Phillipses' home is long and ram-
bling. I made the mistake of going to the
door nearest the driveway, which turned out
to be the entrance to the kitchen. It didn't
bother Gert Phillips, a tall smiling woman
who greeted me like a long-lost relative even
though we had never met before. "Come in.
I'm just cleaning up after supper."

Supper. Such an unpretentious New England word. Gert escorted me into a large
modern kitchen. "I'll call Tom," she said.
"He's playing tennis with the children."

Tom arrived a minute later along with son
Tommy, sixteen, and daughter Debby, nineteen, two tanned, handsome young people.
Gert fixed us all iced tea while Tom mopped
himself dry with a towel. If Gert was aware
of the importance of her husband's position
as president of the state's biggest company,
she certainly did not show it. In fact, she
reminded me of a favorite aunt we used to
visit in the country when I was a boy, who
always wore an apron, smelled of freshly
made bread and cookies, and had the gift of
making everyone feel at home in her kitch-
en.

"You men have things to talk about and
I've got work to do," Gert said as she handed
us tall glasses of iced tea. Tom, towel draped
around his neck, led me through the comfortably furnished dining and living rooms
to a screened-in porch at the far end of the
house. It was an unusually hot night for
New England, the humidity like a heavy
blanket wrapped around me. At Tom's in-
sistence, first the dark gray business-suit
jacket, then my tie came off. He pulled a
wrought-iron ottoman close to the comfortable outdoor settee I sat on.

"Tell me, Chuck," he began, "are you
okay?"

As the President's confidant and so-called
big-shot Washington lawyer I was still keeping my guard up. "I'm not doing too badly, I
guess. All of this Watergate business, all the
accusations — I suppose it's wearing me
down some. But I'd rather talk about you,
Tom. You've changed and I'd like to know
what happened."

Tom drank from his glass and sat back
reflectively. Briefly he reviewed his past, the
rapid rise to power at Raytheon: executive
vice-president at thirty-seven, president

when he was only forty. He had done it with hard work, day and night, nonstop.

"The success came, all right, but something was missing," he mused. "I felt a terrible emptiness. Sometimes I would get up in the middle of the night and pace the floor of my bedroom or stare out into the darkness for hours at a time."

"I don't understand it," I interrupted. "I knew you in those days, Tom. You were a straight arrow, good family life, successful, everything in fact going your way."

"All that may be true, Chuck, but my life wasn't complete. I would go to the office each day and do my job, striving all the time to make the company succeed, but there was a big hole in my life. I began to read the Scriptures, looking for answers. Something made me realize I needed a personal relationship with God, forced me to search."

A prickly feeling ran down my spine. Maybe what I had gone through in the past several months wasn't so unusual after all — except I had not sought spiritual answers. I had not even been aware that finding a personal relationship with God was possible. I pressed him to explain the apparent contradiction between the emptiness inside while seeming to enjoy the affluent life.

"It may be hard to understand," Tom chuckled. "But I didn't seem to have anything that mattered. It was all on the surface. All the material things in life are meaningless if a man hasn't discovered what's underneath them."

We were both silent for a while as I groped for understanding. Outside, the first fireflies punctuated the mauve dusk. Tom got up and switched on two small lamps on end tables in the corners of the porch.

"One night I was in New York on business and noticed that Billy Graham was having a Crusade in Madison Square Garden," Tom continued. "I went — curious, I guess — hoping maybe I'd find some answers. What Graham said that night put it all into place for me. I saw what was missing, the personal relationship with Jesus Christ, the fact

that I hadn't ever asked Him into my life, hadn't turned my life over to Him. So I did it — that very night at the Crusade."

Tom's tall, gangling frame leaned toward me, silhouetted by the yellow light behind him. Though his face was shaded, I could see his eyes begin to glisten and his voice became softer. "I asked Christ to come into my life and I could feel His presence with me, His peace within me. I could sense His Spirit there with me. Then I went out for a walk alone on the streets of New York. I never liked New York before, but this night it was beautiful. I walked for blocks and blocks, I guess. Everything seemed different to me. It was raining softly and the city lights created a golden glow. Something had happened to me and I knew it."

"That's what you mean by accepting Christ — you just ask?" I was more puzzled than ever.

"That's it, as simple as that," Tom replied. "Of course, you have to want Jesus in your life, really want Him. That's the way it starts. And let me tell you, things then begin to change. Since then I have found a satisfaction and a joy about living that I simply never knew was possible."

To me Jesus had always been an historical figure, but Tom explained that you could hardly invite Him into your life if you didn't believe that He is alive today and that His Spirit is a part of today's scene. I was moved by Tom's story even though I couldn't imagine how such a miraculous change could take place in such a simple way. Yet the excitement in Tom's voice as he described his experience was convincing and Tom was indeed different. More alive.

Then Tom turned the conversation again to my plight. I described some of the agonies of Watergate, the pressures I was under, how unfairly I thought the press was treating me. I was being defensive and when I ran out of explanations, Tom spoke gently but firmly.

…"Chuck, I hate to say this, but you guys brought it on yourselves. If you had put your faith in God, and if your cause were just, He would have guided you. And His help would have been a thousand times more powerful than all your phony ads and shady schemes put together."

With any other man the notion of relying on God would have seemed to me pure Pollyanna. Yet I had to be impressed with the way this man ran his company in the equally competitive world of business: ignoring his enemies, trying to follow God's ways. Since his conversion Raytheon had never done better, sales and profits soaring. Maybe there was something to it; anyway it's tough to argue with success.

...I leaned back, still on the defensive, my mind and emotions whirling.... Just as a man about to die is supposed to see flash before him, sequence by sequence, the high points of his life,...key events in my life paraded before me as if projected on a screen. Things I hadn't thought about in years — my graduation speech at prep school — being "good enough" for the Marines — my first marriage, into the "right" family — sitting on the Jaycees' dais while civic leader after civic leader praised me as the outstanding young man of Boston — then to the White House — the clawing and straining for status and position — "Mr. Colson, the President is calling — Mr. Colson, the President wants to see you right away."

For some reason I thought of an incident after the 1972 election when a reporter, an old Nixon nemesis, came by my office and contritely asked what he could do to get in the good graces of the White House. I suggested that he try "slashing his wrists." I meant it as a joke, of course, but also to make him squirm. It was the arrogance of the victor over an enemy brought to submission.

Now, sitting there on the dimly lit porch, my self-centered past was washing over me in waves. It was painful. Agony. Desperately I tried to defend myself. What about my sacrifices for government service, the giving up of a big income, putting my stocks into a blind trust? The truth, I saw in an instant, was that I'd wanted the position in the White House more than I'd wanted money. There was no

sacrifice. And the more I had talked about my own sacrifices, the more I was really trying to build myself up in the eyes of others. I would eagerly have given up everything I'd ever earned to prove myself at the mountaintop of government. It was pride...that had propelled me through life.

...Of course, I had not known God. *How could I?* I had been concerned with myself. *I* had done this and that, *I* had achieved, *I* had succeeded and *I* had given God none of the credit, never once thanking Him for any of His gifts to me. I had never thought of anything being "immeasurably superior" to myself, or if I had in fleeting moments thought about the infinite power of God, I had not related Him to my life....

"How about it, Chuck?" Tom's question jarred me out of my trance. I knew precisely what he meant. Was I ready to make the leap of faith as he had in New York, to "accept" Christ?

"Tom, you've shaken me up. I'll admit that. That chapter describes me. But I can't tell you I'm ready to make the kind of commitment you did. I've got to be certain. I've got to learn a lot more, be sure all my reservations are satisfied. I've got a lot of intellectual hang-ups to get past."

For a moment Tom looked disappointed, then he smiled. "I understand, I understand."

"You see," I continued, "I saw men turn to God in the Marine Corps; I did once myself. Then afterwards it's all forgotten and everything is back to normal. Foxhole religion is just a way of using God. How can I make a commitment now? My whole world is crashing down around me. How can I be sure I'm not just running for shelter and that when the crisis is over I'll forget it? I've got to answer all the intellectual arguments first and if I can do that, I'll be sure."

"I understand," Tom repeated quietly.

I was relieved he did, yet deep inside of me something wanted to tell Tom to press on. He was making so much sense, the first time anyone ever had in talking about God.

...Tom then reached for his Bible and read a few of his favorite psalms. The comforting words were like a cold soothing ointment. For the first time in my life, familiar verses I'd heard chanted lifelessly in church came alive. "Trust in the Lord," I remember Tom reading, and I wanted to, right that moment I wanted to — if only I knew how, if only I could be sure.

"Would you like to pray together, Chuck?" Tom asked, closing his Bible and putting it on the table beside him.

Startled, I emerged from my deep thoughts. "Sure — I guess I would — Fine." I'd never prayed with anyone before except when someone said grace before a meal. Tom bowed his head, folded his hands, and leaned forward on the edge of his seat. "Lord," he began, "we pray for Chuck and his family, that You might open his heart and show him the light and the way...."

As Tom prayed, something began to flow into me — a kind of energy. Then came a wave of emotion which nearly brought tears. I fought them back. It sounded as if Tom were speaking directly and personally to God, almost as if He were sitting beside us. The only prayers I'd ever heard were formal and stereotyped, sprinkled with Thees and Thous.

When he finished, there was a long silence. I knew he expected me to pray but I didn't know what to say and was too self-conscious to try. We walked to the kitchen together where Gert was still at the big table, reading. I thanked her and Tom for their hospitality.

...Outside in the darkness, the iron grip I'd kept on my emotions began to relax. Tears welled up in my eyes as I groped in the darkness for the right key to start my car. Angrily I brushed them away and started the engine. "What kind of weakness is this?" I said to nobody.

The tears spilled over and suddenly I knew I had to go back into the house and pray with Tom. I turned off the motor, got out of the car. As I did, the kitchen light went out, then the light in the dining room. Through the hall window I saw Tom stand aside as Gert started up the stairs ahead of him. Now the hall was in darkness. It was too late. I stood for a moment staring at the darkened house, only one light burning now in an upstairs bedroom. Why hadn't I prayed when he gave me the chance? I wanted to so badly. Now I was alone, really alone.

As I drove out of Tom's driveway, the tears were flowing uncontrollably. There were no streetlights, no moonlight. The car headlights were flooding illumination before my eyes, but I was crying so hard it was like trying to swim underwater. I pulled to the side of the road not more than a hundred yards from the entrance to Tom's driveway, the tires sinking into soft mounds of pine needles.

I remember hoping that Tom and Gert wouldn't hear my sobbing, the only sound other than the chirping of crickets that penetrated the still of the night. With my face cupped in my hands, head leaning forward against the wheel, I forgot about machismo, about pretenses, about fears of being weak. And as I did, I began to experience a wonderful feeling of being released. Then came the strange sensation that water was not only running down my cheeks, but surging through my whole body as well, cleansing and cooling as it went. They weren't tears of sadness and remorse, nor of joy — but somehow, tears of relief.

And then I prayed my first real prayer. "God, I don't know how to find You, but I'm going to try! I'm not much the way I am now, but somehow I want to give myself to You." I didn't know how to say more, so I repeated over and over the words: *Take me.*

I had not "accepted" Christ — I still didn't know who He was. My mind told me it was important to find that out first to be sure that I knew what I was doing, that I meant it and would stay with it. Only, that night, something inside me was urging me to surrender — to what or to whom I did not know.

I stayed there in the car, wet-eyed,

praying, thinking, for perhaps half an hour, perhaps longer, alone in the quiet of the dark night. Yet for the first time in my life I was not alone at all.

Good Morning

AURELIUS CLEMENS

May this morning light illumine
our day and purify our souls.
Let our tongues form no devious words;
let our minds harbour no dark thoughts.

Good Morning, God!

HELEN STEINER RICE

You are ushering in another day
Untouched and freshly new
So here I come to ask You, God,
If You'll renew me, too,
Forgive the many errors
That I made yesterday
And let me try again, dear God,
To walk closer in THY WAY…
But, Father, I am well aware
I can't make it on my own
So TAKE MY HAND and HOLD IT TIGHT
For I can't WALK ALONE!

Let not the sun go down upon your wrath.
Ephesians 4:26, King James Version

Grandma and the Sea Gull

LOUISE DICKINSON RICH

My grandmother had an enemy named Mrs. Wilcox. Grandma and Mrs. Wilcox moved, as brides, into next-door houses on the sleepy elm-roofed Main Street of the tiny town in which they were to live out their lives. I don't know what started the war — that was long before my day — and I don't think that by the time I came along, over thirty years later, they remembered themselves what started it. But it was still being bitterly waged.

Make no mistake. This was no polite sparring match. This was War Between Ladies, which is total war. Nothing in town escaped repercussion. The three-hundred-year-old church, which had lived through the Revolution, the Civil War and the Spanish War, almost went down when Grandma and Mrs. Wilcox fought the Battle of the Ladies' Aid. Grandma won that engagement but it was a hollow victory. Mrs. Wilcox, since she couldn't be president, resigned from the Aid in a huff, and what's the fun of running a thing if you can't force your mortal enemy to eat crow? Mrs. Wilcox won the Battle of the Public Library, getting her niece Gertrude appointed librarian instead of my Aunt Phyllis. The day Gertrude took over was the day Grandma stopped reading library books — "filthy germ things" they'd become overnight — and started buying her own. The Battle of the High School was a draw. The principal got a better job and left before Mrs. Wilcox succeeded in having him ousted or Grandma in having him given life tenure of office.

In addition to these major engagements there was constant sallying and sniping back of the main line of fire. When as children we visited my grandmother, part of the fun was making faces at Mrs. Wilcox's impossible grandchildren — nearly as impossible as we were, I now see — and stealing grapes off the Wilcox side of the fence between the gardens. We chased the Wilcox hens too and put percussion caps, saved from July 4, on the rails of the trolley line right in front of the Wilcox house, in the pleasant hope that when the trolley went by the explosion — actually a negligible affair — would scare Mrs. Wilcox into fits. One banner day we put a snake into the Wilcox rain barrel. My grandmother made token protests but we sensed tacit sympathy, so different from what lay back of my mother's no's, and went merrily on with our career of brattishness. If any child of mine — but that's another story.

Don't think for a minute that this was a one-sided campaign. Mrs. Wilcox had grandchildren too, remember; more and tougher and smarter grandchildren than my grandmother had. Grandma didn't get off scot free. She had skunks introduced into her cellar. On Halloween all loose forgotten objects, such as garden furniture, miraculously flew to the ridgepole of the barn, whence they had to be lowered by strong men hired at exorbitant day rates. Never a windy washday went by but what the clothesline mysteriously broke, so that the sheets wollopsed around in the dirt and had to be done over. Some of these occurrences may have been acts of God but the Wilcox grandchildren always got the credit. I don't know how Grandma could have borne her troubles if it hadn't been for the household page of her daily Boston newspaper.

This household page was a wonderful institution. Besides the usual cooking hints and cleaning advice it had a department composed of letters from readers to each other. The idea was that if you had a problem — or even only some steam to blow off — you wrote a letter to the paper, signing some fancy name like Arbutus. That was Grandma's pen name. Then some of the other ladies who had had the same problem wrote back and told you what they had done about it, signing themselves One Who Knows or Xanthippe or whatever. Very often, the problem disposed of, you kept on for years writing to each other through the column of the paper, telling each other about your children and your canning and your new dining-room suite. That's what happened to Grandma. She and a woman called Sea Gull corresponded for a quarter of a century and Grandma told Sea Gull things that she never breathed to another soul — things like the time she hoped that she was going to have another baby but didn't, and the time my Uncle Steve got you-know-what in his hair in school and how humiliated she was, although she got rid of them before anyone in town guessed. Sea Gull was Grandma's true bosom friend.

When I was about sixteen Mrs. Wilcox died. In a small town, no matter how much you have hated your next-door neighbor, it is only common decency to run over and see what practical service you can do the bereaved. Grandma, neat in a percale apron to show that she meant what she said about being put to work, crossed the two lawns to the Wilcox house, where the Wilcox daughters set her to cleaning the already immaculate front parlor for the funeral. And there on the parlor table in the place of honor was a huge scrapbook; and in the scrapbook pasted neatly in parallel columns, were her letters to Sea Gull over the years and Sea Gull's letters to her. Grandma's worst enemy had been her best friend.

That was the only time I remember seeing my grandmother cry. I didn't know then exactly what she was crying about but I do now. She was crying for all the wasted years which could never be salvaged. Then I was impressed only by the tears and they made me remember that day. Now I know that something happened that day worthier of remembrance than a woman's tears. That was the day when I first began to suspect what I now believe with all my heart; and if ever I have to stop believing it, I want to stop living. It is this:

People may seem to be perfectly impossible. They may seem to be mean and small and sly. But if you will take ten paces to the left and look again with the light falling at a different angle, very likely you will see that they are generous and warm and kind. It all depends. It all depends on the point from which you're seeing them.

Contentment

ALL YEAR I had looked forward to teaching at the summer writers' conference in Cape Cod. The lectures, the talks with students, the new friends made — and in such a beautiful setting. But as the plane nosed down over those blue waters, I could only pray desperately, "Lord, don't let me fail them! Please give me the strength to — hang on!"

My husband and I had just returned from California where he had suffered a serious heart attack. Fear, sleepless nights, weeks of hospital visits, plus the strain of the return trip, had taken their toll of me as well. My husband was better, but I was on the verge of collapse.

I didn't see how I could keep my teaching commitment. But the doctor insisted — "It will be good for you — and better for him."

So, here I was, almost too tired to drag myself to my room.

Then, lying across my bed, I could hear the water. It was like a rhythmic, reassuring voice calling softly under my window. All night it called, and at dawn it seemed to shout, "Come on!"

I rose and ran down to it, plunging into its salty embrace. And, oh! that brisk first slap, waking me up to the thrilling challenge of the day. Giving me energy, joy and faith.

I wallowed and plunged and sang — that first morning, and on the mornings to come. I kept close to the lifeline and waved to the old fisherman who had hot coffee waiting and promised to keep an eye on me. And Isaiah kept singing his comforting words along with me: "When you pass through the waters, I will be with you…when you walk through fire,…the flames will not consume you" (43:2). I had been through the fires, and the flames had not consumed me. Now I was passing through the waters, and they sustained me. God was giving me renewal and strength for a glorious week!

MARJORIE HOLMES

A Cup of Blessing

RALPH WALDO EMERSON

Never lose an opportunity of seeing anything that is beautiful; for beauty is God's handwriting — a wayside sacrament. Welcome it in every fair face, in every fair sky, in every fair flower, and thank God for it as a cup of blessing.

The world is so empty if one thinks only of mountains, rivers, and cities; but to know someone who thinks and feels with us, and who, though distant, is close to us in spirit, this makes the earth for us an inhabited garden.

Johann Wolfgang von Goethe

Greet the dawn with enthusiasm and you may expect satisfaction at sunset.   Author Unknown

To Those Who Are Content

GRACE NOLL CROWELL

To those who are content
I lift my song —
To those who are at peace
Where they belong —

Who rise and question not,
Who go their way
Happily from dawn
To close of day;

Who labor and who earn
The bread they eat,
Who find their rest at night
Is deep and sweet;

Who ask no more of life
Than they can give,
Oh, beautifully fine
I think they live;

Who are content to serve,
To love and pray,
Leading their simple lives
From day to day.

A Day Worth While

ANONYMOUS

I count that day as wisely spent
    In which I do some good
For someone who is far away
    Or shares my neighborhood.
A day devoted to the deed
    That lends a helping hand
And demonstrates a willingness
    To care and understand.
I long to be of usefulness
    In little ways and large
Without a selfish motive
    And without the slightest charge.
Because in my philosophy
    There never is a doubt
That all of us here on earth
    Must help each other out.
I feel that day is fruitful
    And the time is worth the while
When I promote the happiness
    Of one enduring smile.

The Lord is my light and my salvation; whom shall I fear?   Psalm 27:1, Living Bible

Greeting the Day

THOMAS DEKKER

To awaken each morning with a smile brightening my face; to greet the day with reverence for the opportunities it contains; to approach my work with a clean mind; to hold ever before me, even in the doing of little things, the Ultimate Purpose toward which I am working; to meet men and women with laughter on my lips and love in my heart; to be gentle, kind, and courteous through all the hours; to approach the night with weariness that ever woos sleep and the joy that comes from work well done — this is how I desire to waste wisely my days.

...whatsoever things are true, whatsoever things are honest, whatsoever things are just, whatsoever things are pure, whatsoever things are lovely, whatsoever things are of good report; if there be any virtue, and if there be any praise, think on these things. Philippians 4:8, King James Version

Tell Him

PHILLIPS BROOKS

Tell him about the heartache,
And tell him the longings, too.
Tell him the baffled purpose
When we scarce know what to do.

Then leaving all our weakness
With the One divinely strong,
Forget that we bore a burden
And carry away a song.

Cheerfulness and content are great beautifiers and are famous preservers of youthful looks.

Charles Dickens

Invitation

G. A. STUDDERT-KENNEDY

Come sail with me o'er the golden sea
    To the land where the rainbow ends,
Where the rainbow ends,
    And the great earth bends
To the weight of the starry sky,
    Where tempests die with a last
        fierce cry,
And never a wind is wild.

Meditation

ALICE JOYCE DAVIDSON

I sat down by a crystal spring,
My back against a willow tree,
The sound of waters murmuring
Brought peace and restfulness to me.
And letting go of everything
I closed my eyes...so I could "see."
And in that meditative hour,
I knew God's love and felt His power.

Happiness resides not in possessions and not in gold; the feeling of happiness dwells in the soul.

Democritus

Begin the Day with God

AUTHOR UNKNOWN

Every morning lean thine arms awhile
Upon the window sill of heaven
And gaze upon thy Lord.
Then, with the vision in thy heart,
Turn strong to meet thy day.

God's World

EDNA ST. VINCENT MILLAY

O World, I cannot hold thee close enough!
    Thy winds, thy wide grey skies!
    Thy mists that roll and rise!
Thy woods, this autumn day, that ache and
        sag
And all but cry with colour! That gaunt crag
To crush! To lift the lean of that black bluff!
World, World, I cannot get thee close
        enough!
Long have I known a glory in it all,
    But never knew I this;
    Here such a passion is
As stretcheth me apart. Lord, I do fear
Thou'st made the world too beautiful this
        year,
My soul is all but out of me — let fall
No burning leaf; prithee, let no bird call.

The Starlit Hill

RALPH SPAULDING CUSHMAN

There was a night, there was a hill,
    There was a starlit sky;
An upturned face that hardly sensed
    The night wind blowing by.

There was a Voice — no human voice —
    I heard it clear and still;
And since that night, and since that Voice,
    I've loved each starlit hill.

Little Privileges

JAMES M. BARRIE

Happiness is the art of finding joy and
    satisfaction in the little privileges of life:
a quiet hour in the sun instead of a far-away
    journey,
a little outing in the nearby woods instead
    of long trips away,
an hour with a friend instead of an
    extended visit with relatives,
a few pages of a book instead of hours of
    reading at a time,
a flash of sunset, a single beautiful flower, a
    passing smile, a kindly word, a little gift
    bestowed anonymously, a little
    thoughtfulness here and there as the
    days slip by.
Those who bring sunshine into the lives of
    others cannot keep it from themselves.

Lamplighter

ANONYMOUS

He has taken his bright candle and is gone
    Into another room I cannot find,
But anyone can tell where he has been
    By all the little lights he leaves behind.

*One of the most tragic things I know about human
nature is that all of us tend to put off living. We
are all dreaming of some magical rose garden over
the horizon — instead of enjoying the roses that
are blooming outside our windows today.*

Dale Carnegie

Ellis Park

HELEN HOYT

Little park that I pass through,
I carry off a piece of you
Every morning hurrying down
To my work-day in the town;
Carry you for country there
To make the city ways more fair.
I take your trees,
And your breeze,
Your greenness,
Your cleanness,
Some of your shade, some of your sky,
Some of your calm as I go by;
Your flowers to trim
The pavements grim;
Your space for room in the jostled street
And grass for carpet to my feet.
Your fountains take and sweet bird calls
To sing me from my office walls.

All that I can see
I carry off with me.
But you never miss my theft,
So much treasure you have left.
As I find you, fresh at morning,
So I find you, home returning —
Nothing lacking from your grace.
All your riches wait in place
For me to borrow
On the morrow.

Do you hear this praise of you,
Little park that I pass through?

Spring in the world!
And all things are made new!
Richard Hovey

From *Sussex*

RUDYARD KIPLING

God gave all men all earth to love,
    But since our hearts are small,
Ordained for each one spot should prove
    Beloved over all;
That, as He watched Creation's birth,
    So we, in godlike mood,
May of our love create our earth
    And see that it is good.

Legacy

NANCY BYRD TURNER

I had a rich old great-aunt
Who left me, when she died,
A little sloping acre
And not a thing beside.

Nothing else she left me
But a clump of sweet phlox
And an old silver aspen
And some hollyhocks.

A humming-bird disputed
My heritage with me,
And so did a robin
And a gold-backed bee.

A cricket owned a hummock,
He couldn't say how;
Two wrens held a mortgage
On one aspen bough.

A toad claimed a corner
(He said it was a lease).
We learned to live together
In a sort of cheery peace.

Never such an acre
To mortal was given!
My good old great-aunt,
May she rest in heaven!

On the Grasshopper and Cricket

JOHN KEATS

The poetry of earth is never dead:
    When all the birds are faint with the
      hot sun,
    And hide in cooling trees, a voice will
      run
From hedge to hedge about the new-mown
    mead;
That is the grasshopper's — he takes the
    lead
    In summer luxury, — he has never
      done
    With his delights, for when tired out
      with fun
He rests at ease beneath some pleasant
    weed.
The poetry of earth is ceasing never:
    On a lone winter evening, when the
      frost
Has wrought a silence, from the stove there
    shrills
The cricket's song, in warmth increasing
    ever,
    And seems to one, in drowsiness
      half-lost,
The grasshopper's among some grassy
    hills.

A Christian's Joy

PAUL SCHERER

The fundamental joy of being a Christian consists not in being good. I get tired of that. But in standing with God against some darkness or some void and watching the light come. The joy of religion is in having your fling, by the mercies of God, at shaping where you are, as a potter shapes a vase, one corner of his eternal Kingdom.

Wrens and Robins in the Hedge

CHRISTINA ROSSETTI

Wrens and robins in the hedge.
    Wrens and robins here and there;
Building, perching, pecking, fluttering,
    Everywhere!

There are three green eggs in a small brown
    pocket,
And the breeze will swing and the gale will rock it,
Till three little birds on the thin edge teeter,
And our God be glad and our world be sweeter.

Edwin Markham

Young Lambs

JOHN CLARE

The spring is coming by a many signs;
The trays are up, the hedges broken down
That fenced the haystack, and the remnant
    shines
Like some old antique fragment weathered
    brown.
And where suns peep, in every sheltered
    place,
The little early buttercups unfold
A glittering star or two — till many trace
The edges of the blackthorn clumps in gold.
And then a little lamb bolts up behind
The hill, and wags his tail to meet the yoe;
And then another, sheltered from the wind,
Lies all his length as dead — and lets me go
Close by, and never stirs, but basking lies,
With legs stretched out as though he could
    not rise.

The Things I Prize

HENRY VAN DYKE

These are the things I prize
    And hold of dearest worth:
Light of the sapphire skies,
Peace of the silent hills,
Shelter of the forest, comfort of the grass,
Music of birds, murmur of little rills,
Shadows of clouds that swiftly pass,
    And, after showers,
    The smell of flowers
And of the good brown earth —
And best of all, along the way, friendship
    and mirth.

Better and sweeter than health, or friends, or money, or fame, or ease, or prosperity, is the adorable will of our God. It gilds the darkest hours with a divine halo, and sheds brightest sunshine on the gloomiest paths.   Hannah Whitall Smith

No Regrets

AGNES SLIGH TURNBULL

There is only one thing about which I shall have no regrets when my life ends. I have savored to the full all the small, daily joys. The bright sunshine on the breakfast table; the smell of the air at dusk; the sound of the clock ticking; the light rains that start gently after midnight; the hour when the family comes home; Sunday-evening tea before the fire! I have never missed one moment of beauty, not ever taken it for granted. Spring, summer, autumn, or winter. I wish I had failed as little in other ways.

Give Me

S. M. FRAZIER

Give me work to do,
Give me health,
Give me joy in simple things,
Give me an eye for beauty,
A tongue for truth,
A heart that loves,
A mind that reasons,
A sympathy that understands.
Give me neither malice nor envy,
But a true kindness
And a noble common sense.
At the close of each day
Give me a book
And a friend with whom
I can be silent.

Discovery

HELEN BAKER PARKER

Today a man discovered gold and fame;
Another flew the stormy seas;
Another saw an unnamed world aflame;
One found the germ of a disease.
But what high fates my paths attend:
For I — today I found a friend.

Peace in the Heart

CHARLES FRANCIS RICHARDSON

If peace be in the heart
The wildest winter storm is full of solemn
    beauty,
The midnight lightning flash but shows the
    path of duty,
Each living creature tells some new and
    joyous story,
The very trees and stones all catch a ray
    of glory,
If peace be in the heart.

Learn to Wait

AUTHOR UNKNOWN

Learn to wait — life's hardest lesson
    Conned, perchance, through blinding
      tears;
While the heart throbs sadly echo
    To the tread of passing years.
Learn to wait — hope's slow fruition;
    Faint not, though the way seems long;
There is joy in each condition;
    Hearts through suffering may grow
      strong.
Thus a soul untouched by sorrow
    Aims not at a higher state;
Joy seeks not a brighter morrow;
    Only sad hearts learn to wait.

Built Together

RALPH W. SOCKMAN

There are parts of a ship which taken by
themselves would sink. The engine would
sink. The propeller would sink. But when
the parts of a ship are built together, they
float. So with the events of my life. Some
have been tragic. Some have been happy.
But when they are built together, they form a
craft that floats and is going someplace. And
I am comforted.

*The more we love, the better we are; and the
greater our friendships are, the dearer we are to
God.*
                    Jeremy Taylor

At Heart an Optimist

JAN CHRISTIAN SMUTS

This is a good world. We need not approve
of all the items, nor of all the individuals in it;
but the world itself is a friendly world. It has
borne us; it has carried us onward; it has
humanized us and guided our faltering footsteps throughout the long, slow advance; it
has endowed us with strength and courage.
It is full of tangles, of ups and downs. There
is always enough to bite on, to sharpen wits
on, to test our courage and manhood. It is
indeed a world built for heroism, but also for
beauty, tenderness, and mercy. I remain at
heart an optimist.

True Glory

AUTHOR UNKNOWN

The Glory of Life is to love,
Not to be loved,
To give, not to get,
To serve, not to be served;
To be a strong hand in the dark to another
      in the time of need,
To be a cup of strength to any soul in a crisis
      of weakness.
This is to know The Glory of Life.

*You know how I feel
You listen to how I think
You understand...
    You're
      my
        friend.*
                Susan Polis Schutz

When Two People Marry

HELEN STEINER RICE

Your hearts are filled with happiness
    so great and overflowing,
You cannot comprehend it
    for it's far beyond all knowing
How any heart could hold such joy
    or feel the fullness of
The wonder and the glory
    and the ecstasy of love —
You wish that you could capture it
    and never let it go
So you might walk forever
    in its radiant magic glow...
But love in all its ecstasy
    is such a fragile thing,
Like gossamer in cloudless skies
    or a hummingbird's small wing,
But love that lasts FOREVER
    must be made of something strong,
The kind of strength that's gathered
    when the heart can hear no song —
When the "sunshine" of your wedding day
    runs into "stormy weather"
And hand in hand you brave the gale
    and climb steep hills together,
And clinging to each other
    while the thunder rolls above
You seek divine protection
    in FAITH and HOPE and LOVE...
For "DAYS OF WINE AND ROSES"
    never make love's dream come true,
It takes sacrifice and teardrops,
    and problems shared by two,
To give true love its BEAUTY,
    its GRANDEUR and its FINENESS
And to mold an "earthly ecstasy"
    into HEAVENLY DIVINENESS.

In thee, O Lord, do I put my trust.
    Psalm 31:1, King James Version

The White Days of Winter

MARGARET E. SANGSTER

The white days of winter, darling,
    When softly the snow-flakes fall,
Till a royal garment of ermine
    Folds tenderly over all.
Field, and hillock, and valley,
    Hushed in the sweetest sleep,
For the snow comes down from our Father,
    His loving charge to keep.

Under the snow-robe, darling,
    There is wonderful brooding heat,
That is taking care of the daisies,
    And saving the next year's wheat.
And we'd have no flowers, dearest,
    When the spring's green days come
      back,
If the white days did not bring us
    The feathery flakes in their track.

And the golden days, my darling,
    The days of lily and rose,
And the scarlet days of the maple,
    All follow the path of the snows;
For the year goes round, my darling,
    With the sunbeam and the shower,
And our Father's watch is over
    Its every passing hour.

The swift, white day, my darling,
    When the sleigh-bells' merry chime
Is echoing o'er the roadway,
    Is the fun and frolic time.
But the still white eve, my dearest,
    Is sweeter to you and me,
When we have the song and story,
    And the prayer at the mother's knee.

Our little home, my darling,
    Oh, whatever wind may blow,
The south with its quiver of sunbeams,
    The north with its flakes of snow,
Our little home, my dearest,
    Is under the dear Lord's care,
And we fear no ill nor sorrow,
    Lovingly sheltered there.

Cradle Song

SAROJINI NAIDU

From groves of spice,
O'er fields of rice,
Athwart the lotus-stream,
I bring for you,
Aglint with dew,
A little lovely dream.

Sweet, shut your eyes,
The wild fire-flies
Dance through the fairy *neem*;
From the poppy-bole
For you I stole
A little lovely dream.

Dear eyes, good night,
In golden light
The stars around you gleam;
On you I press
With soft caress
A little lovely dream.

Children's Morning Prayers

ROBERT H. SCHULLER

Good morning, God! I am so glad that
you are my friend. Together we make a
great team. I am not afraid of anything
when you are beside me. It will be a
good day if you will think through my
brain, talk through my tongue, and
smile at people through my face. In my
work or play, may my friends and even
        strangers
see that I love you.
Amen.

Good morning, God! Thank you for your
beautiful world! I want to make your
world even more beautiful. So may my
face be like happy sunshine and not a dark
cloud.
Amen.

A Quiet Lane of Happiness

WILL DURANT

Many years have I sought happiness. I
found it first, perhaps, in the warmth of my
mother's breast, and in the fond caress of her
hands, and in the tenderness that shone in
her eyes. I found it again in play; for even in
the pain of defeat I knew the natural ecstasy
of boyhood's games. I found it in first love; it
came to me when a simple girl laid her hand
upon my arm, and her braided hair, sweet
with the fragrance of health, came so close to
my lips that I kissed it without her knowing.
And then she went from me, and happiness
strayed away.

For I sought it next in remaking the lives of
other men. I went forth to reform the world.
I denounced the ways of mankind, and be-
moaned the backwardness of time, and
talked only of glories that were past, or were
to come. I wanted many laws to make life
easier for me, and for youth. But the world
would not listen, and I grew bitter. I gathered anecdotes of human stupidity, and
heralded the absurdities and injustices of
men. One day, an enemy said, "You have in
yourself all the faults which you scorn in
others; you, too, are capable of selfishness
and greed; and the world is what it is because men are what you are."

I considered it in solitude, and found that
it was true. Then it came to me that reform
should begin at home; and since that day I
have not had time to remake the world.

Many years I lost happiness. I sought it in
knowledge, and found disillusionment. I
sought it in writing, and found a weariness
of the flesh. I sought it in travel, and my feet
tired on the way. I sought it in wealth, and I
found discord and worriment.

And then one day, at a little station out on
a wooded cliff near the sea, I saw a woman
waiting in a tiny car, with a child asleep in
her arms. A man alighted from a train,
walked to her quickly, embraced her, and
kissed the child gently, careful lest he should
awaken it. They drove off together to some

modest home among the fields; and it seemed to me that happiness was with them.

Today I have neglected my writing. The voice of a little girl calling to me, "Come out and play," drew me from my papers and my books. Was it not the final purpose of my toil that I should be free to frolic with her, and spend unharassed hours with the one who had given her to me? And so we walked and ran and laughed together, and fell in the tall grass, and hid among the trees; and I was young again.

Now it is evening; while I write, I hear the child's breathing as she sleeps in her cozy bed. And I know that I have found what I sought. I perceived that if I will do as well as I can the tasks for which life has made me, I shall find fulfillment, and a quiet lane of happiness for many years.

Hold Fast Your Dreams

LOUISE DRISCOLL

Hold fast your dreams!
Within your heart
Keep one, still, secret spot
Where dreams may go,
And sheltered so,
May thrive and grow —
Where doubt and fear are not.
O, keep a place apart,
Within your heart,
For little dreams to go!

Good temper, like a sunny day, sheds a brightness over everything. It is the sweetness of toil and the soother of disquietude.
Washington Irving

I Have Everything

JAMES J. METCALFE

However much I have to do,
    However hard I strive,
I always tell myself that I
    Am glad to be alive.
My heart is grateful for the sun
    That keeps my body warm;
And for the comforts of this earth
    Against whatever storm.
I have my friends to cheer me up
    And books to read at night
With boundless beauty to behold,
    Whenever stars are bright.
I have enough to eat and drink,
    And clothes enough to wear;
A normal mind and healthy lungs
    To breathe the best of air.
So why should I object when I
    Have this my job to do,
As long as I have everything
    To help me see it through?

That Quiet Hour

ANNE MORROW LINDBERGH

The church has always been a great centering force for women. Through what ages women have had that quiet hour, free of interruption, to draw themselves together. No wonder woman has been the mainstay of the church. Here were the advantages of the room of her own, the time alone, the quiet, the peace, all rolled into one and sanctioned by the approval of both family and community. Here no one could intrude with a careless call, "Mother," "Wife," "Mistress." Here, finally and more deeply, woman was whole, not split into a thousand functions. She was able to give herself completely in that hour of worship, in prayer, in communion, and be completely accepted. And in that giving and acceptance she was renewed; the springs were refilled.

Happiness

PRISCILLA LEONARD

Happiness is like a crystal,
    Fair and exquisite and clear,
Broken in a million pieces,
    Shattered, scattered far and near.

Now and then along life's pathway,
    Lo! some shining fragments fall;
But there are so many pieces,
    No one ever finds them all.

Sunset Symphony

ALICE JOYCE DAVIDSON

It comes…
every evening
without fanfare or drums
it comes…

it comes softly as a lullaby
beginning with a golden glow
encircling a cloud…

and then the glow begins to grow…
pinks and violets fill the sky
a ball or orange delights the eye
then cymbals crash, the trumpets blare
a symphony has filled the air,
a silent symphony!
Applause! Applause!
a spectacular show!

then the ball of orange, ablaze, aglow,
sinks slowly out of sight…

God has tucked away a day
and ushered in the night!

I have learned, in whatsoever state I am, therewith to be content.   Philippians 4:11

A Little Song of Life

LIZETTE WOODWORTH REESE

Glad that I live am I;
That the sky is blue;
Glad for the country lanes,
And the fall of dew.

After the sun the rain,
After the rain the sun;
This is the way of life,
Till the work be done.

All that we need to do,
Be we low or high,
Is to see that we grow
Nearer the sky.

Since life is short, we need to make it broad. Since life is brief, we need to make it bright.
    Ella Wheeler Wilcox

Lucky is he who can get his grapes to market and keep the bloom upon them, who can carry some of the freshness and eagerness and simplicity of youth into his later years, who can have a boy's heart below a man's head.   John Burroughs

At Eighty-Three

THOMAS DURLEY LANDELS

Thank God for life, with all its endless store
Of great experiences, of hill and dale,
Of cloud and sunshine, tempest, snow and
hail.
Thank God for straining sinews, panting
breast,
No less for weary slumber, peaceful rest;
Thank God for home and parents, children,
friends,
For sweet companionship that never ends:
Thank God for all the splendor of the earth,
For nature teeming with prolific birth:
Thank God for sea and sky, for changing
hours,
For trees and singing birds and fragrant
flowers.
And so in looking back at eighty-three
My final word to you, my friends, shall be:
Thank God for life; and when the gift's
withdrawn,
Thank God for twilight bell, and coming
dawn.

Symphony

WILLIAM ELLERY CHANNING

To live content with small means; to seek
elegance rather than luxury, and refinement
rather than fashion; to be worthy, not re-
spectable, and wealthy, not rich; to study
hard, think quietly, talk gently, act frankly;
to listen to stars and birds, to babes and
sages, with open heart; to bear all cheerfully,
do all bravely, await occasions, hurry never.
In a word, to let the spiritual, unbidden and
unconscious grow up through the common.
This is to be my symphony.

Be at Peace

FRANCIS DE SALES

Do not look forward to the changes and
chances of this life in fear; rather look to
them with full hope that, as they arise, God,
whose you are, will deliver you out of them.
He has kept you hitherto — do you but hold
fast to His dear hand, and He will lead you
safely through all things; and, when you
cannot stand, He will bear you in His arms.
Do not look forward to what may happen
tomorrow; the same everlasting Father who
cares for you today will take care of you
tomorrow, and every day. Either He will
shield you from suffering, or He will give
you unfailing strength to bear it. Be at peace,
then, and put aside all anxious thoughts and
imaginations.

*Finish each day and be done with it.... You have
done what you could; some blunders and absurdities no doubt crept in; forget them as soon as you
can. Tomorrow is a new day; you shall begin it
well and serenely.* Ralph Waldo Emerson

God Is Nigh

AUTHOR UNKNOWN

Day is gone, gone the sun
From the lake, from the hills, from the sky.
Safely rest, all is well! God is nigh.

Memories

WHEN I WAS A LITTLE BOY, I used to tag along with my father to his country churches and listen to him preach. Sometimes, when nobody was looking, I used to slip into one of his churches, put a chair behind the pulpit, and stand up and "preach like Papa." When I was nineteen years old, I was appointed minister to three little country churches, and from that day until this, my dream has been the same — to "preach like Papa."

My father was a minister from 1900 to 1940. During those forty years, his total income was $49,000 — and there were seven children in our family. But all seven of us went through college. We did it because Papa gave us a little money and a lot of inspiration. I'll never forget getting on a bus to go to Wofford College in Spartanburg, South Carolina, and Papa giving me a bus ticket and fifteen dollars. He said, "Charles, I wish I could give you more, but I know you can make it."

During Papa's final illness, he was in the hospital for about six weeks. My brother, John, and I would take turns sitting up with him at night, and one night when I was there, Papa said to me, "Charles, do you know the greatest word in the English language?"

"No, Papa," I replied, "what is it?"

He said, "It is the word *forgiveness*."

They were the last words he ever spoke. Turning his head a little to one side, he breathed his last.

Just before dawn the next day, I was driving to my home about thirty miles away. My radio was tuned in to a country music station but I wasn't aware of the music. I was thinking about Papa.

All of a sudden I saw the first rays of the rising sun. And at that very moment I heard a song on the radio:

"There's a land that is fairer than day,
And by faith we can see it afar."

That morning I found an assurance I had never had before — and I knew Papa was all right.

CHARLES L. ALLEN

Good Night

VICTOR HUGO

Good night! good night!
Far flies the light;
But still God's love
Shall flame above,
Making all bright.
Good night! good night!

Whispering Voices

PETER MARSHALL

There is no disgrace in being homesick. At times I have felt the tugging of those invisible fingers and heard the whispering of those voices.

For I have seen the hills of Scotland moist with mist; have seen the fir trees marching down to the loch-sides; have seen the sheep on the hills and the heather in bloom; have heard the skirling of the pipes down the glen and the gurgling of the burn over the rocks and the familiar music of the kettle on the hob; have seen pictures that will never fade and sounds that will never die away.

I have longed for the northland, to see again the low stone houses, the swelling hills, the white tails of the waterfalls.

I have wanted to hear again the gentle low voices of the women and the music of the Gaelic tongue; to smell the delicate fragrance of bluebells in the spring and the rhododendron; to hear the mavis sing and the lark.

I have wanted to see the long twilights, to look out over the waters of the Firth, and be grateful to God that there was still more of Scotland beyond.

Remembering

JOHN BAILLIE

When I think of my own upbringing, the love and care that were lavished on me in my youth, the kind of home into which I was born, the community in which I was reared, the gracious influences that were brought to bear on me, the examples that were held up before me, the kind of teaching I was given, the signposts that awaited me at every turn of the road, the fences that were set to keep me from wandering from the way, the warnings that were given me against every pitfall, the words in season so often spoken to me — when I think of all these things, and in spite of my shame for having so little profited from them, I must indeed prostrate myself in gratitude before the memory of my parents, my teachers, my wonderful friends, and those who wrote the books I was given to read, who rendered me this inestimable service.

Yet I know that they themselves had it all from Christ. Nothing of it would have been there, if Christ had not come to seek and to save that which was lost.

Thanksgiving Is for Thanking

DINA DONOHUE

When I was a youngster living in New York City, children used to dress up as ragamuffins at Thanksgiving time and beg pennies from neighbors, family or passers-by on the sidewalk. I was about six the year that the custom ended for me.

That year, my older sister, Ruth, and I stood around the corner from the apartment house where we lived. As shoppers approached, Ruth and I each held out a paper bag and cried, "Anything for Thanksgiving?"

People were generous, and pennies, nickels, even some dimes and quarters found their way into our bags. When they were almost half full, we ran home to show our treasure to Margaret, our nurse. Mother was out shopping for the next day's Thanksgiving dinner.

Elated, I cried, "Look at all the money we have!"

"Where did you get it?" Margaret asked.

"From people — for Thanksgiving," Ruth told her.

Margaret, who had come from Hungary a few years before, had often told Ruth and me how lucky we were to be Americans, living in such a rich and wonderful country. Now she was shocked to hear what we had done. "You can't beg for money," she said. "Come with me, you've got to give it back." Taking each of us by the hand, she ordered, "March!" and propelled us out of the house.

"We can't give it back," we pleaded. "Lots of people gave it to us. Besides, it's ours — for Thanksgiving." Tears streaked our faces.

"That's not Thanksgiving — begging for pennies," Margaret answered. "You don't need anything. You have everything — toys, food, clothes. Thanksgiving is to show you're grateful for all you have."

Margaret continued her lecture as we "marched" to wherever she was taking us. "Many children have no toys; some won't even have a Thanksgiving dinner tomorrow, and you can say thank you to God for your good things by giving the money to the poor."

No toys, no food, no Thanksgiving? I may have heard of poor people before, but for the first time I could see a little girl without a doll, a boy hungry. My tears ceased and I stopped lagging behind Margaret.

She led us across the street to Wertheimer's Department Store. A Salvation Army officer was collecting money in a brass pot in front of the store. "There," Margaret said, pointing. "These good people need money to help the poor."

We'd often passed the store, and sometimes my mother or Margaret had given us pennies to put in the pot. But now Margaret wanted us to give away all our own money. I paused, then stepped forward with my bag. Ruth followed.

In the years since, as Thanksgiving Day has approached, I have remembered what Margaret said and I give again — to say, "Thank You, God, for the blessings I enjoy."

Sterling Silver

MARY ELMBLAD

My grandmother died last month. She was almost 90, but she was well and active until she had a stroke and died, just like that.

Her name was Althea. She left her sterling silver to me.

Grandmother's silver chest was open on our coffee table and my brother Bill was counting out the pieces. "Twelve place settings with seven pieces each, that's eighty-four pieces, not counting the serving spoons and all that." He hefted a dinner fork. "And the weight! Listen, Althea, if you sell this stuff you'll get a bundle to put in your grad school fund. Maybe you can even quit waitressing."

Yes, my name is Althea, too, and yes, I work as a waitress and save every cent I can spare for graduate school. I intend to be a professor of history.

We are not a moneyed family. My father got a late start both in marrying and in his insurance business because of his army service in World War II and Korea. He insisted on putting Bill and me through college, but then we were on our own. That was all right. We knew how to work. Bill had a construction job every summer and with that and his expertise at scrounging student loans, he was within two years of an engineering degree. And my graduate school account was rising slowly but surely. I had it all figured out. After six more months of waiting tables I could start the long haul toward a doctorate. I would have to work part-time, but that was okay. I would make it. I wanted it enough to make it.

My father put down his newspaper. "Bill's right, Althea. I talked to Carl Nelson at the jewelry store today. He had a pretty good idea of what the silver is worth." He named a figure that made Bill whistle with surprise.

I looked down at the gleaming silver on the coffee table. A first-class ticket to graduate school. My shoulders sagged with relief. It was only then, when I saw that I could give up my job, that I could admit how much it took out of me. There would be no more heavy trays and demanding customers. No more nights being too bone-tired even to soak my feet.

My father looked over at my mother. "Don't you think she should sell it?"

My mother was sewing a button on one of Dad's shirts. She snipped the thread and then she looked up at me over her glasses and smiled. "Althea will have to decide that."

It was my grandmother who first gave me an interest in history. She was a great reader, but history was her favorite. The way she put it was, "I like to keep in mind when a thing happened." She was born in East Texas, she told me once. "Twenty-five years to the day after Appomattox." Then I had to know all about Appomattox, and before I knew it I had heard a brief history of what my grandmother called "The War Between The States," right down to General Lee's surrender at Appomattox Court House. I liked going to my grandmother's house.

What I liked best was polishing her sterling silver. I remember one Saturday when I was — what? Ten? Eleven?

"Grandmother," I said, "I forget. What does sterling mean?"

"Pure silver, missy. Well, almost pure. Look it up in the dictionary there."

I had to wrestle with the alphabet for a minute, but I found the definition and read it out. "Sterling silver: an alloy of 92.5 percent silver with copper or another metal."

Grandmother explained "alloy" and said, "That's pretty pure, isn't it?"

"Wait, there's another meaning, just for the word 'sterling.' It means, 'of highest quality.'"

Grandmother set the wooden silver chest on the drainboard with a smug little bang. "Of highest quality. Yes. Now, missy, if we're going to get this silver polished —".…

Grandmother unwrapped the first of the purple anti-tarnish cloth bundles and I took a dinner fork and rubbed it with gray polish. That was the best part, watching the pasty rag turn black and letting the sharp smell of the tarnish tickle my nose. "Now, wash it in the soapy water, Althea. Get it good and clean." Then she dipped the fork into the hot water, dried it and held it up to the light.

"This fork, child, is the first piece of sterling I ever owned. The very first."

I already knew the background. She and my grandfather were married just after World War I, when he came home with gas-damaged lungs and enough cash to buy a partnership in the local feed store. He also brought home one sterling silver fork, for my grandmother.

"Missy, that fork was the prettiest thing I had seen in all my born days." She raised it and the light twinkled on the decorated handle. "The Climbing Rose pattern. Yes. We had a little place outside town, you know, with a garden patch and chickens, and I saved up my egg money to buy another fork. I swear, your grandpa and I could eat fatback and turnip greens with those silver forks and think it was the finest meal on earth!"

She took out a teaspoon. "Now, this was one of the pieces your grandpa brought me on the day your daddy was born. He was a proud man that day."

Could she really tell one dinner fork from the others? Did each teaspoon have its own characteristics? Grandmother liked to think it did. So did I.

Grandmother dried the last teaspoon and turned it in her hand. "And this spoon was in the setting he brought to the hospital when our James was born."

"My Uncle Jim?"

"Yes, missy, though you never saw him. Your Uncle Jim."

"Grandmother? Can we do the salad forks now?"

"Oh, I know which one you like!" She took a fork from the purple bundle. "Well, I went to town that day —"

"With your egg money in a handkerchief!"

Grandmother laughed. "That's right, with my egg money tied up in a white handkerchief. I went into Mr. Porter's jewelry store and the screeching and hollering that was going on! It had just come on the radio that Lindbergh had flown his little airplane clear across the ocean and was landed safely in France! Missy, to this day I don't eat a bite of salad that I don't think of Lucky Lindy!"

She picked up another salad fork. "But the radio news was bad when I bought this one, awful bad. It was the week the stock market crashed. October, it was, of nineteen and twenty-nine."

"And then the Depression came, didn't it? What was it like, Grandmother?" I can still remember the surge of curiosity I felt. Even then, I suppose, it was the avid yearning for details, for specifics, that made me want to be a historian.

"Missy, there were weeks when a dollar bill never came within spitting distance of our place. The feed store closed, but we had our garden and we traded off work for what we couldn't grow. Folks would call your grandpa to help with training a horse, say, and pay him off with a poke of meal or a side of bacon. And I could sew a fine seam in those days." She held up her gnarled, slightly palsied hands and looked at them proudly, as if she saw them still as they had been in her youth, white and slim and deft. "A fine seam. But they were hard times, child, hard times. Every day men would come wandering down our road on their way from no place to no place, with no work for their hands and no food for their bellies. Some folks called them tramps and kept a loaded shotgun behind the kitchen door, but we'd help them with what little we could spare. Most of them were good men, just down on their luck. You'll learn about it in school, child."

I did learn about it in history classes, about economic causes and social disruption, but it was from my grandmother that I learned what Depression meant. It meant long gray lines of homeless, hopeless men. And Grandpa trudging home at dusk, bone-tired, with a sack — no, with a poke of cornmeal slung over his shoulder. And Grandmother stitching her fine seam in the yellow light of a coal-oil lamp.

"Why didn't you sell your silver, Grandmother?"

"Oh, child, nobody had money for silver. Once I was going to try to trade it for shoes for the boys, but your grandpa wouldn't have it. 'Even grits taste mighty fine,' he said, 'when you eat them with a sterling silver spoon.'"

Grandmother unwrapped a long bundle. "Your own daddy gave me this carving set on the day he went up to Dallas to enlist. The day after Pearl Harbor. He was saving money for college, but he brought me this set and he said, 'Now, Mama, you keep it polished, you hear? Keep it polished till I come home from the war.' And I did. When he went to Korea, too. I polished it till your grandpa said I'd wear the Climbing Rose off!"

There was another bundle, of a different shape. Sometimes Grandmother would let me help polish the cake server and sometimes she would not. My Uncle Jim had sent it to her just before he shipped out to the South Pacific, to Guadalcanal. No matter how much she polished it, he did not come back.

Twelve place settings of sterling silver. I can remember when new pieces were added. In our family no one ever had to ask what Grandmother wanted for Christmas or her birthday or Mother's Day.

When I was 15 or 16, I finally asked her why. "Grandmother, you and Grandpa weren't rich people. Why did you want all that silver?"

She was startled, I remember, and for a moment she looked disappointed, as if she had misjudged my character. Then she smiled at me. "Why, missy, I reckon I just like to set a pretty table."

When our family gathered for festive meals we gathered at my grandmother's pretty table. I remember a Thanksgiving dinner when my grandfather sat at the head of the table. He asked the blessing and then he raised the Climbing Rose carving set and sliced the turkey with the proud skill of a man working with first-class tools. My grandmother, as always, had to make a minute adjustment in the position of the cranberry dish and to give one teaspoon a quick buff on her apron before she would take her place. The dishes were nothing fancy and the glasses did not match, but that did not bother us. We ate our turkey with sterling silver forks. We were honored guests at the feast, all of us, old and young....

My grandmother took up each piece of silver and told its story, that day when I was ten or maybe 11, just as another woman might take up a pressed flower or a faded photograph. And as she talked I began to understand something about our family. We have produced no famous people, but it is our family and the others like it that make up the fabric of America. Our story is one small thread, but it is woven into the rich tapestry of history.

"Now, you gave me this butter knife, missy, do you remember? It was for my birthday in nineteen and sixty-four."

I remembered. I was seven years old. I saved my allowance and the dimes I was paid for talking to the neighbor's baby when he was in a bad mood, and then my mother took me downtown and I proudly purchased one butter knife.

"And the cocktail forks and these soup spoons came from —"

I knew. They were the pieces my parents gave her on her seventy-fifth birthday. The pieces that completed the set.

"Merciful heavens!" my grandmother said. "I've talked the morning away! Now, child, tell me about your school. Has that new teacher suggested any good books for us to read?"....

"It would be for a good purpose," my father said.

"What? Sorry, Dad, I didn't hear you."

"You would be selling the silver for a good purpose — to pay your tuition."

"Yes. That's true." I touched the silver fork my grandfather brought home from World War I. I picked up the butter knife I gave to my grandmother when I was seven years old. "I'm just not sure."

My brother laughed. "You're not thinking about keeping it! You want to sling hash for six more months?"

"Six months isn't all that long," I said.

"You could always sell it if you got in a bind," my father said.

"I guess I could."

But I guess I won't. I think a time will come when I will show my daughter the salad fork my grandmother bought with her egg money on the day Lucky Lindy landed in France. And when I have a granddaughter of my own (do you suppose that they might name her "Althea"?) I will tell her about the cake server my Uncle Jim sent to Grandmother before he sailed away to Guadalcanal.

You can't sell history, can you?

I straightened my shoulders. I felt strong, suddenly, and sure of purpose. "I'm going to keep the silver."

My father looked pleased. "I'll take care of the insurance for you."

"Thanks, Dad. That means I can keep it and polish it now and again. I don't want to forget which piece is which."

"That's why you want to keep it?" Bill asked. "So you can polish the stuff?"

"No, I'll use it, too. I'm like Grandmother. I like to set a pretty table." I looked at my mother. "Thanksgiving and Christmas dinners, right?"

"Of course," she said comfortably.

"Besides," I said, "I want something to leave my granddaughter."

Richer Today

ANONYMOUS

You are richer today than you were yester-day...if you have laughed often, given something, forgiven even more, made a new friend today, or made stepping-stones of stumbling-blocks; if you have thought more in terms of "thyself" than of "myself," or if you have succeeded in being cheerful even if you were weary. You are richer tonight than you were this morning...if you have taken time to trace the handiwork of God in the commonplace things of life, or if you have learned to count out things that really do not count, or if you have been a little blinder to the faults of friend or foe. You are richer if a little child has smiled at you, and a stray dog has licked your hand, or if you have looked for the best in others, and have given others the best in you.

God's Open Door

A. J. CRONIN

Thirty years ago, when I was a doctor in London, on the point of moving to a special-ist's practice in Harley Street, my health broke down. I was told that I must take a year's rest and that, even so, I might never again be fit to stand the wear and tear of medical life.

What a blow! I liked my work. From the humblest beginnings in a small Welsh min-ing practice, I had slaved to achieve this objective. And now, on the threshold of suc-cess, the door was slammed in my face. My state of mind was such that I could not help voicing bitterness and resentment to my friends.

Soon after, I left for my place of exile, a remote district in the West Highlands. Here

time hung heavy upon my hands. Suddenly, out of the blue, I had an impulse to write. I began a novel, "Hatter's Castle," and I fin-ished it, packed it up, and sent it to a pub-lisher — who accepted it! Out of all reason, a door had opened. A new career lay before me.

So many of us, meeting with sudden dis-appointment, misfortune or defeat, raise a cry of anger and resentment against heaven. Why should God do this to us? To be de-prived of health, miss the chance of promo-tion, to lose one's job, these things are hard to bear, and harder perhaps to understand.

Yet we cannot measure Divine Providence by the yardstick of human mentality. What we think an evil may well be for eventual good.

The demands life makes may seem hard at times, yet we ought not to whine. God never takes without giving something in return. Disappointments and troubles are often the instruments with which He fashions us for better things to come.

Life's Lesson

ELLA WHEELER WILCOX

There are times in one's life when all the world seems to turn against us. Our motives are misunderstood, our words miscon-strued, an unkind word reveals to us the unfriendly feelings of others.

The fact is, that it is rare when injustice, or slights, patiently borne, do not leave the heart at the close of the day filled with a marvelous sense of peace — perhaps not at once — but after you've had a chance to reflect a bit. It is the seed God has sown, springing up and bearing fruit.

We learn, as the years roll onward and we leave the past behind, that much we had

counted sorrow, but proved that God is kind; that many a flower we'd longed for had hidden a thorn of pain, and many a rugged by-path led to fields of ripened grain.

The clouds that cover the sunshine; they cannot banish the sun. And the earth shines out the brighter when the weary rain is done. We must stand in the deepest shadow to see the clearest light; and often through Wrong's own darkness comes the welcome strength of Right.

The Solitary Reaper

WILLIAM WORDSWORTH

Behold her, single in the field,
Yon solitary highland lass!
Reaping and singing by herself;
Stop here, or gently pass!
Alone she cuts and binds the grain,
And sings a melancholy strain;
O listen! for the vale profound
Is overflowing with the sound.

…Whate'er the theme, the maiden sang
As if her song could have no ending;
I saw her singing at her work,
And o'er the sickle bending; —
I listened, motionless and still;
And, as I mounted up the hill
The music in my heart I bore,
Long after it was heard no more.

I May Walk a Little Slower

BOBBIE SOUTAR

Yes, I may walk a little slower
    and old they may call me
But I look a little longer
    at each dawn that breaks for me
I hear a little better
    all the sounds a day can hold
I love a whole lot stronger
    all the worldly births I see unfold

I see a little clearer
    what the world holds out to me
I feel a whole lot deeper
    for another's misery
I dream a lot more often
    of the days that long have past
I acknowledge precious time
    that ticks away so fast

I hold a great deal tighter
    to loving friends' embraces
And oh, how I cherish laughing children
    with life's smudges on their faces
Yes, I may walk a little slower
    and old they may call me
But do you know, I see, I hear and I love
    much better than that young girl
        I used to be.

The Old Man's Dream

OLIVER WENDELL HOLMES

Oh for one hour of youthful joy!
    Give back my twentieth spring!
I'd rather laugh, a bright-haired boy,
    Than reign, a gray-beard king.

Off with the spoils of wrinkled age!
    Away with Learning's crown!
Tear out life's Wisdom-written page,
    And dash its trophies down!

217

One moment let my life-blood stream
    From boyhood's fount of flame!
Give me one giddy, reeling dream
    Of life all love and fame!

My listening angel heard the prayer,
    And, calmly smiling, said,
"If I but touch thy silvered hair,
    Thy hasty wish hath sped.

"But is there nothing in thy track
    To bid thee fondly stay.
While the swift seasons hurry back
    To find the wished-for day?"

"Ah, truest soul of womankind!
    Without thee what were life?
One bliss I cannot leave behind:
    I'll take — my precious — wife!"

The angel took a sapphire pen
    And wrote in rainbow dew,
The man would be a boy again,
    And be a husband, too!

And is there nothing yet unsaid,
    Before the change appears?
Remember, all their gifts have fled
    With those dissolving years.

"Why, yes," for memory would recall
    My fond paternal joys;
"I could not bear to leave them all —
    I'll take-my-girl-and-boys."

The smiling angel dropped his pen, —
    "Why, this will never do;
The man would be a boy again,
    And be a father, too!"

And so I laughed, — my laughter woke
    The household with its noise, —
And wrote my dream, when morning
    broke,
    To please the gray-haired boys.

Old Rugs

JEAN CARPENTER MERGARD

Her rugs are worn, yet she explains,
    That though thick new ones would be
      nice,
It's more like home while she retains
    The old. New rugs at any price
Could not reveal the paths of shoes,
    From babyhood through college days,
Whose footprints have thinned down the
      blues
    And scuffed the golds to burlap maize.
Alone now in her house she hugs
    Thoughts of dear distant ones, and
      sees
In all her faded, footworn rugs
    The mark of heart-bright memories.

To be seventy years young is sometimes far more cheerful and hopeful than to be forty years old.
Oliver Wendell Holmes

You Are Not Old

AUTHOR UNKNOWN

Age is a quality of mind.
If you have left your dreams behind,
If hope is cold,
If you no longer look ahead,
If your ambitions' fires are dead —
Then you are old.
But if from life you take the best,
And if in life you keep the jest,
If love you hold;
No matter how the years go by,
No matter how the birthdays fly —
You are not old.

Good Old Days
GRANDMA MOSES

Things have changed greatly and still are changing, can they change much more? Can you think of any more improvements? My father liked his fireplace the same as I like my old iron stove, and now they have the gas and electric ranges, but I would not be surprised when the younger generation gets old, when people of coming generations, a hundred years from now, will look back upon us as primitives.

And yet I wonder sometimes whether we are progressing. In my childhood days life was different, in many ways. We were slower. Still we had a good and happy life, I think. People enjoyed more in their way, at least they seemed to be happier. They don't take time to be happy nowadays.

The Open Door
GRACE COOLIDGE

You, my son,
Have shown me God.
Your kiss upon my cheek
Has made me feel the gentle touch
Of Him who leads us on.
The memory of your smile, when young,
Reveals His face,
As mellowing years come on apace.
And when you went before,
You left the gates of heaven ajar
That I might glimpse,
Approaching from afar,
The glories of His grace.
Hold, son, my hand,
Guide me along the path,
That, coming,
I may stumble not,
Nor roam,
Nor fail to show the way
Which leads us home.

Secrets of the Heart
PEARL S. BUCK

Mrs. Allenby listened to her daughter's plans for the holiday, and then it was time for her to make her announcement. "I won't be here for Christmas," Mrs. Allenby said, keeping her voice as casual as she could.

Her daughter Margaret stared at her. "What *do* you mean?" Margaret demanded. "It's impossible! Not here for Christmas? Where are you going?"

"I haven't decided," Mrs. Allenby said. She carefully tied a silver bow on a small package. Inside was a brooch for Margaret, a circle of pearls set in gold that she had found only yesterday in an antique shop. When the package was tied to her satisfaction she handed it to her daughter.

"For you — not to be opened until.... I'll deliver the other gifts for all of you, parents and children, to each of your houses before I go."

Margaret, about to leave after an hour of lively talk, sat down again in the blue velvet chair by the fire. They were in her mother's living room. The December sun was blazing through the windows, paling the flames that were crackling in the low grate.

"But, Mother, you've never been away at Christmastime!" Margaret cried.

"So this year I shall be," Mrs. Allenby said, her voice pleasant but firm.

..."Mother, if I didn't know you love us —"

Mrs. Allenby interrupted. "Indeed, I love you all, but I think you should be alone for Christmas, each pair of parents with their own children, the children alone with only their own parents and brothers and sisters. You've no idea —" She stopped.

"Idea of what?" Margaret demanded, her eyes very blue under her dark hair. She was a small creature, but possessed of a mighty spirit. Hot or cold, she was all extremes.

"How peaceful it would be," Mrs. Allenby said rather lamely.

Her daughter looked at her critically. "You

aren't being noble or something, are you? Think we don't want you or something stupid like that?"

"Oh no, indeed," Mrs. Allenby said. "Nothing like that."

…Margaret looked at her mother fondly and then rose. "Well, keep your secrets, but I still tell you I shan't enjoy Christmas for a minute, wondering where you are." She put her arms about her mother and kissed her. "And this present — the package is so small I know it's expensive and you shouldn't have…"

"It's my money, darling," Mrs. Allenby said, laughing.

Margaret kissed her mother again, ran to the door and stopped to look back. "Tell me where you're going," she asked again, her voice coaxing.

Mrs. Allenby laughed. "Go home and tend your children," she said gaily and waved goodbye.

Alone with the fire, the winter sun streaming across the Aubusson carpet, the bowl of holly on the table, the book-lined walls, Mrs. Allenby was suddenly aware of a deep relief. She loved her house, she loved her children and their children, but — but what? She did not know what came after this *but*. Simply that she longed not to be here on Christmas. She would leave early in the morning of Christmas Eve. That would see her at the cabin in Vermont by nightfall. Now she rose, gathered some bits of silver cord and wrapping paper which she threw into the fire, and went upstairs to pack.

By eight the morning of Christmas Eve she was in her car and headed north. Snow threatened from a smooth gray sky, and in Vermont, the radio told her, it was already snowing. They had often gone skiing in Vermont in the old days, she and Leonard, before they were married. And it was to Vermont that they had gone for their honeymoon, but in October, and too early for skiing. How glorious it had been, nevertheless, the mountains glittering in scarlet and gold!

"In celebration of our wedding," Leonard had said.

It was because of him, of course, that she wanted to have Christmas alone, and in Vermont. They had always come here alone. It had been his demand.

"Let's never go to Vermont with the children — always alone," he had said.

"Selfish, aren't you," she had teased, with love.

"Plenty of other places to ski with them," he had retorted.

"Of course we mustn't let them know — they'd be hurt," she had said.

"No reason why they should know this place even exists," he had agreed.

That was just after they had built the cabin and now it was the place essential to her, for there she could refresh, revitalize her memory of Leonard. She was frightened because she was forgetting him, losing him — not the sum total of him, of course, but the clarity of detail of his looks, the dark eyes and the sandy hair. He had died so heartbreakingly young, the children still small, and their own children never to see their grandfather — see the way he walked, his tall spare frame moving in his own half-awkward, curiously graceful fashion. The memory came strong at Christmas, especially — he had loved sprawling on the floor with his children, showing them how to play with the toys he chose for them with such care.

The snow was beginning to fall now, a few flakes, growing heavier as she drove out of the traffic and toward the mountains. She would reach the cabin this evening late. Leonard had designed the cabin before any of the children were born so it had only three rooms. He had not wanted children too soon.

"Let's be solid with each other first," he had said.

They had come to the cabin often during the first years of their life together, as often as he could get away from the laboratories where he worked as a research scientist. After the children came, it was less often and at last, when he was dead, not at all — that is, she had never come back alone. Yet she had not thought of selling it. Gradually she had not thought of it at all, though she knew now she had not forgotten it.

The hours sped past. She was a fast driver but steady, Leonard always said, and it was she who usually did the driving when they went to the cabin, the quiet hours giving him time to think. He had said gratefully, "What it means to a man like me not to have to talk —"

Yet, some laboratory problem solved, he would be suddenly gay with lively talk. They had good talk together, and it was not until his voice was stilled in death that she realized how good the talk was, and that there always had been something to talk about.

The day slipped past noon, and the snow continued to fall. Before darkness fell she reached the village and there she stopped to buy food for a day or two.... She drove on then in the dusk, up the winding graveled road to the top of the snow-covered hill....

She got out of the car and lifted a flat stone. Yes, the key was still there, too, the big brass key.

"I hate little keys," Leonard had said. "They lose themselves on purpose."

So they had found the huge, old brass lock, a heavy and substantial one. She fitted the key into the hole, and the door creaked open. Dear God, it couldn't be the same after all these years — but it was the same.

"We must always leave it as though we were coming back tomorrow," Leonard had said.

It was dusty, of course, and it smelled of the forest and dead leaves. But it had been built so solidly that bird and beast had found no entrance. The logs in the great fireplace were ready to light, and in the bedroom the bed was made — damp and musty, doubtless, but there it was, and the fire would soon drive out the dampness. She would hang the bedclothes before the chimney piece.

She lit the fire and the big old lamp, then she unpacked the car, and sat down in the old rocking chair to rest a few minutes before preparing food. So here she was, unexpectedly really, for she had made no long-standing plans to come here. It had come over her suddenly, the need to find Leonard somehow, even to remember him, and this had happened when she was buying the brooch for Margaret. It had taken a little time to find it.

"Are you looking for something for yourself?" the young woman in the antique shop had asked.

"No," she had replied, "I'm just looking."

"A tie pin for your husband, perhaps?" the young woman had persisted.

"I have no husband," she had replied, shortly. Then she had corrected herself. "I mean — he died many years ago."

But her instinctive reply had frightened her. No husband — was she forgetting Leonard? Impossible — but perhaps true? And here it was Christmas again, and if ever he was not to be forgotten it was at Christmas, the time he loved best. And suddenly all her heart had cried out for him. Yet where was he to be found, if not in memory? And suddenly she needed to be alone this Christmas. The children, grown into men and women, and their children, whom he had never seen, were strangers to him, and living in their midst, she had almost allowed herself to become a stranger to him, too.

...She pulled the small drop-leaf table before the fire and set out her supper, a bowl of bean soup, bread and cheese and fruit, and she ate with appetite. When she had eaten she folded the table away against the wall. Then she heated water and took her bath in a primitive tin tub. It was all so easy, so natural, to do what they had done, she and Leonard, here alone in the forest. Clean and warm in her flannel nightgown, she went into the bed, now warm and dry, but still smelling of autumn leaves, and fell into dreamless sleep.

She woke the next morning to sunshine

glittering upon new-fallen snow. For a moment she did not know where she was. Here, where she had always been with Leonard, her right hand reached for him instinctively. Then she remembered. It was Christmas Day and she was alone. No, not alone, for her first thought summoned Leonard to her mind. She lay for a moment in the warm bed. Then she spoke.

"I can talk out loud here — there is no one to hear me and wonder."

She heard her own voice and was comforted by its calm. "I can talk all I want to out loud," she went on.

A pleasant peace crept into her heart and body, as gentle as a perfume, and she smiled....

She filled the big kettle now with water from the kitchen pump and hung it on the crane above the fire. When the water was hot she washed and dressed, putting on her red dress, and sat down at the table for breakfast. And when she finished eating and washed the dishes, she put on Leonard's lumber jacket, which hung as usual behind the door, and went out to cut a tree — a very tiny one, just to set on the table. The tree ornaments were where Leonard had put them, years ago, in the wall drawer under the window and she tied them on the tree. Then she found the gift she brought for herself in her bag, and she tied it to the tree.

"A year or two and perhaps there'll be more than the two of us," Leonard had said, on their third Christmas. "We've had over two years alone. Now let's have our children — four of them — close together while we're still young. They can enjoy each other and us, and there'll be years for us alone after they've grown up and don't need us anymore."

"We can't bring a baby to this cabin in the middle of winter," she had said.

"We'll take Christmas where we find it," he had told her.

And sharing his desire, as she loved to do because she loved him, by the next Christmas they had a son, named for his father but called Lennie. He was three months old that Christmas and they spent it, the three of them, in their first house, a modest one on a quiet street in the small Connecticut town where she still lived.

"I'm sure he sees the tree," Leonard had insisted.

Lennie, lying on the rug, had stared steadily at the glittering tree, still not a very big tree but one loaded with gifts. Then he had smiled, and both she and Leonard had laughed and reached for each other's hand.

"I'm glad we're alone, the three of us," Leonard had said. "It's selfish of me not to want to go to either of our parents, but we have our own home now, you and I and our child. That's the trinity of life, my love."

In less than two years they had their daughter, Margaret.

"Another one and we'll need a bigger house," Leonard had said on Christmas Day.

...They had started to build their new house that next spring. By November it was still not quite finished but they moved in anyway to celebrate Dickie's birth.

"It was such an occasion," she said aloud now, smiling.

...That first Christmas in their new house had been a blessed one. Two little children ran about the room, shouting with delight, and Dickie sat propped on the couch. Lennie had his first tricycle and Margaret her first real doll. She loved dolls from that day on, and from them learned to love babies — nowadays her own. But little Dickie....

The tears were hot against her eyelids now and she bit her lip. There was more than joy to remember. There was also sorrow. Dickie had died before the next Christmas. Death had come suddenly, stealing into the house. She had put him to bed one night, a few days before Christmas, and in the morning had gone to wake him and had found him dead. The beautiful little body was there, white as the snow outside the window, and the blue eyes were still closed as if in sleep. Unpredicted, unexplained, and she still wept when she thought of it.

She wept now as if she had lost him only yesterday. Back then she had known she must try to comfort Leonard, although in weeks upon weeks, he would not be comforted. But for his sake she had been compelled not to weep, compelled to seem brave when she was not brave.

"Don't even speak of Christmas," he had said that dreadful year. And against every beat of her own aching heart she had persuaded him.

"Dearest, there are the others. They've been looking forward to Christmas Day. We must go on as usual — as best we can."

"You are right, I know," he had said at last. "But don't expect too much of me."

They had both been glad when Christmas Day was over, that heartbreaking day.

"Oh, how did we ever,..." she whispered now and sobbed.

...She and Leonard had endured that terrible Christmas, and in the spring she was pregnant again.

By the next Christmas Day, Ronald was born and two years later Ellen.

"Enough," Leonard had told her, laughing. "You produce wonderful babies, my pet, but enough is enough."

So there had been no more and thereafter her Christmas Days became a blur of happiness, the kinds of celebration varying only with the ages of the children, gifts changing from toys to adolescent treasures and at last to young adult possessions.

"I wish, Leonard darling, that you could have seen the first grandchild," she said now, her gaze fixed on the peak of the mountain, glowing in early sunset.

That would have been their happiest Christmas, the year Margaret's first child, Jimmy, was born, a little bundle of joy and mischief. Impossible to believe that now he was in college!

"You would have laughed all day, my darling, at his antics," she said aloud and laughed to herself at the very thought of what had never been.

When the children were almost grown came the years when Leonard took her with him on business trips. He was the head of his own company by then and they had traveled to Europe and sometimes even to Asia. It had seemed to her that everyone treated her as though she were a queen, and that was because he was the king. But they had always managed to be home for Christmas, what with the children growing up and getting married and she had talked of the grandchildren coming along, though Leonard had laughed at the idea of her being a grandmother.

"Didn't I tell you it was right for us to have the children when we were young? Now we can enjoy ourselves, doing whatever we like, for years to come."

Not so many years, at that, for nineteen years and thirteen days ago Leonard had come home at midday saying that he felt ill. His heart, so robust an organ all his life, had developed its own secret weakness, had suddenly stopped, beyond recall.

She stared out the window now, as the shadows of evening crept over the landscape. There was nothing more to say, for long ago all questions had been asked and answered, in some fashion or other. Only the eternal *why* remained and to that there was no answer. She sat in silence but strangely comforted. She had wanted to remember him clearly, and in remembering, he had come back to her.

At this moment she heard a knock on the door. With no sense of alarm she opened it and saw a man standing there, a man with a graying beard.

"I'm Andrew Bond, ma'am, a neighbor. My wife says she saw smoke here and I thought I'd better come over."

She put out her hand. "Why, Andrew Bond, your father used to look after the cabin for us. You've forgotten."

He stared at her. "No, I haven't forgotten — but are you here alone, ma'am?"

"Yes, for the day, that is. I came just to — well, I just came."

"Yes, ma'am. So you aren't staying?"

"No, if you'll dig me out tomorrow morning?"

"Yes, ma'am, I'll be glad to."

"Will you come in?"

"No, thanks. Wife's got supper on and she doesn't like to wait!"

"Well, thank you for coming, Andrew. And I hope you had a Merry Christmas."

"Well, my wife and me, we've had a happy Christmas, anyway. Our son come home from Vietnam — wounded, but alive."

"I'm glad he's alive," she said fervently, as though he were someone she knew. But she was really glad.

"Thank you, ma'am," he said. "I'll see you in the morning, ma'am."

"I'll see you in the morning," she echoed.

She closed the door and lit the lamp and heaved another log on the fire. She decided she would eat something and then go to bed early. Tomorrow she would be home again, ready to see them all, the children and their children. She had had her day, her Christmas Day. She went to the window and stood looking out into the gathering darkness.... Happy? Who knows what that is?

No, wounded — but alive!

Embers

HENRY WADSWORTH LONGFELLOW

Good-night! good-night! as we so oft have said,
    Beneath this roof at midnight, in the days
    That are no more, and shall no more return.
Thou hast but taken up thy lamp and gone to bed;
I stay a little longer, as one stays
    To cover up the embers that still burn.

Blessed Is the Giver

ANONYMOUS

It is in loving — not in being loved —
    The heart is blest;
It is in giving — not in seeking gifts —
    We find our quest.
If thou art hungry, lacking heavenly food,
    Give hope and cheer.
If thou art sad and wouldst be comforted,
    Stay sorrow's tear.
Whatever be thy longing and thy need,
    That do thou give;
So shall thy soul be fed, and thou, indeed,
    Shall truly live.

Be glad of life because it gives you the chance to love and to work and to play and to look up at the stars.
Henry van Dyke

Shining Hour

GRACE E. EASLEY

Tell me again of days gone by,
Help me recall the sounds and songs,
What matter if we can't return,
Back to the place where the heart belongs!
Waste not your sighs on years grown old,
Weep not for faces of the past,
Speak not again of long lost dreams,
And sands of time that flow too fast!
Within the power of all men,
The vision of a shining hour,
In every memory there clings,
The sweetness of a faded flower!
And what the heart has loved the most,
CAN NEVER BE MISLAID OR LOST!

INDEX of Authors

INDEX

INDEX of Titles and First Lines

231

This book was created by the same staff that prepares *Guideposts*, a monthly magazine filled with true stories of people's adventures in faith.

If you have found inspiration in *Dawnings*, we think you'll find monthly help and inspiration in the exciting stories that appear in our magazine.

Guideposts is not sold on the newsstand. It's available by subscription only. And subscribing is easy. All you have to do is write Guideposts Associates, Inc., Carmel, New York 10512. A year's subscription costs only $4.95 in the United States, $5.95 in Canada and overseas.

When you subscribe, each month you can count on receiving exciting new evidence of God's presence — His light shining through the darkness in life.